NUCLEAR
AFTERNOON

NUCLEAR
AFTERNOON

True Stories of Atomic Disasters

CLYDE W. BURLESON

Thunder's Mouth Press
New York

NUCLEAR AFTERNOON:
True Stories of Atomic Disasters

Copyright © 1978, 2007 by Clyde W. Burleson

Published by
Thunder's Mouth Press
An imprint of Avalon Publishing Group, Inc.
245 West 17th Street, 11th Floor
New York, NY 10011
www.thundersmouth.com

AVALON
publishing group incorporated

First printing, April 2007

Library of Congress Cataloging-in-Publication Data is available.

ISBN-13: 978-1-56025-996-1
ISBN-10: 1-56025-996-5

9 8 7 6 5 4 3 2 1

Book design by Bettina M. Wilhelm

Printed in the United States of America
Distributed by Publishers Group West

CONTENTS

AUTHOR'S NOTE

The stories in this book are true. The facts have been checked and rechecked. All names, dates, locations, and descriptions of places as well as events are as accurate as available documentation can make them. The dialogue comes from official transcripts and news reports contemporaneous with the event, or a close approximation of what was actually said at the time. Eyewitness testimony was combined with thousands of pages of documents to develop and refine these accounts. Some of the information was classified as Top Secret by one government or another.

Nuclear Fission and Chain Reactions Have Occurred Naturally

The day began like any other. A rising, hot equatorial sun warmed a dense haze of water vapor. Stirred into motion by solar energy, the mist rose in swirls, then congealed into thick clouds. Lifted to higher levels, the clouds cooled, releasing rain that fell onto the saturated ground below. Gale-force winds rolled over the low brown plains, gusting toward distant blue hills. The land was barren. Only the most primitive plants grew in the highlands. It would have been impossible for man to have lived on the bleak, storm-torn prairie.

But there were no men. They, and all of their inventions, would not arrive for more than a billion years.

The Precambrian storms engorged streams that became freshets, then masses of roaring water spilling down slopes to lakes and oceans. In places the rain fell onto porous rock that allowed air and moisture to filter deep into the earth. At one location, the seepage encountered a rich vein of uranium. In the presence of oxygen, uranium dissolves in water. So the trickle became enriched with this unusual element. Water also has the effect of slowing the neutrons thrown off by the uranium. Spinning at their usual high velocities, the neutrons would have just glanced off any atoms they might have encountered. But moderated by the water to a more sedate speed, the neutrons struck with exactly the right amount of force.

So it happened. One atom, wayward and mindless, rocked in its ordained orbit as its nucleus was smacked by a passing neutron. A positively charged proton, agitated by the crude jolt, moved ever so slightly aside, only to be quickly joined by another proton that had been similarly assaulted. Repelled by their positive charges of electricity, they reeled apart and, like drunks staggering backwards, bumped into still more of their fellows, not to mention a horde of other neutrons. Excited by the possibilities of the situation, the neutrons sped away to look for more of this impact-and-collision action.

A balance so delicate as to be immeasurable was upset. The single wanton act of the wayward neutron caused the entire nucleus of the uranium atom to fly asunder. It released all its particles in a hot, infinitesimal flash of energy. Broken and homeless, their stable community destroyed, the remnants of the shattered atom flew outwards, propelled by their death thrust and doomed to flee until their velocity paled or they made contact with others of their kind. This nuclear imbalance became sufficiently large to ensure, on the basis of chance alone, that even more atoms would be affected.

The reaction flared. Like a sputtering damp match, it gained flaming intensity. An observer on a super-microscopic level would have seen giant suns collide, blaze brightly, then spin off, only to ram the suns of other universes. But the fragile flame caught. And a chain reaction started.

As the impacted splitting atoms released their energy, heat built up at an alarming rate. In the briefest possible time, the layers of uranium contained a fire without flame of enormous intensity. The molten mass spewed off huge amounts of radioactive materials into our young atmosphere as it charred its way deeper and deeper into the earth.

Extremely high temperatures instantly flashed the water into steam. While water slows neutrons, steam does not. So the faster-moving particles lost the ability to split atoms into their components. And the chain reaction was dampened.

This natural phenomenon occurred about 1.8 billion years ago. It happened on at least fifteen occasions in what is today a uranium mine called Oklo in the country of Gabon, situated on the Atlantic coast of central Africa. This is the only discovered instance of a completely natural, spontaneous nuclear reaction. It shows us atomic power is not a new or exclusively man-created phenomenon, not solely a product of our technology.

Eons passed after the last Oklo flare-up. Time makes little difference, as the earth abides. Then we did what nature had done before us. Only we made it explode. A bomb. Alamogordo, Hiroshima, Nagasaki, Atoms for Peace, then so many more nuclear events that people lost count. We tried to control in a decade what it took the entire history of man to decipher. In a way we failed. In a way we succeeded. But we still know little of the impact of what we wrought.

Born in wartime tumult and terror, our newest advance has problems that disturb even the most knowledgeable. But we are trying. And each year we come closer to a full understanding of a force beyond the fanciful dreams of the most imaginative alchemists and sorcerers. Through it all, we too abide. How well, is the question. And where it will lead us is the quandary.

The atom offers us an enormous source of energy, for which our global society has a voracious need. Our very comfortable lifestyles are dependent upon the consumption of massive amounts of low-cost power. None of us wants to give up conveniences that have become necessities. The average American has a quality of life in many ways better than what royalty enjoyed only a hundred or so years ago.

Our science has defined the nuclear force, contained it, and harnessed it to do our bidding. But there is still some question as to who is really in command. There is a glimpse of unseen fury in every atomic pile. We try to be careful, we try to be safe, and we try to plan for the contingencies that will be the certain result of our eventual mistake or failure. Even so, one fact is clear.

The production of any source of energy involves risks. Miners die digging coal. Roughnecks have fatal accidents in the oil fields. Refinery workers are killed every year. So it would be foolish not to believe there will be deaths stemming from nuclear activities. And there will be accidents that release radioactive materials into our environment. Scientists are concerned, politicians are concerned, civic leaders are concerned, and because of all the hubbub, the people are concerned. Sometimes. When they are directly affected.

An antinuclear group has appeared on the international scene singing songs of annihilation, holocaust, and the end of man. They are countered by the pronuclear army, which answers these claims of Armageddon with an "atomic power is as safe as a powder puff" philosophy.

Both extremes give telling arguments. Yet neither is entirely right. The tiny atom can provide us with needed energy and, in so doing, possesses a dangerous potential. But disaster does not have to be a certainty if we manage our affairs properly. And there is the key question: Have we done a good job of nuclear management?

One way to gain sufficient insight to judge is to take a close inside look at some of the atomic events and happenings that have caused headlines in the world's press. The stories to follow have a common moral, best summed up by an old engineering adage called Murphy's Law: "If it can break or go wrong, it will. At the worst possible time. And in such a fashion as to cause the worst consequences and make repair the most difficult." Murphy was an optimist.

Perhaps the most intriguing aspect of these major events that happened in our time is how few people remember them. This alone says something interesting about the society in which we live.

Has out-of-sight out-of-mind become a dominant feature of our twenty-first century culture? There is sound reason to argue this is the case. If so, the worldwide resurgence of nuclear power, and the resulting increase in publicity, can kindle old fears. Recounting our past mistakes may help us avoid repeating them.

ONE

The Afternoon the Bomb Fell on America

At dawn, the Strategic Air Command flight line was an eerie place. In that first gray light, flight lines looked much the same anywhere in the world. Low buildings formed a barrier along one edge of an endless expanse of concrete that served as taxiways, runways, aircraft parking areas, and service roads. The knife-edged wings of B-47s, standing one to a pad, threw savage shadows onto the pitted ground.

On this particular day, Tuesday, March 11, 1958, at Hunter Air Force Base outside Savannah, Georgia, those B-47s were the center of intense activity.

A blue truck, engine roaring, pulled alongside one of the droop-winged aircraft. Brakes squealed, and two uniformed men jumped out. They moved with practiced rapidity, connecting ground wires to prevent a spark of static electricity from igniting the JP-series fuel that would be pumped into the tanks. Both men were watchful and merely nodded to a passing Air Police guard, who marched by slowly, M-1 A-1 carbine slung over his shoulder.

A ground crew, servicing the plane, talked in low tones. There was tension in the air, a feeling of suppressed power and activity.

It was almost as if the noise and hurricane violence of a thousand jet engines had left an imprint of their sound and fury in the rough texture of the concrete.

The first of the spring warmth had brought some color to the southern soil, and it promised to be a fine day.

Down the flight line, in the area reserved for B-47s of the 308th Bomb Wing, the towering empennage of one of the huge aircraft bore the number 876.

The plane had been fueled, its systems checked, and a single nuclear bomb, called a "pig" by the airmen who worked on it, had been loaded under maximum security conditions. The Strategic Air Command was proud of its procedures. Each of its men felt a special responsibility. They knew together they formed the most powerful deterrent force in the history of the world. They were America's first line of defense and its most feared offense.

A mission was on. But that was nothing new. There was one every week. Training was a way of life in SAC. So much so that some men, fed up with the constant regimen, would ask to transfer out. As with membership in any elite, there were costs. But there were also compensations: Promotions came fast, and there was a feeling of belonging to the best.

The B-47 marked 876 was assigned to fly in a phase of Operation Snow Flurry. That was a curious name for a series of field maneuvers that would take the aircraft and its crew, along with others in the squadron, to one of four bases in North Africa. Like all SAC missions, this one would simulate combat conditions. The plane would fly in its optimum trim. The pig on board would be "live"—a real atomic bomb, not a dummy. Also according to SAC rules, a plug-like detonator, the single component needed to arm the weapon, would be on board in its locked safety container. Orders were not to insert the device and activate the warhead until a special code signal was given and acknowledged.

By 10:00 AM, 876 and her sister ships were pronounced ready. Paperwork, telling the condition of the aircraft, had been properly checked and initialed.

The mission briefing went well. Officers, wearing the bars-and-leaves insignia of lieutenants, captains, and majors on their olive-green flight suits, lolled in chairs. Casual postures belied the rapt attention they paid to the presentation of the many elements of their flight plans.

Meteorology: no problems over the Atlantic but some fine winds aloft. Navigation: checkpoints here, here, and here. Radio frequencies for both air-to-air and air-to-ground. Estimated times of departure and arrival. Maps. The assembled pilots and aircraft observers made detailed notes, checked watches, and turned the dials of their E6B circular slide rules to estimate fuel consumption. Rendezvous points: here and here. Abort instructions. God forbid anyone would have to abort and not fly the mission. SAC was hell on that, and somebody's head was certain to roll. But if it became necessary, in the mind of the aircraft commander, then the procedure would be as outlined.

An astounding amount of information was offered and absorbed. The officers, all pilots and air crew, sat through the session smoking cigars and making notes in their three-ring books. An occasional scuffing foot or squeaking chair distracted the listeners, but there was no conversation aside from a few whispered remarks when the final destination was revealed. In a row halfway back, Captain Earl Koehler paid particular attention.

At the end of the questions, the briefing closed, and the crews adjourned for a light lunch. Air crews who are going to spend endless hours in the air at high altitude eat carefully. Intestinal gas is not a joking matter at thirty-five thousand feet, and since there is not much room to stand in a B-47 cockpit, whoever gets it just has to sit on it. It may sound funny, but the pain can be severe.

After lunch a few of the married officers made short phone calls to their wives. They knew their destinations but were unable to reveal them. All they could indicate was roughly how long they might be away. This one looked like an extended trip.

Several modes of transportation were used to transfer the men to the flight line. A private automobile or two, which would be picked up later by someone with clearance, carried a few. Others used the blue-and-yellow shuttle bus out to the edge of the airpark, then took the flight line trolley to their ready room.

The crews began to form themselves into separate units as they took care of final departure details. Maps were folded; lunches and cans of CoCo Malt were packed in briefcases; flight helmets, visors, and oxygen masks were inspected; parachutes drawn; aircraft assignments taken; radio frequencies given a final check; and other minor problems attended to. The men's room did a steady business.

Then, almost as if there were no way to delay further, they straggled out into the bright afternoon sun in groups of two and three, chatting casually. After stowing a small mountain of equipment in the open car of the trolley, they clambered aboard. With a squealing jerk, they began rolling along the now-noisy and active flight line.

The small tractor pulling the open cars halted momentarily at each parking ramp, and at every stop, three green-suited men hurriedly jumped off, tugging at their gear. Finally, it pulled up in front of 876 and three officers, wearing the railroad-track double silver bars of captains, climbed out.

They stood a minute in the soft glare of the spring sun as the tractor engine gunned. With a lunging creak and a cloud of blue-white smoke, the vehicle rolled on down the endless line.

The three men acted with great precision. Gathering their leather bags, parachutes, flying helmets, survival packs, and other gear, they made their way across the warm concrete toward the silent plane. One captain carried a locked, marked briefcase containing go-code orders and actual targets.

A ground crewman, assigned to fire guard, stepped from the dark shadow under the nose of the ship. On the fuselage above his head, someone had painted a neatly lettered name, "City of Savannah." He saluted informally and presented the Form One, which the aircraft commander scanned. Folding the gray plastic cover back over the document, he tucked it under his arm.

The three captains continued on to the plane and started their walkaround inspection.

They moved slowly around the towering aluminum structure, checking the condition of rivets in the main spar of the wings, the cleanness of control surfaces, the dark recess of the nosewheel bay, and other vital signs that, to their experienced eyes, would tell clear tales about the anticipated reliability of the ship on its long flight.

Satisfied at last, the three loaded their gear, donned the harnesses locking them to their parachutes, and climbed into the belly of the ship.

The B-47 was not a spacious aircraft. Its vast size belied its interior room. Sophisticated systems did the jobs normally assigned to several air crewmen so three highly trained aviators could operate the massive six-engine bomber. In a quest for speed, it was built almost like a single-seat fighter. The aircraft commander and the pilot sat one behind the other under a Plexiglas bubble high up on the nose. The aircraft observer's station was below them in the belly of the fuselage.

There were the usual gruntings and squirmings as they settled themselves, completing hookups for oxygen and radio contact. The aircraft commander, Earl Koehler, tried the intercom. From his seat forward, he couldn't see the pilot, Charles Woodruff, who was strapped in directly behind him. "You read me, Charlie?"

"Ah, roger."

"You, Bruce?"

The aircraft observer paused in his task of setting out his maps and calculation devices. "Roger, Captain. Five by five."

The title of aircraft observer was a euphemism for the man whose job it would be to actually drop the bomb. It was revived from the last stages of World War I. In the three-man crew of the B-47, he was charged with navigation, acted as bombardier, and was also the electric countermeasures (ECM) officer operating the gear designed to foil enemy radar and prevent detection. The plane was much faster than existing fighter aircraft so it had no weapons facing forward. The ECM officer was also charged with control over the swiveling tail gun.

Captain Bruce Kulka usually had his hands full on a flight. On this one, he was really going to be busy because the mission was complex. As he worked over the maps and set his radios to assigned frequencies, he could hear the two pilots above him run through the checklist, an item at a time.

Finally the intercom crackled again. "You 'bout got it, Bruce?" The aircraft commander's voice had the flat sound of the Illinois farmland.

"Ah, yeah. I've about got it all set. You ready?" The intercom popped again.

The pilot, from his position forward and above the observer, could see the ground crewman holding up the safety pins used to secure the landing gear in the down position. The man held the long steel rods up, one at a time, so the crew on board could count them. The red streamers attached to the ends fluttered lightly in the breeze, making them look like banderillas used in a bullfight.

Woodruff was completing the before-starting checklist and Koehler raised the tower, testing the radio. The response came with the time and barometric pressure to be dialed into their altimeters.

The B-47 was an unusual airplane. Ungainly on the ground, it flew like a dream. As the first fully operational strategic jet bomber, it was still considered a major plane of the line even though the newer B-52s had more range and outright speed.

Sounds filled the small interior of the ship as the ground crew used the auxiliary starter to begin spinning the huge rotors in the port engines. As soon as they reached critical RPMs, they thundered into life. The starboard power plants followed.

From the outside, the droopy-winged aircraft sounded like two trains fighting a tug of war. Noise was muffled in the cockpit, however, and the pilot was conscious only of the thrust of the jets as they gulped huge quantities of fuel.

Jet aircraft are terribly inefficient in the dense atmosphere below ten thousand feet. Their engines, which depend on passing thousands of cubic yards of air through the gaping intakes, burn fuel at a prodigious rate during taxiing and takeoff, so things were planned to get them off the ground as quickly as possible after startup.

All down the flight line, engines fired and settled into their whistling roars. Ground crews pulled back, driving the portable generators at more-than-authorized speeds to get away from the noise and stench of burned fuel that shrouded the field. Heat waves shimmered from tailpipes of the now-rolling airplanes as they made their cumbersome way out onto the taxi ramps.

Inside the *City of Savannah*, Koehler ran his engines up and kept a close eye on the gauges indicating tailpipe temperature. Behind him, the pilot jiggled the control column to signify he had the ship under his guidance. Brakes off, it taxied forward.

Below, Kulka monitored the various transmissions requesting permission to taxi and lined up his first rendezvous points. He checked the press-to-test lights on the ECM control panel. All the carefully-thought-out devices, designed to ward off radar detection and send enemy missiles astray, indicated ready, so he reported this fact to the commander, who noted it on his checklist.

The B-47 was once described as a fuel tank with wings, a small bomb bay, and just enough room to tuck in three midgets to fly it. It doesn't sound comfortable, and basically, it wasn't. It took some getting used to. Every square inch of space around the crewmen was filled with gauges, switches, circuit breakers, plug-ins, and flight controls. There was enough room for a man about five foot, ten inches, with a sitting height under thirty-four inches, to stretch, slightly, before his head came into contact with the clear plastic canopy or the thin aluminum sheet covering the side armor plate. The seating position was limited, and while there was room to rotate the upper torso, in-flight gymnastics were pretty much out of the question.

Cleared for takeoff, the silver and gray bomber proceeded into position at the end of the main runway. The concrete strip stretched endlessly ahead, and even Koehler, in the front seat, could not see the end as anything but a brown line over a mile away. He exchanged comments with ground control, checked the tower frequency, and on command, started his takeoff roll. The oily smell of the cockpit became more pronounced as he opened the throttle.

Acceleration came slowly as the huge jet engines beat inertia and began to rotate faster and faster. Finally, at about the five-thousand-foot marker, the nose of the plane rotated upward, and with a shudder, the big ship broke clear of the runway. North Africa was more than six thousand long miles away.

———

Florence, South Carolina, was thought of throughout the country-side as a pretty big place. With a population of about thirty thousand, it was then the largest town between the capital, over in Columbia, and Fayetteville, up in North Carolina.

Florence was known to the people of the area for two things. First, it had at least one whorehouse. Generations of "good ol' boys" had driven in from Kingstree and Timmonsville and even from as far away as Darlington for an evening on the town—and then driven back, long past midnight, belching bourbon whiskey and filled with tales of their prowess in the squeaky, narrow beds.

Florence's second claim to fame was the railroad. In its large marshaling yards, several lines made up their trains. Major repairs were performed when needed on both engines and cars. And judging from the number of people employed by the various companies, the need was both frequent and pressing.

Working for the railroad had some rewarding side benefits. Since crews traveled across country, a man might be on duty for five days, then have a week off at home with his family. Saturdays and Sundays, normal periods of relaxation for most of America, might be spent on the road, forcing other weekdays to become family times. School schedules got altered for the children to take advantage of dad's layovers, and the people in the area made adjustments where needed.

Out from the main part of Florence, a few miles back in the piney woods, the land had a feeling of freshness. It looked, in many ways, about the same as when the English settlers first arrived. Far enough inland from the coastal plain to be a little hilly, the rolling terrain was green with the fresh growth of spring.

Many of the people who worked in Florence preferred to live away from the bustle of the noisy rail yards. Commuting was especially easy for the train men. Their hours were as erratic as their workdays, so they could travel on the roads while most people were asleep or at their jobs.

Mars Bluff wasn't so much a town as a place, about ten miles north of Florence. At one time, in years gone by, it was a general store and post office. Little had changed. But the land around the tiny settlement was now owned by people who were employed in the small city to the south. Not too much real farming was done anymore.

Walter Gregg, thirty-seven, married, a World War II paratrooper, was one of those landowners. As a conductor on the railroad, his comings and goings were dictated by the needs of the line. Bill, as his friends called him, made good money and was able to afford the comfortable, roomy gray-shingled house at the end of the short road from the main highway. He lived out where the living was good.

On March 11, 1958, Bill was at home with his wife, Ethel, working in a shed behind the main house. Walter, aged six, one of a pair of twins, was playing outside the open door. The other twin, Helen; his older daughter, Frances; and his niece, Ella Davies, were involved in a game.

It was a pleasant day, not particularly distinguishable from any other. Bill had a few jobs to do around the house. He and his wife, along with the kids, planned to cook out later. Their conversation would often focus on adding a swimming pool out back, toward the edge of the property. They had discussed it for some time.

Involved in his task, he didn't notice the sound from the engines of the B-47s. Flyovers were such a normal event, with the base being located as near as Savannah, that they no longer attracted much attention. Especially since number 876 had already attained over twelve thousand feet in its on-course climb. Bill Gregg softly whistled the opening bars of the latest Theresa Brewer hit as he reached for another tool on the workbench.

The visored pilot tilted his head slightly to include the altimeter in his scan. Now 13,500 feet. His eyes found the heading indicator.

On course. They shifted to the rate-of-climb instrument. He touched the trim-tab control on top of the stick with his thumb, and after a second's hesitation, saw the white needle inch up to five hundred feet per minute.

All this was done unconsciously. Every motion connected with flying the B-47 had been repeated so many times it was automatic. His mind was filled with early-mission fidgets. He was uncomfortable in his seat. The thought of the bologna sandwich and can of CoCo Malt in the box lunch made him grimace. He tried to relax. He was going to be in the saddle for hours.

Altimeter: 14,000. Air speed: 450 knots. Heading indicator: he corrected slightly; on course.

Suddenly he was jolted from his reverie. The sight of a bright red light on the console hit him like an electric shock. He triggered the radio intercom button on the mike with his left thumb, without removing his hand from the throttle.

"Charlie." There was no special emotion in his voice, but he was tense.

"Got it, Earl. Malfunction light on the bomb-lock circuit."

"Roger that."

Neither man appeared to hurry, but both worked quickly.

"Circuit breakers OK."

"Flip it in and out a couple of times."

"Did."

"OK. Bruce?"

"Roger?"

"Got a malfunction light on the bomb-lock circuit."

Kulka started wrestling with his shoulder harness. Removing it in the tight confines of the aircraft observer's cockpit was difficult. "I hear you. Want me to take a look?"

"Ah, yeah. Roger that."

"Gotcha. I'll be off intercom."

"Right." The aircraft commander's eyes scanned the panel with practiced ease. It now recorded 14,250 feet. Things had taken only a few seconds. The red light continued to glow brightly.

Bruce struggled free of his straps. Using his arms, he scooted himself back toward the narrow crawl way. The dimness of the interior of the B-47 made him pause until his eyes, accustomed to staring into the sharp light of his console, adjusted. Inching along in the confined space, he scrambled to the hatch, which opened easily. He squeezed through into the floodlighted bomb bay. In the place where he was standing, the Air Force–blue paint had chipped away, revealing yellow undercoating.

With the advent of the nuclear age, the bomb load had reduced itself to a single cylindrical unit of polished steel over one hundred inches long and about five feet in diameter. It hung, suspended above the fragile bomb-bay doors, from a single steel shackle attached to a main spar of the aircraft fuselage. In the bright light it looked like what it was—a gleaming seven-thousand-plus pound carefully machined weapon of total war.

Kulka paused for a minute. No matter how many times the ground crew tried to relieve tension by calling it the "pig" or the "ham hock," it always took a second to overcome the feeling of awe in its presence. The bomb seemed to radiate malevolence.

Working space in the bomb bay was tight, and he had to step with care so as not to place any of his weight onto the bomb-bay doors. Cautiously, he withdrew the stainless-steel safety-locking pin from its gray plastic case on the stanchion above the bomb. The shiny surface glittered in the single spotlight, and, holding an awkward stance, Kulka sought the narrow hole with its tip. Once inserted through the shackle, the pin would hold the weight of the weapon even if the electric locks failed.

He was working at arm's length, above the level of the bomb's body, when he first noticed a slight shift of the long steel canister.

It was a sort of wobble along the main axis. The pig, which should have been statically secured, was rocking.

Realizing something was desperately wrong, he fished frantically for the insertion hole of the mechanical lock. He changed position, and holding on to a perforated stanchion with one hand, leaned further forward.

There was a metallic "snick" clearly audible over the flight noises of the still-climbing airplane. Then, with a click as the electrical locks failed and the shackle opened, the bomb suddenly fell free.

Horrified, Kulka watched as the weapon struck the thin bomb-bay doors. It paused, then its weight and inertia overcame the door locks and they burst open, freeing the weapon into the blindingly bright blue sky below.

It disappeared from the astonished captain's eyes in an instant, and before he could react he was fighting for his life. The pressure from air rushing over the skin of the aircraft at speeds close to five hundred miles per hour was tremendous. The gaping bomb-bay doors allowed the maniacal force to whip into the small space where Bruce Kulka was standing. A hurricane wind tore at him with unbelievable power, trying to suck him out into space. Instinctively, he'd gripped the stanchion next to his body when the bomb started to fall, and now, standing in the midst of the screeching maelstrom, it was all he could do to hang on. Slowly, an inch at a time, he pulled himself back toward the manual bomb-bay-door control-switch console where he fought against the blast as he wrestled with the safety latch.

In the flight cabin the aircraft commander, who had been watching the red light indicating problems with the electrical bomb lock, twitched slightly. The plane bounced, and a second light, showing a malfunction with the bomb-bay doors, glared ominously.

"What th—?" He started to speak into the intercom to the pilot behind him, then stopped as the plane gave another lurch. This time the sensation was more familiar. "Charlie, did you feel that?"

"Roger. Like a shockwave radiating up from the ground."

There was a long silence, and the two men stared at the lights, flying by reflex.

It took most of Kulka's strength to hold on near the manual bomb-bay-door activator switch. Prayerfully, he cycled the control. The doors drew closed, shutting out the screaming wildness. Stepping with caution, he crossed the narrow space to the exit hatch and squeezed through into the confined tunnel on the other side. The silence after the mad noise of howling wind made the normal sounds of flight ring in his ears. He sat for a long moment, catching his breath, then headed slowly back to the crew stations.

"Earl."

The aircraft commander, startled at hearing a voice close behind him, turned in his seat. He wiggled the controls in the age-old pilot's signal. "You've got the aircraft, Charlie." Koehler looked at Kulka.

"The bomb. It broke loose."

There was a long silence. "Oh, my God." Koehler reached for the radio channel selector and dialed in a predetermined three-digit code. His voice was calm as he spoke, "This is Garfield 13. Aborting the mission. Repeat. Garfield 13. Aborting mission."

The sound of Bill Gregg's whistling was imitated, lightly, in the air high above the house, as the bomb, descending with the streamlined precision intended by its designers, gathered momentum.

On the ground, Gregg first heard a far-off whine. The whistle died on his lips. The noise grew louder, intensifying into a shrill, piercing scream. Seconds before the note attained its final crescendo, Bill's son shouted to his father, who quickly scanned the sky.

A sudden shockwave, pushing quickly ahead of the rumble of the blast, struck with the intensity of a tornado. Timbers flew out and knocked Bill off his feet. The children were tumbled down as if playing some game of their own devising. The house, subjected to immense forces, gave up its structural integrity. Wallboard, plaster, splintered wood, and dust mixed with flying glass to fill the air with lethal shrapnel. The roar of the blast, arriving in its own good time, battered the ears of the fallen people and covered the lesser sounds of destruction.

The shockwave pressed onward and out. Cars on a nearby road were thrown off course and spun around. The Mount Mizpah Baptist Church was twisted by the force. Homes as far as a half mile away were damaged. A new landmark had appeared in the peaceful countryside. A crater about thirty feet deep and more than seventy feet across had been created out of the muddy ground. Tendrils of steam curled up from the wet black sides. Trees in the surrounding area were stripped of their limbs or knocked flat.

According to Gregg, "It blew out the side and top of the garage just as my boy ran inside with me. The timbers were falling around us. There was a green, foggy haze, then a cloud of black smoke. It lasted about thirty seconds. When it cleared up, I looked at the house. The top was blown in and a side almost blown off." The screams and sobbing of the frightened, bleeding children were counterpoint to the jumble and confusion of broken furniture, debris, and tumbled interior fixtures thrown out by the blast.

Gregg was shaken but able to see clearly. "I saw the other children on the other side of the house. About a hundred yards from where the bomb hit."

It was some time before a complete inventory of damage could be taken. At McLeod Hospital in Florence, all the children but one were found to have only minor physical injuries, mostly cuts and scrapes. The visiting niece required a total of thirty-one stitches to close the slice on her forehead. Miraculously, none of the adults was seriously hurt. But the house was a total loss.

The bomb had landed and, according to plan, the chemical "trigger" designed to set off the nuclear warhead had exploded with the power of several hundred pounds of TNT.

But the atomic portion of the device, locked into its safety mode, did not ignite. The components of the weapon were vaporized by the intense heat of the chemical explosion, throwing a wide ring of radioactive contamination around ground zero. This was the only nuclear consequence.

Reaction was immediate. As soon as the B-47 landed, its crew was rushed into a nightlong debriefing. An experienced air force public relations team swung into action to handle press matters on a local, state, and national basis. A special disaster crew was formed and ordered into the stricken town under the personal direction of Maj. Gen. Charles B. Dougher, commander of the 38th Air Division at Hunter.

The first step was to close the area to curiosity seekers and souvenir seekers. Even though the nuclear portion of the bomb had been destroyed by the heat of the explosion, radioactive material had been blasted outward from the crater's center and presented a potential threat.

Careful monitoring and a complete physical check of each member of the Gregg family indicated they had suffered no radiation exposure. A radiological group headed by Major Jack Wilt was dispatched to the crater, and it began a "mopping up" operation within hours of the original blast.

Exhibiting true concern for the stricken family, an air force colonel was sent to the hospital. Years later, the only badly injured member of the group, the young cousin, recalled the visitor rather fondly because he brought her ice cream and talked for a while.

The incident gained immediate attention in the press. The Florence paper reported the situation in a strictly local context, including comments by the mayor. Nationally, headlines blared notice of the event and stories were aided by an official air force release that gave scant details but offered assurances there had been absolutely no danger of an atomic explosion. The foreign press went wild.

In England and other NATO countries, where flights by manned, atomic-armed B-47s were as common as they were in this country, comments became bitter. War and its destruction were still fresh in their memories, and they wanted no part of such potential disaster.

The British were especially vocal in their opposition to continued flights over their country by U.S. military planes carrying nuclear armaments. The House of Commons went into full debate, and both the Labor Party and the Trades Union Congress came up with demands to halt all such missions.

Italy, Greece, Holland, India, and other nations, according to their press, remained somewhat cooler than their British neighbors, but obviously no one was delighted by the idea of the now-proven possibility of an accident.

The Soviets, acting quickly to capitalize on the situation, launched a propaganda program using radio as well as print. Their theme, designed to maximize the seriousness of the incident, centered on a single concept. The accidental dropping of nuclear bombs could well lead to the issuance of an attack order by "some irresponsible official," who would choose to blame the Soviets for the error rather than admit his own mistake. Their theme even offered a cure. "From all this, we can draw only one conclusion," one of their commentators said in a Greek-language broadcast. "An end must be put to flights of aircraft with nuclear weapons. The flights," he went on, "threaten the life of many men and they create a danger for peace all the world over."

The reaction in the United States, however, was pretty much business as usual.

In Florence, the mayor, David McLeod, speaking at an open forum attended by air force dignitaries, said, "We all realize that we live in periled times, and our nation must be prepared to defend itself at a moment's notice. There are dangers in such defense, and this is one of the dangers."

Neil McElroy, then–secretary of defense, also spoke of the risks of our age. "I can only say these are perilous times and that as a part of our security measures, strategic bombers are on twenty-four-hour training. It was one of these bombers that accidentally, due to mechanical malfunction, dropped an unarmed nuclear device near the city of Florence."

Gregg himself, after being assured the government would cover his loss, also placed a bright note on the incident. "I always wanted a swimming pool," he said, "and now I've got the hole for one at no cost. I may open it to the public. Charge them for swimming in uranium-enriched waters."

The air force acted as fast as possible with the hearings, and they immediately ordered all planes equipped with nuclear bombs to manually and positively "lock in" their weapons while on practice combat runs.

Within seventy-two hours, radioactive materials had been scoured from the crater and all surrounding terrain had been checked and declared free of contamination. A few days later, Col. William Byers arrived in his role as damage claims officer. To support the payment process, a congressman, John L. McMillan, entered a bill exempting the Gregg family from the federal law that restricted claims to $1,000.

This point brings up an interesting quandary. What if the bill had never been introduced or had failed to pass? Would Gregg's total compensation have been fought on the basis of a maximum

$1,000 loss reimbursement? This is a question that still affects us today.

Within the same week it took for Col. Byers to arrive to handle financial matters, the press had forgotten the incident and gone on to other news. It was all over but the actual payments needed for final settlement, which required a full two years to complete. The $50,000-plus finally received by Gregg was far less than the amount for which he had asked, but with Mrs. Gregg in a state of near collapse, the family took the cash but maintained some degree of bitterness. Many years later, the bad feelings remained.

"That bomb came within fifty yards of wiping out my whole family," Gregg was quoted as saying. He also kept his wife and children away from visiting reporters, sending them inside their new house when photographers came around.

Among the statements made at the time by apparently responsible people, some are remarkable in retrospect.

South Carolina congressman John J. Riley of the Second District said the bomb dropping was "something that wouldn't happen again in a million flights." The congressman was probably unaware that the military was still searching for a nuclear bomb jettisoned at sea off Savannah Beach, Georgia, when a B-47 collided with a jet fighter at thirty-five thousand feet only a month before. Or the May 22, 1957, accident in which a B-36 lost a pig while flying over a New Mexico desert.

In the final analysis, the incident boiled down to this: Mistakes can and do happen. The best we can hope is that most systems will work properly and be operated by individuals with personal integrity who will exercise all possible caution.

The score this time?

One safety precaution worked; the atomic portion of the weapon did not explode. But one "foolproof" device failed and the bomb was released.

After the hubbub quieted down and the air force completed its investigation, additional safeguards were developed. Everyone shrugged, and things returned to normal. More or less.

TWO

Military Nuclear Incidents

The Mars Bluff incident, if an atomic bomb falling into someone's backyard can be relegated to the category of a mere incident, is far from the only case of an accidentally dropped or lost nuclear weapon.

Since February 1950, when the world's first nuclear weapons accident occurred, through 2006, there have been dozens of documented instances of American military-related atomic problems. These range from the complete disappearance of a B-47 carrying two nuclear weapons while on a mission over the Mediterranean Sea to a B-52 crash near Thule Air Force Base in Greenland, which scattered fragments of three hydrogen bombs on the ground and dumped one into the sea.

Adding in the nuclear accidents incurred by the military of various nations, problems aboard nuclear vessels, missile mishaps, atomic weapons testing, and other related armed forces situations, the number is far, far larger. No accurate count can be made because the tabulations are hidden behind veils of national secrecy.

The Soviets, propagandizing about Mars Bluff, raised an interesting point. Could we be launched into a nuclear exchange because of the accidental detonation of a lost weapon? It's a possibility our side has considered at some length. In a classified study, this scenario was given serious attention. The conclusion? There might well be, at some time in the life of our republic, a leader with a sufficiently severe sense of insecurity to allow escalation of hostile events rather than accept responsibility for the accidental destruction of several square miles of populated land. Strong safeguards have been taken against this possibility. The go/no-go system that allows for the arming of our operational nuclear warheads is elaborate—and as fail-safe as man can make it.

So the chance of an unintentional or mistakenly started atomic war is almost nil. The word "almost" is troublesome, but as the mayor of Mars Bluff said, we live in periled times.

Even the best systems, however, are subject to failure. Often it is the ingenuity and quick thinking of the servicemen and women involved that prevents a disaster. Examples of resourcefulness include parking an armored vehicle on top of a Minuteman III intercontinental ballistic missile silo at Warren Air Force Base near Cheyenne, Wyoming, which stopped an actual launch caused by a computer glitch. Then there was the alarm bell that dispatched pilots to their nuclear-armed aircraft during the Cuban missile crisis. That audio alert meant a real shooting war with the Soviet Union had begun. The mistake was caught by the command center in time to abort the jets' take-off.

The air force is not alone, as a military branch, in having problems. The army, for example, has had a number of mishaps with its tactical atomic artillery warheads. These devices, although smaller in size and lesser in power than the strategic bombs, represent a considerable explosive force.

One incident concerned a private first class who, through a series of misunderstandings, was called upon during a European maneuver involving NATO forces to direct from a zone headquarters the movement and deployment of atomic artillery.

By his own admission, the man, whose security clearance was limited to "rumor" status, was responsible for the issuance of orders for the placement and simulated firing of nuclear field artillery shells on a several-hundred-mile front.

American forces engaged in the operation carried live atomic warheads. When the private was found to have no clearance for this activity, the officer in command dealt with the situation in traditional army style. He marched the enlisted man down to the proper authorities and ordered, in a loud but somewhat shaken voice, a temporary "Top Secret" classification. His demand was complied with at once.

The navy, more deeply involved than the other services in nuclear energy, has special difficulties. All the military now rely on atomic warheads to an extent far greater than imagined by the public. The navy, in addition to bombs, artillery warheads, torpedoes, and other explosive devices of various sizes, also has nuclear-powered vessels. According to recent reports, a certain amount of casualness in the operation of these ships and boats has occurred, leading to potentially dangerous situations.

The *Norfolk Virginian-Pilot* newspaper reported several crewmen from the U.S.S. *California*, a nuclear cruiser, who cited abuses including the falsification of atomic data to impress inspectors and overt acts of sabotage or negligence. Examples offered included an incident in which someone tampered with a saltwater condenser, a situation where cereal was tossed into a steam generator, and a crew game where one man playfully squirted another with a squeeze bottle full of reactor coolant water while shouting, "You're contaminated." Drug abuse poses another singular dilemma. One entire submarine crew was reassigned because of this problem. The seriousness of these breaches at sea is nothing compared with the potential threat they pose in the crowded confines of a major port.

The armed services of all atomic nations create a special difficulty because of the large numbers of devices in their stockpiles.

As of July 1, 2005, the United States is credited with having 1,225 strategic nuclear delivery vehicles, including 550 land-based intercontinental ballistic missiles (ICBMs), 432 submarine-launched ballistic missiles (SLBMs), and 243 active bombers. We can deliver 5,966 independently targeted nuclear warheads.

Best estimates of the Russian capability, also as of July 1, 2005, indicate they have 955 delivery systems: 585 ICBMs, 292 SLBMs, and 78 strategic bombers. The delivery vehicles have about a 4,380 nuclear warhead capability.

But the ten-thousand-plus strategic devices are only a small portion of the arsenal. Between the U.S. and Russian armed forces, there are a large number of tactical weapons. Many of these smaller units pack more power than the original bomb that destroyed Hiroshima. All together, among the total number of countries known to have atomic explosive devices for military use, there are well over sixteen thousand warheads of all types. And a significant portion of them are on "ready" or alert each day.

Those numbers are substantially lower than in the 1970s. And the safety record in handling this assorted weaponry has been adequate. No known incident has caused a disaster.

Still, some accident descriptions defy the imagination. A mobile, land-based United States Corporal missile, fully armed with a live nuclear warhead, was reported to have "rolled off a truck into the Tennessee River." A heavy salvage job was needed to retrieve it.

There is also disaster potential in any further proliferation of atomic weapons—or from the expanding base of individuals trained to use such weaponry. It would be difficult to estimate the number of Russians and Americans who have been taught to operate nuclear reactors or detonate atomic warheads.

Military use places another problem before us. There is no holiday from warfare. Once engaged, convenient stopping points cannot be decreed. The likelihood of combat or precombat pressures placing a strain on the maintenance schedule, say, of an atomic pile, is a real possibility.

It is interesting to note that the only U.S. reactor ever to attain critical mass and explode was one of a military design, intended for a military mission. The SL-1, located in Idaho Falls, Idaho, had been giving trouble for a couple of months. Then, on the evening of January 3, 1961, while being attended by three service-trained maintenance operators, it went off. In less than a single unguarded second, atomic piles can increase their energy output a billionfold, resulting in a possible explosion from trapped steam or a rapid release of highly radioactive material into the atmosphere. SL-1 did this. The three men died.

During times of war, all equipment is called upon to perform at the absolute limits of its reliability. And on many occasions, when the need is great, history shows us almost miraclelike instances when machines were driven beyond reasonable stopping points. In all probability, a field commander, somewhere, sometime, will have to call on his nuclear staff for more than they believe they are capable of delivering. But this time, if they fail, or if there is a malfunction, or if the weapon won't stand the extra stress, the results will be drastic.

Military planning takes this concept into consideration and sets specific limits on the use of atomic apparatus. But rules are broken every day by people with less reason than a hard-pressed or besieged general officer who is responsible for the lives under his command.

Likewise, there is no development program sufficiently rapid to deliver new weaponry at a rate fast enough to satisfy a military force engaged in an armed confrontation. Even the requirements by a government for defense preparedness can place time constraints on a project that result in too much being attempted too soon.

It was just such a situation that caused what may possibly be one of the worst man-made disasters in the history of the world.

THREE

Ural Mountains Catastrophes

In the days following April 25, 1986, the news media focused global attention on the horrendous situation at Chernobyl. The event was called the world's worst nuclear reactor accident.

It was. But that didn't make it the worst nuclear disaster of any kind. When that happened, there was no press coverage. In the halcyon days of the Union of Soviet Socialist Republics, tight governmental control over all sources of information was an accepted fact, which allowed unfortunate incidents to be completely hidden. What had taken place, along with the extent of damage, remained a guarded secret.

The events, which occurred over several years, reached a climax on September 29, 1957. Collectively, they give an entirely new meaning to the concept of atomic havoc. Few outside of Russia were even aware that the series of catastrophic nuclear incidents had taken place.

The first public indication of the disaster came under a somewhat suspect circumstance. A dissident Russian scientist, allied with the community of exiled Soviet scientists, arrived in London, England.

In his field, Zhores Medvedev was considered to be a first-class geneticist. While outlining the growth of genetics-related fields of study in Russia, he mentioned the impetus given to the science and the new importance placed upon it by that government. The cause of this greater interest? A nuclear accident.

His statement drew immediate attention. When asked to amplify his comments, the researcher obliged. He described what he believed caused the catastrophe. And he offered his assessment of the magnitude of the damage.

The possibility that there was a motive behind Medvedev's revelations arose when he was shown to have close ties to an English scientific group. That group had expressed strong opposition to a plan for the establishment of a shallow nuclear waste disposal/burial area in the northeastern part of the British Isles.

Shallow burial of nuclear wastes, mostly from power plants and breeder facilities but with some spillover from plutonium production centers, had been a subject of scientific debate for many years. One side maintained low-activity wastes could be safely trenched underground at depths of several feet. The opposing camp, with many references and experiments to the contrary, held that shallow burial was asking for long-term trouble. They felt the only successful disposal method was super-deep bedrock burial or special container dumping in the depths of the deepest oceans.

Since a material with a several-thousand-year half-life is at least a part of what is being disposed of in these centers, it's a little hard to come back to correct any mistakes, although a few centuries are barely enough time to determine if an error was made in the first place.

Medvedev's alliance with the anti-shallow-burial group cast doubt on his story because, coincidentally or not, it was this same shallow burial he blamed for the Soviet mishap.

The pro-shallow-burial group dismissed his references to the disaster with great disdain. Chairman of the United Kingdom

Atomic Energy Authority, Sir John Hill, called the argument against shallow burial "rubbish." He maintained the type of low-activity waste being buried "could not possibly give that sort of explosion." He also stated that the commission, which was in close touch with its counterpart inside Russia, had never even heard a suggestion of such a happening. He felt, therefore, that the report was inaccurate or incorrect.

The story would have died out had it not been for a second scientist, Leo Tumerman of Israel, who suddenly came forward. Tumerman maintained he had actually driven through a devastated area in the Ural Mountains.

His comments more or less agreed with Medvedev's, but he attributed the damage to a different cause. According to Tumerman, faulty reactor cooling at a manufacturing plant located in an atomic weapons arsenal resulted in an explosion. He did not rule out the possibility that the accident might have stemmed from storage of waste matter, but seemed more inclined to a reactor failure.

Additional controversy came from a report in the *Los Angeles Times* in November 1976, in which two unidentified but separate intelligence sources were given. Both reported a 1957 or early 1958 accident as having been caused by an out-of-control plutonium production reactor in a nuclear weapons complex several hundred miles northeast of the Caspian Sea near the southernmost Ural Mountains.

News of this disastrous event, it seems, had been leaked across to U.S. intelligence sources for nearly two decades. But there was no way to obtain formal confirmation or denial.

According to the *Times,* our top-secret radiation sensors detected the incident shortly after its occurrence. The knowledge was classified and kept secret to avoid showing the Soviets the sensitivity of our atomic detection systems. Decades later, on learning through the Freedom of Information Act that the CIA had satellite intelligence revealing the disaster, antinuclear groups claimed the facts were suppressed as an aid to the nuclear industry in America.

One incident cited by the CIA was an explosion at the radioactive materials plant located in the restricted area of Kyshtym, which was devoted to atomic research. A reactor at Techa and a radiological institute at Sungul combined with the processing facility to make the Kyshtym zone one of the major nuclear centers of the world. After the blast, stores selling milk and other produce closed, and people existed in a state of raw panic from fear of radiation effects.

Another report held there was a severe blowup of an atomic nature that had strength enough to "shake the ground." Trees and other vegetation died following this event.

Today, newly available facts indicate that a series of events, each a disaster of noteworthy magnitude, occurred in a brief period of years. While it is difficult to judge which was the most horrific, the 1957 incident immediately killed the most people. Taken together, since they all involved a single Soviet nuclear facility, they make up the worst atomic disaster in history.

The mystery of what really happened was finally solved during the summer of 1989 when scientists, along with American reporters and three members of the U.S. Congress, were invited to the Soviet Kyshtym plutonium production facility as part of ongoing arms control negotiations.

Between 1945 and 1948, a huge plutonium processing facility had been constructed by the Soviet government to make nuclear weapons. Five reactors were built and placed into operation. Called Chelyabinsk-40, it was one of the best-kept Russian secrets.

Trouble had plagued this site since its inception. One reactor, with its pile constructed of graphite, had generated and contained enormous amounts of heat. During one period of operation, a critical point was reached, then exceeded, resulting in a skyward-booming rush of incandescent gases. This radioactive flare caused the deaths of several workers inside the installation compound. It also released lethal amounts of radiation high into the atmosphere where it was tracked by U.S. air-sampling planes patrolling the Soviet borders. People in a nearby settlement were exposed to damaging amounts of alpha and gamma particles. Illness and death followed.

The reactor itself was so radioactive it was useless. Contamination levels were such that no humans could safely linger in the area. Rebuilding the facility was out of the question. Annoyed at the loss of the unit, which had to be covered over by such a huge amount of dirt it resembled one of the Ural foothills along the distant horizon, Soviet scientists learned what they could from their mistake. Then they plunged ahead into construction of a new and improved plutonium producer at an adjacent site.

From this location, between 1948 and 1956, a massive amount of radioactive waste was dumped into the Techa River. Some estimates hold that over one hundred thousand people were exposed to various levels of radiation. This disposal method was halted when radiation was detected flowing into Arctic waters.

Other waste was pumped into various lakes in Siberia. During an unusually hot summer, one lake dried up and storm winds scattered radioactive dust over a massive area.

The harm from those incidents should not be taken lightly. But the seriousness pales when compared with two other far more devastating occurrences.

———

The first event may well have been the source for Medvedev's statements in England.

Blagoveshchensk is a settlement located on the European side of the Urals. Life in the little community had continued without change for hundreds of years. Wars and czars came and went. The village was too small to be fought over, too insignificant to be included in anything other than a cursory political list, and too unimportant to be considered for any projects of consequence.

All that changed one day in the early 1950s. Accord had been reached on the use of shallow burial techniques as one way of disposing of low-level wastes. The next question was where to build a disposal site. An ideal location had to pass two tests.

First, it should be in geographical proximity to the reactor. Not too close, because the earlier incident had shown the wisdom of dispersing assets far enough apart so that damage to one would not cause abandonment of others. But not too far either, allowing for easy transport of the radioactive materials.

Second, it had to be in a sparsely settled area, yet near some existing town where labor could be found and the disposal experts housed while quarters were constructed on the burial site.

Detailed maps were studied, and Blagoveshchensk was selected. The location fit both requirements. The people of Blagoveshchensk neither knew of its coming nor cared. The dump compound was far enough away, as long as the strangers kept to themselves, to ensure the villagers' traditional tranquility.

For the first disposal activity, a large trench about ten meters deep was scratched into the earth by a special machine. Then an underground tank was constructed out of steel and concrete. This was filled with hot debris, then covered over by a bladed bulldozer. Ground surface readings were taken. No indication of leaking radiation was found, so the burial depth was deemed to be sufficient.

In the 1950s, Soviet engineering tended to depend more on the empirical result of actual tests as opposed to theory. Once the technique seemed to prove itself, the trucks really began to roll in. Hot waste, which had been temporarily stored, was sorted out and allotted for immediate disposal. Eagerness to use the new facility caused carelessness. Not all the matter was of the specified low grade. Since the plant had been jammed with waste containers for some months prior to the opening of the burial site, a certain amount of transuranic and extremely hot matter got mixed in with the original low-level materials.

The expanding nuclear weapons operation was producing a great deal of throw-off and demand for immediate removal and disposal was constant. Winter or summer, through snow or clear weather, the trucks continued to roll, using the old main highway and network of newly constructed roads to service the run between the Chelyabinsk-40 installation and the dump.

Monitoring at the burial site must have produced strong indications that some of the arriving waste was too highly radioactive to be casually interred along with the lower-risk materials. If objections were made, they were ignored. Everyone was acting under a time schedule that would permit no significant delays. The government wanted no excuses. The plutonium facilities ran on a twenty-four-hour basis, producing the strategic material day and night, and waste disposal problems increased in direct proportion to manufacturing efforts.

Trucks came and went. The deep snows of winter covered older burial mounds but new trenches were visible as precise black grooves in the whiteness of the blanketing ice.

Site monitoring continued on a regular basis with careful notes taken of the condition of every disposal location, from the original ditch to the newest in the geometrically placed series.

Haste meant progressively less and less care being exercised in the selection of the various levels of radioactive wastes included for burial. Even the trained scientific staff made poor decisions. As in the United States, real understanding of the potential danger of the debris from plutonium production was lacking. Everyone knew it was hazardous, but the material just didn't seem so menacing.

A couple of minor incidents developed among the unskilled workers due to their lack of knowledge about nuclear contamination. These came to little: minor burns and the need for long, hard scrubs in the showers augmented by light medication.

A year passed. Then two.

The original burial site, where the initial consignment of hot material had been covered over according to the best available knowledge at the time, began to generate critical amounts of heat. Measurement sensors noted a temperature buildup, but the coldness of the winter days, together with a growing nonchalance on the part of the technical staff, combined to dull their minds to the seriousness of the information.

The end came with frightful suddenness. On an overcast afternoon, with a minimum of noise, the original trenching site simply shook itself awake and, with a single release, spewed radioactive gas and earth up into the sky in a kind of nuclear belch.

What had happened was as simple as it was devastating: The high-level and transuranic wastes, which had been carelessly mixed into the low-level matter destined for burial disposal, had reached a point of critical mass. The ability of the various materials to interact was known to be so great that during production, enriched uranium might be placed in trays side by side, but never stacked one on top of the other.

The result of this unintentional and ignorant mixing of hot materials was a chain reaction resulting in enough heat to actually melt and vaporize the frozen earth. The containment ditch had been close to this crucial point for days, perhaps even months. Then the single, final nucleus was shaken apart by the invisible bombardment, and the mass became instantly unstable.

There was no explosion in the traditional sense of the word. The ground shook but a loud blast was missing. With more a rumble than a bang, it erupted "like a kind of a volcano" and shot virulent radioactive gas and debris into the air.

As was normal, a wind was blowing from the still plains toward the frozen heights of the Urals. This time, though, instead of bringing dust or droplets of rain in towering thunderclouds, it picked up the particles of the spewing nuclear waste and spread it along a narrow corridor.

It took over an hour for the first of the deadly material to reach the edge of the village of Blagoveshchensk some twelve kilometers away.

At the dump installation, personnel were in near panic. All scintillation counters indicated such high readings there was no way to approach the still-steaming burial trench. Almost everyone on the staff had received doses of sufficient strength to turn the film in their personal radiation detectors black. Telephone calls rattled at emergency speed up and down the wires to both the plutonium reactor plant and the seat of science in Moscow. Indecision due to surprise and disbelief was rampant.

The wind continued to blow over the area and pick up additional emittants. Not as deadly as the first releases, they were nonetheless damaging to humans and continued to spread at a steady rate.

In the settlement, there was no sign of anything amiss. Villagers moved around outside their houses, going about their business as usual. The air looked no different, felt no different, and smelled no different.

But each breath they took contaminated their systems.

The breeze passed on, and as the radioactive materials sailed along, the natural currents of wind dispersed the dust and vapor over a larger and larger swath of land. One by one, other villages in the surrounding area were engulfed by the lethal atmosphere.

Instructions finally came to the dump site. The open trench must be covered over by a large mound of dirt taken from the emergency pile that formed a huge mountain near the center of the installation.

Brave men, some of whom realized they had already faced a life-threatening dosage of radiation, sprang into action. Trucks, backed by bulldozers with huge ten-foot blades, started to work. In a matter of hours the open trench was capped and the release of the pollutants into the atmosphere halted.

The seriousness of what had happened was not immediately evident to the scientific community. News of the remarkable event was contained within the bounds of a narrow group. Geneticists and other specialists of different technological backgrounds received no information on the disaster. Secret debates over possible courses of action considered the next steps. The outcome was an order to send field investigating teams into the countryside to determine the extent of radiation fallout.

Organization of these survey crews took days. No previous thought had been given to the need for such units outside the wire-fenced compounds where radioactive materials were regularly handled and stored. No one had anticipated a disaster requiring the study of several hundred square miles of land.

Before the first crews were in the field, early symptoms of radiation sickness had struck the less physically fit. Preliminary signs—nausea, vague malaise, and headaches—would be followed by more ominous physical indicators in a matter of days.

The dump site itself was closed. Studies of the buildings and equipment made by the technical staff assigned to the burial center indicated that the zone was far too hot for human habitation. Vans were outfitted to carry exposed patients without danger of contamination to the drivers, and the station was vacated.

The plutonium reactor operation, faced with no disposal area, was forced to curtail its output, and more time was expended on devising interim ways of handling low-level wastes to meet production goals. Failure in this activity, which was watched by the highest governmental sources as well as the military, could result in the early termination or ruination of a promising career. A massive water-cooled storage tank was constructed to hold thousands of tons of dissolved nuclear waste.

Informed members of the Soviet hierarchy took an expedient view of the matter. What was done was done. The important thing was to salvage the reputation of Soviet science. No word of the disaster must leak out. Until the field survey was complete and a real understanding of the seriousness of the incident had been obtained, no one should take any action at all.

Over a few days, nuclear dust and debris settled from the air. In places where the wind had formed eddies, concentrations were high enough to cause serious injury to animals and humans.

Survey teams were astonished at the levels of radiation they found. Exposed ground, water in wells, snowdrifts on the back sides of hills and hummocks, building walls, and the people themselves—not known for their propensity to bathe during the long, dark winter months—were contaminated sufficiently to cause occasional off-scale readings. The devastation was complete.

High scientific and governmental circles were now faced with a vexing problem. Medical aid could be sent in for only short periods of time. Inhabitants of the drift area could not be evacuated en masse without causing the situation to become noticeable.

Sickness had already set in. To prevent individuals from leaving or running away before a decision was made, checkpoints on the only roads through and around the perimeter were established. Guards were instructed to be humane but firm to contain the residents in the area. All outside traffic was halted. Even cars intending merely to pass through were rerouted. The pretext was a scientific experiment supposedly in progress.

Experts in radiation therapy were called upon to give their best opinions about the potential injury suffered by individuals in the disaster zone. Many specialists had questions put to them as if the problem were only theoretical. They did not realize they were ruling in a life-or-death matter.

Coldly objective again, the government decided to set up health centers for the least exposed individuals in the areas inside the zone where radiation was at its lowest. These field hospitals could house and treat those with non-lethal doses. Construction of large medical facilities was rejected because an installation might lead to speculation about a problem.

For the less fortunate, two solutions were accepted. The first, which covered the village of Blagoveshchensk and others in the area of highest contamination, was to cut off all communication to the outside world. Then events were allowed to take their course. Massive relocation was out of the question due to the need for secrecy. Besides, the damage had already been done. Measures were being taken to examine and more closely monitor the other shallow burial trenches. There was no reason to needlessly alarm the populace concerning an event that would never occur again.

In short, government policy dictated that the people exposed to the heaviest dosages of radiation be left to live or die. Some medical aid would be offered, but no one could be moved. It would be far better for the event to appear as if it had been caused by some unknown and powerful epidemic than for the truth to leak out. Besides, observation would provide valuable information on the effects of high-dosage radiation exposure among humans.

Weeks passed. Daily monitoring of the area, done surreptitiously, indicated no decline in the number of hot spots or their relative strengths. The entire countryside was deadly if a person remained inside its perimeter for a sufficient length of time.

The members of the medical staffs who were treating the less severely injured were rotated, and their number was cut to an absolute minimum. As patients at the small treatment centers recovered, they were transported away from their traditional homes and relocated in nearby large cities. Some were given jobs. Others, too ill to work, were placed on the state rolls. They had all been told the same story. They were the fortunate ones. What had caused the illness was unknown, but they were the sole survivors of a pestilence that made the Black Death of the Middle Ages look like the common cold. The disease was so strong, the buildings of the small towns in the infected zones had been burned to the very ground in an effort to stop its spread.

This, in fact, was being done. Recognizing that the contamination would linger past the memory of any living man, the decision was reached to raze the area. As soon as a family died or was relocated, their dwellings and out-buildings went up in smoke. The entire countryside was methodically put to the torch to create an area of visible devastation that matched the invisible menace to be found everywhere.

During this same period, teams of cleanup men were sent into the contamination zone to bury the dead and dying domestic animals. Even those that had remained relatively healthy were dispatched and piled into shallow graves.

In two months the work was complete. All checkpoints had been turned into permanent establishments, the last of the villagers were gone, and the wind, now free of radioactive particles, was able to blow across an area of about six hundred square miles, unimpeded except for an occasional still-standing stone chimney. Even compared with the great deserts farther to the southeast, this once-fertile land was bleak and barren. Unlike the cold, sandy wastes, it was deadly poison to all living things.

The size and audacity of the cleanup and relocation program was unprecedented, but, as is likely to happen when such a huge undertaking is attempted, it was impossible to prevent people from talking.

Medical staff members knew the truth. They quickly realized they were not treating some kind of contagious bacterial or viral disease. Treatments they were instructed to prescribe were for radiation sickness. Like all humans, they told what they knew to colleagues, friends, and family.

Before the operation ended, word was making the rounds of the rumor mills. A major atomic accident of some mysterious nature had occurred in the far-off area north of the Caspian, in the fringes of the Urals.

The controlling governmental body could do little to squelch the persistence of the story. The general level of ignorance, due to the newness of the whole atomic field, provided some protection because most of the population did not have any idea of the possibility of a nuclear disaster on such a scale. Everyone had heard of the bomb, but no one knew much about contamination from other sources.

Some effort was made to handle the cover-up without taking official notice of the circulating story. *Pravda* ran an article that, without citing the cause of the prevalent tale, outlined the safety and efficiency record of the Soviet nuclear industry. The story also touched on techniques of disposing of low-level wastes and their fine success record in this effort. Within sixty days of the incident, work was back to normal at the plutonium production center. Then came the next blow.

On September 29, 1957, the gigantic holding tanks that contained dissolved waste had a problem. Their cooling system either failed or was shut off inadvertently. Accident or breakdown, it does not matter. The result was an atomic explosion estimated to be in the range of seventy-five tons of TNT. At least two hundred people died from the blast or exposure to intense radiation. Ten thousand people who had not been exposed during the previous incident—some maintain the number was many times greater—were evacuated from their homes. Later estimates hold that no less than four hundred seventy thousand people were exposed to radiation. Secrecy again ruled. Nothing appeared in news media. Normalcy will be a long time in returning, however, to the wasted land.

In June 1961, Leo Tumerman, then–professor emeritus at Weizmann Institute in Israel, and several other scientists were driving along the main north–south highway in the foothills of the Ural Mountains on their way to visit the construction site of the first major Soviet atomic plant at Beloyarsk in the northern part of the mountain chain.

The car in which he was riding reached a point on the highway where large billboard signs had been placed, cautioning drivers to roll up their windows and proceed as rapidly as possible through the area. No stopping was allowed.

Curious, Tumerman questioned his driver about the cause of the warnings. He was informed there had been "a tremendous explosion several years before and ever since then it had been like this."

According to Tumerman, they drove for miles through utter devastation. "On either side of the road there was nothing. An empty land. There were trees and grass, but where there once were villages and herds and industry, there was nothing." The professor said they drove for twenty miles noting each side of the road was a vast wasteland.

"It must have been sixty square miles that we could see in the valley, and we were not really close to where the explosion occurred. The entire area was hot, very radioactive. The other scientists were discussing which was more dangerous to eat in the area, the fish or crabs. I asked the driver to stop so that I could drink some water and he told me it was forbidden."

When questioned about the cause of the disaster, Tumerman said the accident, as far as he could ascertain, was due to a mishap at a military plutonium deposit "either from burying atomic waste or from processing plutonium to make bombs."

He was certain of one thing: "The explosion was the result of the negligence of officials. They were careless and a catastrophe occurred."

It should be made clear, however, these incidents were not of the type that might happen in the far tamer nuclear power–generating station. The plutonium manufacturing process was, at the time, in its early stages, and much has been learned since. In addition, the type of installation utilized for electrical power production is different from a graphite-cored unit designed to produce radioactive materials.

No real thought, up to the time of the Ural accident, appears to have been given to even simple matters such as evacuation routes and temporary shelter for displaced people. Here in the United States, emergency plans are a part of every application for a license to construct an atomic power station. These same contingency programs exist around each of our plutonium manufacturing and weapons production centers, as well as every other site where atomic materials are processed in any great amounts.

One of the most intriguing aspects of the Chelyabinsk-40 disaster happened decades later. It is testimony to the total devastation that occurred. In need of money, the Russian government repealed a ban on the importation of nuclear waste. The Russian Atomic Ministry (Minatom) has asked to be allowed to store other nations' nuclear wastes for a fee. The proposed site is the destroyed area. The price under discussion with eight nations to dispose of a total of several thousand tons is more than $20 billion.

If the lessons of the past have not been learned, a still greater disaster could be in the making.

FOUR

External Threats

One of the most difficult variables to consider in estimating potential nuclear plant disasters does not result from internal equipment failures. It is the threat from external sources—the direct, deliberate, premeditated attempt to sabotage an atomic installation.

Planning for such an assault would have taken all safety contingencies into consideration. Fail-safe mechanisms would be bypassed or double-faulted so as to surmount them. Deliberate sabotage is unforeseen as far as the moment of its occurrence.

Who would be insane enough to try and sabotage an atomic installation? Apparently there are many people. As difficult as it is to imagine, any number of separate attacks have been made on nuclear power stations alone. These have happened in various countries around the world. Many have taken place right here in the United States. Additionally, numerous threats have been recorded and dozens of vandalism or deliberate sabotage cases have been made public. None of the above includes incidents in which vital security breaches have taken place or the number of U.S. companies that have paid fines for noncompliance with nuclear security regulations.

Altogether, between 1966 and 1978, there were sixty-four notable incidents worldwide. The brunt of these took place after 1974. More have occurred since 1978. Surprisingly, few big news stories have come out of all this.

The number of assaults is clearly increasing as proliferation of atomic energy continues and procedures for handling materials and their various potentials become better understood by nonscientists.

The government long ago recognized this vulnerability and mandated stricter security controls at all nuclear power plants and other installations. According to an early report issued by Morris K. Udall (D-Ariz.) and Paul E. Tsongas (D-Mass.), on behalf of a House subcommittee, the Nuclear Regulatory Commission (NRC) acknowledged security deficiencies, but many had not been corrected.

In the Udall and Tsongas report, the commission was especially troubled about the possibility of attacks by three or more "well-armed, well-trained persons who might possess inside knowledge or assistance." The document further stated, "The Commission believes that such groups might possess explosives, machine guns, anti-tank weapons, and helicopters." What made this possibility so alarming was that the sum total of defense and fire power possessed by the average nuclear installation at the time consisted of only a few guards "armed with .38 caliber revolvers and shotguns."

A letter from then–NRC Chairman Marcus A. Rowden revealed security deficiencies at every one of the fifteen installations handling plutonium or highly enriched uranium.

In a more recent situation, a reporter posing as a contractor sent the air force $5.30 and received detailed plans of a nuclear weapons depot through the mail. He then personally visited two sites, where he was shown a guardhouse and told the routes and approximate timetable for trucks carrying atomic bombs to waiting aircraft. The only identification required of him was a driver's license and a few credit cards. Apparently no one checked to see if he was actually a contractor. As a result, Donald R. Cotter, a Pentagon weapons chief, was reported to have ordered an immediate investigation of Defense Department procedures.

Partially as a result of the House subcommittee report and partly due to a growing concern of several members of the NRC, strict new rules were proposed to safeguard all atomic installations. These requirements, set forth early in 1977, recognized the need for greater care both at power production and nuclear manufacturing sites and while materials were in transit.

News accounts of the revised proposals made it clear the NRC had given some thought to direct terrorist or guerrilla intervention by armed force into the premises of the many civilian-operated nuclear facilities. Owners and operators of these plants were ordered to submit new and more far-reaching plans for increased security and protection of vital equipment and controls.

The NRC's action set off a mad scramble for development of the required programs within a ninety-day limit granted by the committee. According to one utility executive, the speed demanded by the body's action "did not leave much time to really think about all the questions."

By the week of June 13, 1977, twenty-eight U.S. utility companies had turned in security programs for their forty-four nuclear reactor power stations. They were granted until August 1977 for the NRC's approval and complete installation of various devices they felt were needed to defend themselves against a determined effort by a small but heavily armed and knowledgeable force. The same deadline was set for the addition of manpower outlined in the various proposals.

The cost of this added security was and is high. Estimates indicate these tighter requirements opened up a $100 million market, in 1978 dollars alone, ranging from closed-circuit surveillance TV to special fences with barrier alarms. All told, about 90 percent of atomic power plants in the United States needed additional security-related products to comply with new regulations.

James R. Miller, once the NRC assistant director for reactor safeguards, estimated a plant's investment back then would be about $2.5 million for initial setup, and another $1.5 million annually for maintenance. Compared with security costs in other industries, that was not an unreasonable amount.

In addition to increasing the number of guards at each plant to a minimum of ten and requiring two hundred hours of specialized training for every man, bullet-resistant glass was specified for selected areas. Tamper-proof locking systems, for which no key can be duplicated, perimeter intrusion alarms, massive fencing, extra command posts, and remote-area television surveillance were also part of the package.

But security consists of more than guards and gadgets. It is an attitude. And for many years, this necessary mindset was lacking. The reasons are clear. First, utility companies operating most of the nuclear-powered generators have long been associated with the production of electricity by more conventional means. Coal, gas, or oil-burning plants have never been a serious target for terrorist groups here in the United States. To a large extent, the business of producing electricity had been isolated from the mainstream of violence. In short, due to past experience, management attention, just a few years prior to 9/11, had not been adequately focused on protection.

The second major reason for a lack of security concerns stems from the rather cursory treatment given to this matter by the U.S. government and regulatory bodies.

It was not until July 18, 1973, that the American National Standards Institute issued ANSI Standard N 18.17 entitled "Industrial

Security for Nuclear Power Plants." This document established the first detailed measures for protection of a reactor installation. Later, in the November 13, 1974, issue of the Federal Register, the then-active Atomic Energy Commission (AEC) proposed rules for the protection and physical security of nuclear power plants and materials. These first steps were general in nature, expressing the necessity and advisability of security, but few specific requirements were established.

This was the state of readiness until recently. In the time between publication of the original ANSI Standard and the later revised NRC requirements, the AEC, through on-site visits and a review of security systems, was able to begin development of tighter controls. Ample material was available for detailing these safeguards, but the AEC was phased out of existence, and the NRC became heir to its work in this area.

Some of the NRC's action regarding safeguards may have been spurred by a series of reports from the Government Accountability Office (GAO) that were highly critical of previous security requirements. The GAO, acting in an investigative mode, sent its auditors to one installation where they gained access to vital areas by picking door locks with pieces of discarded wire and an old screwdriver. They also learned, as their study progressed, of a plant protected only by an eight-foot wire fence, of incidents in which full-time guards had been given less than four hours' actual training, and of situations where the security force could not operate TV scanning equipment or find the main control room.

The GAO recommendation eventually went so far as to suggest giving nuclear plant police the right to "shoot to kill" in some conditions. That brought forth the frightening prospect of a private army whose ranks are filled with men granted privileges above the law.

In acknowledgment of the utilities' past faults, Phillip J. Cherico, ex-director of security for the New York State Power Authority, said, "Security has not had the priority it should have had, particularly among private utilities. It does not," he continued, "contribute to the generation of either power or profits."

Part of the security problem has been eased by available technology. In addition to the expected TV cameras and electrical barriers, the use of reliable walk-through metal detectors and gas sensors to spot guns and explosives allows for quicker screening.

Steps toward better safeguards are still being implemented. Renewed focus on the security of both atomic installations and the transportation of radioactive materials has brought about more stringent regulations. Clearly, recent actions by the Nuclear Regulatory Commission have produced an atmosphere in which considerations of site protection play a much larger role in facility-management thinking.

No clear indications are available as to the effect these new security measures will have on armed attempts to take over atomic installations. Judging from the thoroughness of current rules, especially as compared with the almost nonexistent prior regulations, a terrorist organization will have to expend a lot more effort to intrude into a nuclear power station.

Since 9/11, everyone in the industry understands the inherent danger in complacency. No security, no matter how well formulated, will ever be enough to cope with all possibilities of an attack.

During the Vietnam confrontation, the effectiveness of an assault by a determined force was proved beyond all hope of rebuttal. A team of specially trained Americans was flown to Vietnam with the mission of destroying the only nuclear reactor in South Vietnamese control. The mission was to prevent the Vietcong from obtaining radioactive materials that could be fabricated into weaponry. The task was easily and quickly completed. One official source holds the reactor itself was destroyed. Others maintain that only the nuclear fuel was removed from the body of the pile. This operation required specialized equipment, trained individuals, and support teams to evacuate the group after the attack was executed.

While expensive, none of these requirements is more than could be met by any one of several terrorist groups in existence today. There are, throughout the world, ample targets for such operations. Perhaps the only reason one has not yet been successful is due to the attitudes of insurgent groups toward atomic energy. The argument that terrorists want to create only the kind of havoc that produces a large audience is a weak one. If the group is after absolute negotiating power, there is probably no more effective way to achieve it than attainment of some form of nuclear weapon. As far as getting attention, modern mass media will see to it that the event, whenever and wherever it occurs, will be brought to the public's attention, unless governmental security is clamped tightly in place.

But there is yet another threat to the basic security of any atomic installation. A desperate or deranged individual, acting out of a strong religious conviction or in a moment of panic, could end the lives of thousands of people. It sounds farfetched. Pro-atomic forces have scoffed at the idea, and once more, the critics have embraced it. Yet long before the destruction of the World Trade Center, such an event actually took place. The participants successfully held an atomic installation for ransom and caused the evacuation of the most prestigious nuclear operation in the United States. They did it in what was then a surprising and prophetic manner, using a technique we now all fear.

The drama made headlines for a single day back in the early 1970s and is now largely forgotten. It shouldn't be, because it demonstrated that what possibly can happen, will, and in a most unlikely fashion. Three men were involved. They had no special training, no particular knowledge of nuclear facilities, and, fortunately, no strong purpose other than the attainment of a large sum of money. Security measures utilized today, including the X-ray machines, TV systems, electronic sensors, metal detectors, and armed guards did not stop them. They came in on the blind side. From the air.

FIVE

Skyjacking

The terrorist attack on the twin towers of the World Trade Center in New York was a truly horrible event. But it was not the first time a stolen passenger-filled commercial airliner was used as a weapon—nor the only time that weapon was aimed at a vulnerable American target.

The first occurrence began on Friday, November 10, 1972. It became the longest skyjacking in history. Had the three desperate men involved carried out their threat, the resulting devastation would have dwarfed the September 11 disaster. Their intended target was the nuclear reactor of the Atomic Energy Commission's research installation at Oak Ridge, Tennessee.

When Southern Airways Flight 49 left Birmingham airport, bound for Montgomery, Alabama, and then on to Orlando, it seemed like another slightly dull, normal trip. High above the Alabama countryside, ripping through the blackening twilight, none of the plane's crew sensed what was to come. The ground below, dotted by individual lights from scattered farmhouses, looked much like the star-strewn sky above.

The jet, which could seat seventy-five, was about one-third full, and the two flight attendants were moving through the cabin caring for their charges. The passengers had just settled down from the disquiet brought on by takeoff, and were ordering beverages.

Flight 49 was on course and on time. Tension drained from the cabin. Three of the passengers, however, were still uptight. One of them nervously kicked the satchel he'd slipped under his seat, then leaned back and tried to relax. Twenty-one years old, Melvin Cale had been in a number of difficult situations. Since his escape from the minimum-security rehabilitation program to which he'd been sentenced in 1971, he'd been on the move, avoiding notice. Now, on board with his half-brother, Louis Moore, and Moore's insep-arable companion, Henry Jackson, both also fugitives, he was about to make world headlines.

Moore and Jackson had been through a lot together. They'd run a restaurant, "Lou and Smooth's Soul Palace," and they'd done okay for a while. But then things turned sour, and they'd given it up. There wasn't any money in the two-bit place anyway. And it sure took money, because the real color of segregation was green, baby, not black.

Karen Chambers, one of the two attendants, passed in the aisle again, and Louis Moore followed her with his eyes. The Detroit cops had hit them with charges of rape. He'd gone down to the sta-tion with "Smooth" Henry Jackson to lend his friend a little moral support. They went everywhere together. Then that sassy little lady cop knocked on them, and next thing, they were charged with rape. Them. They'd made speeches before the Detroit City Council and were on their way inside the system to be somebody. The scene at his home with his wife crying and the two kids looking scared had been awful. Hell, he'd make it up to them after this little number.

Smooth Henry sat beside him. One thing about Smooth Henry. He didn't have a bad home life. His wife was an ex–Playboy Club Bunny and did go-go dancing when her old man needed bread. He knew Henry's tastes ran to cold liquor and hot women, so there was little question in his mind what he'd do with his split of the ransom.

Taking the money wasn't stealing, either. The money was coming from the same city that once had the gall to offer them $25 in settlement of their $4 million suit for police brutality.

Melvin Cale sat alone, apart from his two companions across the aisle. It had seemed natural, when boarding, to let the pair sit together. They did everything together.

Cale twisted to find a more comfortable position. He was edgy, and it was hard to keep from fidgeting a little. The flight attendant's voice startled him.

"Can I get you anything, sir?"

Cale shook his head. "No, nothing." He looked across at the partners, who were staring back at him. Not time yet. He tried again to relax.

He was wound tight since he'd fled the jail-release project in Nashville. He'd been in trouble with the law much of his life, and the last episode had ended with a five-year sentence for larceny. When the opportunity had come to run, he did.

The droning of the aircraft was soothing, and he glanced across the narrow aisle at the other two. They were shrewd. Real dangerous cats from up north in Detroit. And running from the law, too, no matter what they said. It was their scheme, really. He'd been called in to help and had added some ideas, but it was their deal from the start.

More out of nervousness than anything else, he leaned down and, unzipping the canvas flight bag resting on the floor, peered inside at the chrome-plated steel barrel of a revolver. Satisfied, he re-zipped the bag and straightened in his chair.

Not long now. They'd discussed it and decided to give things a few minutes after takeoff to settle down. Time to get the airplane away from the field—where no one could interfere.

Melvin Cale got up and out into the aisle as he saw Jackson start forward. Lou Moore remained in his seat but was cradling something against his stomach.

In the forward part of the cabin. Donna Holman, one of the attendants, was filling a cup with hot coffee. The captain always liked to have it served immediately after takeoff, and a happy captain meant a happy crew.

Turning toward the flight deck, she saw the stocky, round-faced man walking up the aisle. His Afro haircut and mustache marked him for a Northerner. She paid little attention to him as she tried not to spill any of the steaming liquid. The man approached her, talking excitedly, before she could move. She attempted to turn away, but he slipped his arm around her. The barrel of his fancy .38-caliber Smith & Wesson dug into her neck. She resisted for a second, then stopped.

Midway back in the cabin, Louis Moore, seeing the attendant safely captured, stood up in his seat and began waving a black World War II Luger pistol in the air.

In the rear, striding swiftly, Melvin Cale, who had started for the back as Jackson headed forward, grabbed the other attendant, Karen Chambers. He shoved a cheap .22-caliber Saturday Night Special into her so hard she winced.

Jackson's voice carried through the cabin, overcoming the noise of the engines and the rushing air outside. "Nobody move. We're taking over. And let's not have any heroes. Because they'll be dead heroes."

The frightened passengers reacted in a variety of ways. A man started to rise, then, thinking better of it, settled back in his seat under the watchful muzzle of Lou Moore's automatic. A woman seated next to her teenaged son grabbed his arm and, speaking in a low voice, tried to reassure him.

Jackson, apparently familiar with the routine of the plane's crew, moved rapidly. With his strength and threatening pistol, he forced the flight attendant to the narrow door leading to the flight deck.

Following standing airline orders, she did not resist. At the door he spoke to her urgently and motioned with the gun to the lock. They stood for a moment in conversation, then, with a look of resignation, she took out her key and opened it.

On the flight deck, Captain William R. Haas, a veteran pilot, and Billy Johnson, his second officer, were at the controls. Haas, forty-three, was a calm man with great flying experience. He was on Flight 49 as a favor to another pilot. It was his day off, but he had shifted his schedule to accommodate a friend who needed the free time.

The on-course climb out had gone according to plan, and the two flyers had no inkling of the action behind them in the passenger area. They had just finished making normal course corrections during the leveling-off procedures when the door burst open.

Turning, expecting to see the stewardess with a cup of hot coffee, almost a ritual for Haas, he was shocked to find a wild-eyed man holding her captive and waving a pistol. An icy composure descended over the captain, and he faced the situation squarely.

The girl, Jackson's arm still around her neck, spoke quickly. "This is a hijacking. He's not kidding."

Haas looked intently at the man, realizing the seriousness of the situation. He held his voice down, maintaining a placid exterior. "Keep calm. We don't want anyone hurt. We'll obey your instructions."

Jackson, confused by the array of gauges and controls and made anxious by the tight confinement of the cockpit, was wary.

Haas's demeanor, however, put him at ease. Sensing the captain was telling the truth, he released the flight attendant and sent her back into the cabin where Lou Moore was standing on one of the seats, waving his pistol at one after another of the passengers.

Jackson waited until the girl was gone before speaking again. "Get this plane to Detroit. We want ten million dollars from the city of Detroit or we're gonna start killing people."

Capt. Haas, a native of Moscow, Tennessee, and copilot Billy Johnson, who, when not flying, served as mayor of College City, Arkansas, were experienced men. They had the full responsibility of the crew and passengers' lives in their hands and were well trained in company policy dealing with hijack attempts. With Jackson, Moore, and Cale clearly in control, their orders were to cooperate until rescued or released.

Haas, trying to lead Jackson into conversation, outlined the problems of changing course for Detroit. First, there was the FAA and a flight plan. They would have to be cleared for a corridor that would take them there. Then there was the matter of insufficient fuel. They would have to stop somewhere to refill their tanks.

He and Jackson spoke for several minutes. Haas outlined radio procedures necessary to put out the ransom demand, get clearance, and the number of airports where they might find the right kind of fuel for the DC-9. Jackson went back into the main cabin, and keeping an eye on the two flight officers, motioned to Lou Moore, who came forward. They talked briefly, then Moore headed back to the waiting Cale to explain their plan. Jackson returned to the flight deck.

He and the pilot exchanged a few more words before a decision was made. They would refuel at Jackson, Mississippi. No one nor any vehicle, except a gas truck and the driver in his undershorts, would approach the plane.

Haas went back to the radio and the flight continued its way through the night.

———

The guard shift had changed at Oak Ridge Atomic Laboratories, and the new men had taken the positions vacated by the retiring group. It was almost Saturday, November 11, and the endless displays of television surveillance pictures continued their regular mindless pattern across the battery of cathode-ray tubes. The routine of the day remained unchanged.

The DC-9 was rerouted from its original course and given immediate clearance to Jackson, Mississippi. Word went out as soon as the hijacking of Flight 49 became known, and agents of the FBI met with Southern Airways representatives within an hour after receiving notice. Demands of the three were discussed, as was the impossibility of attaining large sums of cash at 7:00 in the evening. A long chain of events was set into motion, and many, many tense hours would pass before it came to an end.

Conversation between the pilot and the armed men was terse. Knowing it might take some time to gather up the demanded money, the three planned to keep the aircraft aloft as much as possible where interference would be far less likely.

Shortly before 8:00 Friday night, the plane rolled to a halt on one of the runways at Jackson. The refueling operation took a minute to start, and one of the two guarding the main cabin came forward and passed the hijacker in the flight deck a heavy object. Pulling the pin, Henry Jackson held a hand grenade next to the ear of Capt. Haas. The pressure of his fingers on the narrow safety handle kept the primed bomb from exploding. His meaning was clear. There were to be no tricks.

The people inside the aircraft stayed away from the windows, and two of the three bandits remained on watch constantly as the truck approached to hook up its fire-preventive static discharge wires. The hand gripping the grenade remained near Haas's head, and Jackson watched the operation with intense concentration. There was little conversation.

On the ground the authorities had rushed two agents to the scene, but they were unable to approach the aircraft. Identification of the three hijackers was made, however, and on the off chance some good might be done, Cale's wife and daughters were sought so they could be brought to the Knoxville airport. Authorities hoped she would talk to him over the radio and dissuade him from killing anyone on board.

In the main cabin, all male passengers had been ordered to strip down to their underwear in an attempt to keep them under control by embarrassing them.

After about an hour on the ground, during which time the fuel truck had topped the big airplane's tanks and driven away, Jackson grew impatient. The increasing number of radio transmissions and his unfamiliarity with speaking over the microphone, along with the tension created by being on the ground, caused him to react.

"Take off." His voice showed his stress, and Haas responded quickly. Tower and runway control permission had already been granted, and he spurred the ship into immediate motion. They rolled quickly down the long runway and were airborne in minutes.

Once aloft the three skyjackers seemed more relaxed. Jackson, working with exaggerated care, replaced the pin in the grenade and passed it back to Lou Moore. They were on their way again. An air route was chosen, and air traffic control cleared a flight corridor for the plane toward Detroit.

The three were joking and singing but continued their close scrutiny of the crew. One male passenger was looking ill, and the flight attendants saw to his needs as best they could.

Several radio messages were exchanged as the plane flew northward. To calm the situation, progress reports on arrangements for the ransom were made as if the full amount were being raised.

A major mobilization was going into effect. The FBI had alerted its field agents over a large zone, and the U.S. Air Force offered the use of military jets to assist in the hunt.

Once in the Detroit area, Jackson and Moore ordered the pilot to place the ship into a circular holding pattern. It was like having their own special scenic cruiser as they gazed down at their city from a majestic height. They had arrived back in style and were safe from the police miles below.

A meeting of law enforcement groups, representatives from Southern Airways, and members of the Federal Aviation Administration (FAA) had produced a plan. The situation while the plane was in the air was hopeless. Short of shooting it down, there was no way to abort the flight. But once they had the craft on the ground, even in the open spaces of an airport, there was a chance. One or more of the men might expose himself to specially trained sharpshooters. Or a team might gain entry by a ruse. As long as the ransom collection could be delayed—and the hijackers continued to believe there was a possibility they would be paid—things could be held in suspense.

The three on board, keeping the passengers in a state of terror, had ordered the liquor locker opened. Inside, small bottles of scotch, bourbon, vodka, and gin were rummaged though, and the hijackers began to drink.

In an aisle seat, eighty-three-year-old Alvin Fortson, a farmer who had been showing signs of breathing difficulty, now seemed to be having a heart attack. One of the passengers requested and received permission to come to his aid and helped him lie down across three seats. After loosening his tie, belt, and shoes, the man massaged Fortson's legs to help circulation. But his condition worsened. Finally, the flight attendants asked if they might give him oxygen from the emergency equipment. Cale agreed.

Radio messages continued to be exchanged, and the three

armed men talked among themselves. They brought up different ideas to confuse authorities about the number of hijackers actually on board. Unknown to them, a previously agreed upon emergency code was being used to keep ground stations posted. Southern Airways representatives continued to assure the men work was progressing on the roundup of the required $10 million, but were quick to add it was taking time.

The scene in the cockpit of the jet was strained as they circled the city. The three bandits, taking turns standing guard, were an ominous presence. The captain and his second officer, consuming cup after cup of steaming coffee, were feeling the demands of irregular operations and hours spent at the controls. The two had done everything in their limited power to ensure the passengers of their individual safety, but the sight of the ship's officers under gunpoint was demoralizing to everyone on board.

As soon as the basic desires of the three terrorists had been clearly understood by the FBI, they developed a plan. Money would be used as a lure to bring the big airplane to earth. Since the ransom had been demanded from the city of Detroit, it seemed an ideal place to try the trick.

Detroit Mayor Roman Gribbs was contacted and told of the men's requirements. Surprised and incredulous, he replied, "Are you kidding? That much money? Why would they want it from the city?" When he was given a brief outline of Henry Jackson's and Lou Moore's previous records, Gribbs understood. After consultation with Southern Airways spokesmen, he proceeded with quick effectiveness. A midnight emergency session of the city council was convened and a loan of $500,000 was immediately approved.

Gribbs's decisiveness and action provided the FBI with the bargaining tool they needed. They now had a large amount of cash and could try to trade with the three hijackers.

But as rapidly as things had been done, they had taken valuable time. After circling for almost two hours, the DC-9 was again low on fuel. Now the three desperate men were running low on patience. Cleveland was chosen as a satisfactory landing site for refueling. Without much warning, the DC-9 altered course, and the pilot called for a new flight corridor. The authorities, sensing an opportunity, quickly rushed a squad to the Cleveland airport in an effort to prevent a takeoff.

By radio, the three men, still trying to confuse the issue of how many were really in their group, asked for food, additional drinks, and ten parachutes. These were to be put on the aircraft while the refueling operation was in progress.

The short flight from Detroit to Cleveland hit a new high in tension. Fortson, the eighty-three-year-old farmer with lung and heart problems, had taken a turn for the worse. In spite of the attentions of one of the passengers and the attendants, it seemed he might be dying. Oxygen was given on a continual basis. Melvin Cale, gun in hand, in an act of either bravado or attempted humor, would grip the old man's wrist and study his watch, as if timing his heart rate. Then he would smile and nod sagely. He apparently liked playing doctor, but obviously didn't know how to take a pulse reading.

Special agents reached the Cleveland airport ahead of Flight 49 and held a quick conference to go over various attack possibilities. A rapidly mounted operation went into effect as the large aircraft shut down its engines at the end of one of the concrete run-up areas. While refueling took place, a specially trained team tried to make visual contact with the hijackers by bringing food and water on board. The sight of the armed hand grenade dissuaded this group from any action, but they tried to hold the skyjacker's attention while FBI marksmen slipped within shooting range.

The ploy failed. One of the terrorists, posted as lookout, saw the men advancing across an open area of the runway about a hundred feet away. The hijackers' response was instantaneous and directed not toward the crew and passengers held captive, but against the attacking agents.

Yelling from one of the small windows in the flight cabin, a single voice was heard over the noise of the refueling truck: "Get the hell back or we'll throw a grenade."

Convinced it was no idle threat, the sharpshooters retreated. At this point, things relaxed a little. With replenished fuel, food, water, and ten parachutes, the men were buoyed. Aside from the aborted try to recapture the aircraft, no resistance was in evidence. It was apparent they were going to be very hard to stop.

Less than an hour after landing, the DC-9 was in the air again.

Jackson discussed matters with his two associates, then gave Haas a new destination: Toronto, Canada. The radio once again was busy with messages. Confident of their newfound bargaining ability, the three became more insistent about their desire for immediate payment of the ransom. Jackson, speaking to Haas, sounded more intense than ever. "Tell 'em," he said in a threatening tone, "that they goddamn better have the money there."

What had up to this point been a national problem now reached the status of an international incident. Communications between Canadian law enforcement officials and U.S. forces were established. Air hijacking was a problem of concern to all countries. The Canadians were glad to help.

A long series of conversations ensued between the FBI and the bandits. Montreal was agreed upon as the place the ransom would be paid. Time was beginning to favor the police. The plane had been in the air over twelve hours, and even with food and water resupplied, the flying officers had to be getting weary. This also brought on renewed concern for the passengers.

A total of $500,000 in small bills, the amount Southern Airways had borrowed from the city of Detroit, was delivered in a courier plane. A Canadian police officer with an exceptional record of service offered to strip to the skin and present the money in person so the three on board could see there was no trickery. His proposal was made and refused. Negotiations were continued as the plane once again touched down and was refueled.

There was no chance the three men would settle for a mere $500,000. Their original demand for a full $10 million was renewed, but this time in a tone that made it clear the high spirits the hijackers had when leaving Cleveland were gone. Threats against the lives of the passengers and crew were repeated.

In about fifty minutes the plane was airborne again. Heated exchanges flew over the radio. There was no question in the minds of law enforcement officers the matter was taking a nasty turn— just how nasty no one yet knew.

The three hijackers were at a loss. It was obvious to them the flight officers, who had now been at the controls for more than twelve hours with only minor breaks allowed for trips to the lavatory, were approaching their limits of endurance. And the passengers, fatigued by the constantly oppressive fear, were becoming inured to the danger of the situation. Somehow, the threat the three held over their lives, as well as the valuable airplane, had not been enough to get action. Something far more drastic was needed.

Jackson, Moore, and Cale conferred briefly, keeping a careful lookout for any sudden activity by the captain or the crew. The weather outside the DC-9 was as wild as the scene inside. Wind, rain, and snow swept the plane and caused it to bounce like a cork in rippling water.

No one is certain which of the three came up with the idea, but Cale had lived in the Oak Ridge area and knew of the fear, and thus a powerful potential for negotiations, attached to the atomic reactors installed at the nuclear facilities. The instigator is unimportant, however, because all three men agreed to the following course of action.

Jackson's voice over the radio was firm. The reaction in the aircraft control tower in Toronto was one of stunned silence. "We're tired of all this bull. No more foolin' around. We're taking this f . . . er to Oak Ridge and dive it into a nuclear reactor."

From the brief conversation between the startled tower personnel and the now-committed men, two things emerged. First, Jackson, Moore, and Cale were sincere. If they didn't get the $10 million, they would crash the plane into the Oak Ridge atomic installation. Second, they gave a deadline, after conferring with the captain about flight time, of 8:00 AM for arrival in the area and a 12:00 noon ultimatum. Either they got their money by then or they would deliberately crash into one of the nuclear reactors. What had been a threat to the lives of twenty-seven passengers and four crew members now became a promise of potential national disaster with the well-being of innumerable people in the balance.

Top-level meetings were convened. The Oak Ridge staff was alerted to the danger, and new, harsher measures were considered for trying to capture the three hijackers. Through the early hours of the morning various experts and field agents were consulted, while frequent radio transmissions continued to promise quick delivery of the ransom.

On schedule and tracked all the way by FAA radar, the DC-9 arrived in the Oak Ridge area and began another of its unending circles. When the call came through from Canada to the Oak Ridge guardroom, the man on duty at first thought the story he was hearing was a hoax. Then, slowly, his disbelief changed to horror. He contacted his superiors, and orders went out immediately for a meeting of all key personnel to consider possible emergency action.

The ultimate threat had been made. And there was no defense

possible. If the three men on the plane could overcome the pilot's resistance to crashing directly into one of the reactors—and this seemed highly likely—no one was certain how much damage would result.

Everyone agreed on one thing. If the crash actually occurred, the impact could rupture the protective shell and there would be a massive release of radioactivity into the environment. That was the least of the projections. The worst indicated the possibility of a core meltdown and the issuing forth of enough contamination to make the day one that would long linger in the memories of man.

Evacuation of the Oak Ridge laboratories did not extend to the nearby communities. Government spokesmen, acting on the least serious damage projections, issued a calm statement to all news media indicating there would be little or no release of radioactivity if the three men should succeed in their plan. Controversy was eventually to arise out of this statement and the actions of the concerned officials of the Atomic Energy Commission.

After circling for two hours, waiting for the final 12:00 noon deadline, the three hijackers were once again told by Capt. Haas that they were low on fuel. Lexington, Kentucky, was chosen as a stop, and they landed. The fill-up was made without incident, and in less than thirty minutes the ship was airborne again.

The attitudes of the people aboard Flight 49 had gone from calm acquiescence to near panic. Everyone grew progressively more anxious as the three made their plans clear. No one present doubted their seriousness.

Twelve noon was approaching rapidly as the relentless circling began once more. The air force offered planes to the FBI and several fighters were sent aloft. They were under no specific orders, but could, if called in time, make a pass or two in hopes of shooting the DC-9 down before it could actually dive into one of the atomic structures. The authorities, wrestling with the morality of killing all thirty-one innocent people on board to possibly spare the lives of many thousands, were close to action but not yet ready to take the final step to order an attack by the jets.

Still convinced money was the answer, a continuous battery of assurances was broadcast. The money was on its way. Hold on. Don't do anything rash.

But the three men on board were in a highly agitated state. Lou Moore, talking to the passengers, revealed his position clearly. The situation was getting hopeless. Death might be the only way out. And a far better alternative to prison. "I was born to die," he said, "and if I have to take all of you with me, that's all right with me."

Haas, concentrating his tired mind on precision flying, realized a climax of sorts was being reached. All through the long night he had done his best to cheer the weary passengers and encourage them. But things were looking more and more hopeless.

Finally at 12:00 noon, with no real progress made on a delivery place and time for the ransom, Jackson acted. He pointed his .38 at Haas and said in a low, serious tone, "Dive it into a reactor."

Haas thought as quickly as his fatigue would allow. "I can't," he replied slowly. "There's an overcast beneath us and there's no way to tell where the reactors are."

He was convincing, but Jackson was undeterred. His mind was made up. Then, the first break occurred. Haas told Jackson, and apparently was able to convince him by his discussions over the radio, that there had been a mix-up in the times due to crossing from the Eastern to the Central Standard Time zones. The money was coming, but everyone thought they had until 12:00 Central, not 12:00 Eastern Time.

The ruse worked. Haas gained another hour, which was to become the critical factor.

Jackson, with some of the tension off for a moment, dictated a radio message that the copilot, Johnson, sent to the area ground stations. "The one o'clock deadline isn't far off. We must have the money, seven bulletproof vests, helmets, and a document from President Nixon granting us the ten million. We must have stimulants for the crew, food, a six-pack of Pabst Blue Ribbon Beer, coffee, water, and cigarettes for the passengers. If the conditions are not met, we take this thing into an atomic energy plant."

Down below, through broken overcast, the sound of the circling plane could clearly be heard as it passed over the now almost deserted Oak Ridge facility. Evacuation of nonessential personnel from the site had gone according to plan, and nothing stirred on the usually busy streets. In nearby towns, the natives went about their normal routines. There was some extra traffic out of the area, but by and large people maintained their regular schedules. Many did not know until later about the seriousness of the threat.

The clock ticked time slowly away while the interval between noon and 1:00 PM lessened. The radio crackled with progress reports and promises, but the three hijackers seemed to be in another world. They were going to get their money or die. If the alternative was to die, they would take a lot of others with them. Haas had done his best. He'd worked against hope to gain the last possible time extension, and now it was running out.

More air force pilots were alerted. The shoot-to-kill order had not been passed down but could come at any moment. No one was certain who would take responsibility for the final attack command, but Acting FBI Director Patrick Gray was in personal contact with the field forces. He knew every situation had limits, and when they were reached, few if any courses other than violence were possible or advisable.

Jackson, who had his first order to crash thwarted, renewed his resolve. As they approached 1:00 PM, he became more agitated. This time it was for real!

The management at Oak Ridge, alerted through their security team around midnight, set up a command post in the AEC building inside the installation. Realizing the threat was serious, a group of specialists from the major contract operator, Union Carbide Corporation, Nuclear Division, was alerted and called to duty. Shortly after 7:00 AM, they ordered a shutdown of all plant operations that could be curtailed without "massive effect." Three research reactors in Oak Ridge were closed and many of the operations deemed hazardous in the Y-12 weapons plant were stopped. The gaseous diffusion plant, however, continued to function.

Communication links were installed between the command post and local, state, and national law enforcement authorities. Contact was also established with the Knoxville Airport control tower, which was capable of receiving the hijacked aircraft's radio transmissions.

The public information section of the installation's staff drafted a short basic statement to answer incoming queries. It consisted of a single question and answer.

Question: "What would happen if a commercial airliner were to crash into one of your plants?"

Answer: "If an airplane should crash into an Oak Ridge AEC facility, it would have similar effects compared to the same kind of crash into any large industrial complex. Such a crash could not cause a nuclear explosion. In the case of certain facilities, a crash of this nature could be accompanied by a localized release of radioactive materials, but this would not be a hazard to the public outside the plant affected."

To appreciate the full impact of this statement, some idea of the complexity of the installation is necessary. Oak Ridge was a ninety-five-square-mile site near Knoxville, Tennessee, that contained a community of about thirty thousand people and three plants. The Oak Ridge Gaseous Diffusion Plant was the biggest of the three and covered almost a square mile of land. In addition, this one installation had five large processing centers, each between twenty and forty acres in size, plus another seventy auxiliary buildings. The Y-12 plant was located on a separate five-hundred-acre tract and served primarily as a nuclear weapons manufacturing, test, and design center. Some Oak Ridge National Laboratory activities were also carried out on this site, but the laboratory had its own five-hundred-acre development nearby, containing several small research reactors, chemical processing plants, particle accelerators, waste disposal test operations, and other nuclear-related activities.

The massive size of the area provided the hijackers with an ample selection of targets if they could identify the functions of the various buildings from the air. But it was felt the very magnitude of the installation, unless highly unusual atmospheric conditions might accidentally prevail at the time of the crash, would confine the damage caused by the radioactive plume to the Oak Ridge area. This basic concept was a part of the early planning for the site and was justification for the statement "but this would not be a hazard to the public outside the plant affected."

All during the threat, AEC management maintained a calm front in reaction to the crisis. They did not believe the hijackers would actually manage to drop directly into a reactor, but could tell, by monitoring conversations between the three men and the tower, that the situation was "deadly serious."

Evacuation of the various plants, while not an everyday occurrence, took place routinely. (Only a month after this incident, 5,800 workers in the Y-12 weapons facility were called out again. This time, it was a bomb scare. The ensuing search proved fruitless.)

The constant drone of the aircraft overhead, as it slowly

circled, served to shake up the residents of the area. The AEC requested additional telephone operators as a part of their emergency plan, and more than ten thousand calls were handled during the five to six hours the situation lasted. The local radio station began to broadcast the official release to ease the populace's concern and had the good sense to refuse the services of an unidentified scientist who offered to come down to the station for the purpose of "evaluating" the threat to the community.

Prompt action by the AEC staff rapidly mobilized the installation. After a flurry of excitement, during which people were required to perform their tasks quickly and well, they were faced with the hardest chore of all. What could be done on their part had been. The only thing left was to wait it out. And so tension mounted. Conversations between the hijackers and the authorities became progressively more heated. As the final minutes of the extended deadline drew nearer, the three skyjackers became more determined. They realized they had made the ultimate threat, and if they failed to follow through, the effectiveness of further coercion would be badly weakened.

On board the aircraft, the situation was desperate. Jackson, Moore, and Cale stalked the aisles. Passengers were threatened, but no one was actually assaulted. The vexation of the three was clear for all to see as the deadline approached. Later, one passenger, who had remained calm throughout the ordeal said, "There is no question about it. They were going to do it."

The skyjackers maintained a constant battery of questions over the radio concerning the ransom. They pulled the pins on their hand grenades and showed them to the thoroughly frightened passengers and crew, promising immediate annihilation. Jackson, gun in hand, stepped forward into the cockpit as the minutes ran out and pointed his pistol at Capt. Haas. The time had come for the final act.

The staff in control of Oak Ridge was in a high state of apprehension. As the 1:00 PM deadline drew near and time ran out, more experts had been called in to give professional assessments of the potential damage the huge aircraft might cause. They agreed with the issued statement but could not achieve unanimity on the amount of radioactive gas that might eventually find its way into the atmosphere. The meteorological staff was able to provide reports on potential direction and velocity of drift from various places on the site where the final thrust could come, but had trouble in estimating the total effect of winds aloft on the outcome.

Jackson, in the closing minutes of time allotted before he would be called upon to make good his threat, acted with great deliberation. Thwarted once, he had, during the past hour, bolstered up his nerve. He was determined to go through with his part of the drama. Haas, still working against all hope to save both his people and his plane, waited while controlling the DC-9 in a precise circle some twenty thousand feet off the ground.

The climactic moment had been reached. No time was left. Jackson was on the verge of giving the crash order when, without warning, the radio broke into static, and a voice came through. The three skyjackers had won. Their wishes were in the process of being granted, and a Southern Airways plane was en route to Chattanooga, Tennessee.

Jackson and his friends were skeptical. They had been lied to once and were not going to be taken again. Additional radio messages were exchanged. The three kept asking how much money was on board, and if their other desires had been met.

Finally, Haas asked the question. "We don't know how much money you've got on board, and the people want to know."

"Are you checking the amount?" Haas was forced to ask again.

"We have the amount requested on board. Repeat, the amount requested."

At this point, jubilation broke out among the three. The $10 million was on its way.

The truth, however, was the Southern Airways plane was carrying only $2 million in cash. They had helmets, bulletproof vests, and other items agreed upon but were $8 million short of the needed ransom. It had been no small feat to collect $2 million over the weekend, but the airline had managed. At the advice of authorities, who felt the ship would rapidly depart for Cuba as soon as the money had been transferred, the $2 million was considered to be sufficient. The three on board would have little time to count such an immense amount of cash in small bills.

As Capt. Haas started a letdown toward Chattanooga, southeast of the Oak Ridge complex, he made a valiant plea for the release of the other hostages. He personally offered to stay aboard and fly the men to any destination they desired but argued for immediate freedom of his passengers while they were on the ground. An agreement was reached, but as they approached the airport, the three were spooked by seeing thousands of people gathered on hilltops and nearby shopping-center parking lots to view the spectacle.

"Pull down the shades," Moore was shrieking as he ran down the aisle. The plane was on final approach to landing. "Get your heads between your legs. No talking." He was strident in his demands.

Looking out the windows, the three, in their imaginations, saw a potential law enforcement agent behind every man, woman, and child. Earlier elation changed to agitated fear. They realized their safest course was to be airborne as soon as possible. Offloading passengers would take time and expose them to the view of crowds and agents. So they decided no one would deplane and the final transfer and refueling would take place quickly.

According to prearranged plan, a fuel truck and a smaller

vehicle convoyed with deliberate slowness to where the plane had stopped. The area around the end of the runway, far from the terminal building, had been selected because of its isolation.

Jackson, gun and grenade in hand again, had taken station in the DC-9 cockpit, where he could observe, watch Haas, and hear all incoming signals over the radio.

In the terminal, there was mass confusion. One eyewitness said the activity of agents, coats flapping open, showing their pistols as they ran from place to place, was constant. Passengers awaiting flights were restricted to certain areas, and efforts were made to place lookouts at every available point.

Action in Oak Ridge, while calmed by the landing, remained intense. There was no guarantee the hijackers, disappointed by not getting the $10 million, would not resume their deadly circling when they took off again.

Hundreds of people in the Chattanooga terminal, aware of the drama on the concrete runways outside the air-conditioned building, pressed for a look at the scene below.

Fred Vogt, stripped of his clothing and wearing only undershorts, climbed into the cab of the yellow refueling vehicle. He started his engine and, followed by the smaller truck, commenced the long, slow, crawling drive out to the waiting DC-9. In the control cabin, Jackson and one of the other men waited with growing annoyance. Their plan called for everything to be passed up to the open copilot's window, thus prohibiting anyone from actually coming aboard.

As the fuel truck pulled alongside the wing to position itself for filling the first tank, the smaller vehicle rolled to a stop. From an elevated platform used to load food service and maintenance personnel into a parked aircraft, Vogt handed through bundle after bundle of currency and requested materials. On the wing, the worker with the fuel hose was anxious and slipped, allowing the steel nozzle to bang on the main spar. Deciding the refueler was an agent in disguise, Jackson cocked his .38 and took aim.

"I'm gonna kill him." He spoke in an excited voice, and Haas, still in his captain's seat, answered, "He's just nervous in this situation." Then, taking a chance, he leaned forward into the field of fire and called out the window to the man, "Take it easy. You won't get hurt. Just fill the tank."

When the last of the bundles came aboard, the three were ready to leave and watched the lone fuel truck operator carefully. Was he delaying them? It seemed so, but there was no hurrying the pumps that delivered the JP mixture to the waiting tanks.

Then, after an eternity, it was done. As soon as the nozzle was removed, Jackson gave his order. "Let's go. Take her to Havana. And tell them we want Fidel Castro waiting at the airport."

With the ground wires still connected, the engines burst into a roar of life, and the plane was taxiing again. The copilot, Johnson, duly transmitted the last demands over his radio headset.

The takeoff was given immediate clearance, and a corridor was cleared for the DC-9 by the most direct route to Cuba. The plane began its long takeoff roll.

Inside the terminal, agents on duty realized their prey was about to escape and a shout rang out. Emergency vehicles filled with armed men were quickly started, and tires howling, went screaming after the ship. Several officers who had tried to get close enough for a sniper shot were left stranded as the plane, in a shimmering wave of heat and kerosene-smelling black smoke, accelerated farther and faster away from them.

A brief chase ensued. Agents in cars and an ambulance, which had been commandeered on the off chance there might be an opportunity to board and remove the passenger who had suffered a heart attack, sped through the bright afternoon. But it was too late. They watched the jetliner gather speed, rotate into a takeoff attitude, then lift into the air.

The hijackers had slipped away again, this time to potential sanctuary.

The story doesn't end here. The plane, with the same complement of passengers and crew, flew to Havana, where Castro was waiting in a terminal building office. He refused to see them, however, leaving all dealings to a middleman to whom he passed instructions.

On the way south, Jackson, Moore, and Cale were jubilant. Their gamble had paid off. Wearing the helmets and flak vests, they paraded in the cabin before their captive audience. Threats were still made, but this time not aimed at Oak Ridge. Now they were declaring they would don parachutes, set off a couple of hand grenades in the confined space to demobilize the flying ability of the aircraft, then bail out into the sea. But these boasts turned out to be idle.

The money, about $2 million, was spread out "all over the rear seats," and the three, when not shouting or bragging, would run their hands through it with glee. It was more cash in one spot than any of them had expected to see.

Time and again they offered and gave money to passengers. One man, who received $250, had no idea what to do with it and stuffed it into his shirt pockets.

The skyjackers started a party, washing down amphetamines, which had come aboard as stimulants for the two pilots, with small bottles of liquor from the unlocked cabinets. This combination was later to put them through a bad series of elations and depressions.

One of their prize possessions was a "grant" from the president of the United States, stamped with a variety of impressive seals, and totally worthless. Moore, waving it in the air, said over and over again, "Ain't this great? We're millionaires. The money's ours."

The various sacks and bags seemed to intoxicate the man, and on a wave of emotion, drugs, and alcohol, he turned benevolent. "Folks, we ain't got nothin' against you. Some of you businessmen have missed a day's work. You all have things you want to buy, and you've got payments on your houses. We're gonna share the wealth." With that, he began another round of passing out dollars. The passengers were afraid to refuse.

Moving into the cockpit, he began piling bills around Jackson and Cale. By the time he had reached more than $200,000, the money was so deep Capt. Haas had to request he stop because it was interfering with the controls.

The hijinks went on for the entire trip. During the time in the air, the men would go from high spirits to deep depression. The radio remained in constant use, relaying progress notes on their whereabouts and conversation among the hijackers, pilot, and authorities on the ground. The three remained firmly in control. As they neared Cuba and Haas began to make his clearing turns for José Martí Airport, Moore became more cautious. Again he demanded all shades be drawn and that the passengers bend over, heads between their legs.

The reception of the skyjackers in the Cuban capital was less than cordial and far less than the men had expected. Whatever deal they had intended to discuss was forestalled by the hostile actions of the Cuban troops who surrounded the plane. Moore and Jackson, carrying pistols and hand grenades, climbed down out of the aircraft by throwing an escape rope out the cockpit window. A great deal of shouting ensued. Apparently none of the Cubans spoke English and neither of the hijackers could communicate in Spanish. Instead, in an effort to use volume as a substitute for understanding, they yelled at one another. The Cuban guards and officials began to close in on the two men, who scared them back by waving their guns and showing the grenades.

It was a hard climb back up into the aircraft, but the two made it. Then in a fit of rage at not having been welcomed to the Communist island as heroes for having hijacked a capitalist airplane, Jackson stuck his head out the window and gave vent to his bitterness.

"Get me Fidel. And get me a fuel truck, or we're gonna start throwin' dead people out of this airplane."

Moore, meanwhile, was talking to the passengers. "Those people wanted to arrest us," he said indignantly. "Can you believe that? Why, they're nothin' but a bunch of Spanish-speakin' George Wallaces."

A single passenger on board could speak Spanish, and he was brought to the cockpit. In an emotional plea, he spoke with the tower asking for fuel and stating the seriousness of the situation. "For the love of God, comply with their demands," the man said passionately. "This situation has been going on over twenty-two hours and the hijackers are desperate."

The Castro forces, in answer to this request, furnished the jet with a minimum of fuel, and the plane was quickly airborne again. With only partially filled tanks, it could not remain so for very long.

A debate commenced, and after several radio transmissions, a landing at the U.S. Naval Air Station at Key West, Florida, was agreed upon. This was one of the closest places where the type of JP fuel compatible with the DC-9's engines could be found. Time on the ground was brief, and the fully refueled plane was once more in the air.

Jackson, holding wads of money in his hands, instructed the pilot to take the plane to Switzerland. That nation's record of neutrality seemed to make it the only possible haven.

Capt. Haas, however, vetoed the idea by explaining the DC-9 did not have the necessary range for a transatlantic hop, and that their engines were running low on a special oil. Still not convinced,

Jackson ordered the plane to land in Orlando, Florida, to "get what you need."

On the ground, a major gamble took place. FBI agents, under orders from Acting Director Patrick Gray relayed through his agent-in-charge at McCoy Air Force Base in Orlando, were instructed to stop the plane from taking off again at any cost. The decision was made to shoot out the tires and then, when the ship came to a halt, board, using techniques a special team had been practicing all day long.

Although J. Edgar Hoover had had a long-term understanding with the Air Line Pilots Association about action without the pilot's prior knowledge or consent, Acting Director Gray decided not to contact Haas and use the code to tell him of his plans. He felt this decision was justified because he did not consider the pilot and copilot "free to exercise their best judgment."

In any event, the FBI and other authorities wanted the plane grounded before another Oak Ridge incident could occur. There was a good possibility the trio, having once been successful with that ploy, might try again—and this time might actually crash.

While refueling was going on, fifteen agents crept through the darkness and gained sanctuary under the fuselage at the rear. As the fuel truck roared away, they opened fire on the tires of the DC-9.

Dim pops were heard inside the soundproofed cabin, and the aircraft lurched off to its left as the tires on that main gear were blasted away. Although possibly hit, the nose wheel and right main gear tires were not flattened.

Moore and Jackson, standing at the open cockpit door, were at first puzzled by the noise and sudden tilting of the plane. Then, realizing what had happened, they went wild. They fired at the rapidly departing fuel truck, then shot again through the cockpit windows, past Haas's and copilot Billy Johnson's heads.

Insanely angry, they started shooting through the galley floor at the men they knew were lurking under the aircraft. This is when the only incident of intended injury to passenger or crew occurred.

In a complete rage, Jackson pointed his pistol at Johnson, who bad been handling radio communications with the tower, and started screaming. "We're gonna start shootin' people and throw 'em out the window. And you're first, Harold." He had been mispronouncing Billy Halroyd Johnson's name for hours. "You did it," he screamed again, "You told 'em to do it, and we're gonna kill you."

Johnson resisted as the two hijackers dragged him out of his seat and into the main cabin. He flung himself to the floor between the second and third rows and Jackson fired. The first shot exploded in the confines of the passenger space, and the bullet blasted through one of the seats into Johnson's arm. The copilot screamed in pain, and as Jackson tried to fire another shot, he rolled partially into view. Jackson's pistol failed to go off the second time he pulled the trigger, and before he could try again, Lou Moore stopped him. "That's enough, man. Don't kill him. We may need him. Let's get out of here."

Mollified, Jackson motioned with the barrel of the gun. Johnson, pale-faced, with blood pouring from his wound and staining his once-white shirt, climbed slowly to his feet. Jackson pushed him roughly into the cockpit, and began hollering again to "Take off."

Haas argued the impossibility of such a maneuver with the tires blown away, but was again faced with a threat. "Get into the air, or we'll start killing people. Harold will be first."

Haas slammed on the power, and the agents under the aircraft were blown away by the force of the jet wash. One man rolled and tumbled half the length of a football field before he could stop himself. When he stood up, his clothes had been torn away.

The plane, lurching drunkenly, rumbled down the runway until, with a great reeling bounce, it was airborne. Treads from the flailing tires were sucked into the engines as they flew off the wheels, and the rims, trailing showers of red-orange sparks, dug parallel lines in the hard concrete surface.

The odyssey, which had now gone on for more than twenty-four hours, was still far from ending. The plane, with no rubber on the left main gear and engines badly strained by ingestion of flying parts of the shot-away tires, had only one landing left. Haas, who had been at the controls the whole time, was now without the assistance of his copilot, who had a shattered bone in his arm.

The hijackers, still in a temper, tried to talk to the president but refused to converse with Secretary John A. Volpe of the Department of Transportation. Some thought was given to crashing into the Key Biscayne home of Nixon, but the money and the possibility of better treatment in Cuba drove them to their final selection of a field. They ordered Haas to return to Havana.

Using the passenger who spoke Spanish to request a foam-lined landing surface, they were amazed to learn there was not enough fire-preventing material to cover an entire runway. They would have to be met by a foam-fire truck when they stopped their forward motion on the ground.

Capt. Haas, after orbiting the José Martí field long enough to burn away almost all remaining fuel load, brought the plane in safely.

The three hijackers, Moore, Jackson, and Cale, stuffed plastic flight bags with money. Each waited by an exit to make a fast getaway as soon as the plane stopped.

The stress imposed on the airframe during the landing was enormous. Flying with exceptional skill, Haas brought the tireless left gear in first, throwing up a cascade of sparks from the concrete. Then, holding direction perfectly, he lost more speed and eased the ship down onto its good gear. Metal screamed as it tore and the plane shrieked with the twisting fuselage. Then, after a rush of noise, there was silence. They were down. The three hijackers burst from the plane and ran, trying to hide in the tall weeds near the runway. Three minutes later, they were prisoners of the Cuban government.

The passengers were personally greeted by Castro, who was sincerely glad for their safety. They were treated well, and after a good night's rest and medical care for those in need, were allowed to return to their homes. Castro, speaking through an assistant, complimented Capt. Haas on his abilities as a pilot. Haas, known as "Billy Bob" to friends, continued his flying career, which spanned twenty-nine years.

As for the hijackers, they appear to have been arrested in Cuba and held there for eight years. Then, in 1980, the trio, back in the United States, reportedly faced charges in Birmingham, Alabama, and were sentenced to jail terms of between twenty and twenty-five years.

The ordeal, which holds some kind of record for skyjacking, lasted twenty-nine hours and twelve minutes. The plane flew more than four thousand miles, landed nine times, crossed and recrossed the borders of three countries, and at one time or another had over one thousand people involved in some phase of either flight direction or apprehension.

The threat to the Oak Ridge complex caused great anxiety for a prolonged period, and almost became a full-fledged nuclear incident.

All in all, it was some ride for the thirty-one passengers and crew aboard Southern Airways Flight 49. Everyone involved will remember it for a long time. Especially the people at Oak Ridge— because they came close to being involved in a disaster of biblical proportions.

SIX

Worldwide Proliferation

In the first decade of the twenty-first century, nuclear proliferation has reached a hazardous level. The main cause for this growth can be traced back to policies and actions taken more than sixty years ago by the U.S. government. A step-by-step tracing of U.S. nuclear political history since the early 1950s more than supports this view.

"Atoms for Peace" was established in 1954. Under this program, any nation more or less favorably inclined toward the United States could have a nuclear reactor erected in a location of its choosing. The Atoms for Peace plan was viewed as a powerful tool by which the United States could control the spread of nuclear weaponry and at the same time support the economies of world nations by making a positive contribution to their desire for energy. It was eventually to produce somewhat opposite results.

No one can dispute the need for Atoms for Peace. Nuclear reactors were and still are very expensive. One, erected in Arizona years ago, reportedly cost more than the total assessed value of the city of Phoenix at the time. If the underprivileged, technically less-experienced nations were ever to share in the bonanza of atomic energy, a highly developed nation—and that meant the

United States, the only real atomic power of that era—had to come in and help.

Few political hooks were attached to the grant of a nuclear reactor. Few were needed. The Atomic Energy Commission (AEC) regulated more than 90 percent of all supplies of enriched uranium utilized by the non-Communist countries of the world. Control of that one vital element gave the United States practical dominance over American-donated installations. Inspections were on our terms, as was enforcement of regulations concerning disposal of radioactive waste materials like plutonium. In short, that which the United States had granted, the United States could also take away, by reducing or cutting off the flow of uranium. The deal was too good to last.

As early as 1953, then-President Dwight D. Eisenhower suggested the creation of an international uranium holding organization. Such a move would have maintained U.S. control over fissionable materials for years. However, Cold War concerns defeated that concept.

The situation remained static until the early 1970s. Then the Nixon Administration began a series of steps that would eventually result in massive proliferation of atomic reactors outside the control of the U.S. government. Under a loose program known as "privatization," commercial vendors were encouraged to become suppliers of nuclear materials, and the federal powers pulled back to reduce the importance of the Atomic Energy Commission. And the 1970 Nuclear Non-Proliferation Treaty gave nations an "inalienable right" to develop and use atomic energy.

These policies resulted in the 1974 shutdown of the AEC, which became, in part, the Nuclear Regulatory Commission (NRC). And the supply function for all previously regulated atomic raw material was turned over to large publicly owned corporations. Sensing a period of potential price instability and fearing cost increases when the uranium industry was freed of government control and subsidy, a last-minute panic among nuclear power plant operators doubled orders for enriched uranium. This run tied up all then-available AEC supplies. An artificial shortage ensued, and the price of most atomic elements rose with sudden sharpness in world markets.

Coinciding with this seemingly accidental problem was the unforeseen activism of environmentalists and others working in unison against the construction of new nuclear facilities. A groundswell of public response occurred almost as if in reply to a single signal. Overnight, groups were vocally and visually active in numerous countries, causing both politicians and private businessmen to proceed with caution. The outcome was a dramatic slowdown in the growth of new nuclear installations and a reappraisal of the long-term prospects for atomic power. By the late 1970s, industry estimates showed no American plans for construction of more reactors after 1985 or '86.

Several major companies had responded to the apparent uranium shortage by investing millions to develop process plants that produced nuclear fuel elements. The end of new domestic reactor construction left them in the untenable position of having made large capital outlays to produce materials for which there was declining demand.

According to industry reports, General Electric and Westinghouse had laid out more than $500 million each in pursuit of this phantom market. Others, in joint projects, had lesser but still significant dollar investments. Combustion Engineering and Babcock & Wilcox are reported to have had combined costs of over $150 million.

One of the most difficult business problems comes from making a major capital outlay for a production facility and then not using it. Normally, there are possible conversions that, providing funds are available, can be made. Almost every industrial and chemical process lends itself to some flexibility. In fact, initial design usually takes a duality of purpose into consideration, so a large plant is seldom constructed without serious study given to alternative uses for the complex.

A nuclear facility, however, is different. Federal and scientific safeguards, along with the ever-present problems stemming from radioactive contamination, render the design single-purpose. In other words, if a company invests hundreds of millions of dollars to construct an operation for the production of enriched uranium, what the company ends up with is precisely that, and nothing else. The buildings cannot easily be switched to the manufacture of alcohols or ammonia.

Faced with a hard decision, business firms that had joined in the Nixon-supported privatization began to look for ways to generate some return on their now-doubtful investments. Fortunately, just before the demise of the AEC, two U.S.-based nuclear brokerages were established. These were designed to bring buyer and seller together in an open trading forum.

The World Nuclear Fuel Market (WNFM) came first, and the Separative Work Unit Corporation (SWUCO) followed. These two firms arranged sales across international borders. SWUCO, with headquarters in Maryland, operated as a listing service. A seller listed a commodity, and a buyer posted needs. With this information available, deals were consummated.

WNFM acted more as a consortium. In 1976, there were seventy-nine business organizations, ranging from construction contractors to power utilities, as members. Thirty-eight were U.S. companies, and the forty-one remaining were from other countries. A report at that time indicated SWUCO had assisted in the dissemination of enough plutonium to construct eight or nine atomic weapons. One shipment was said to have been sent from a U.S. company to an overseas buyer.

The existence of these two firms provided interested U.S. companies with world markets for their nuclear produce. Some of the nations buying considerable quantities of atomic materials would have been held in check by the old AEC. The new NRC had no responsibility in that area. In short, there existed a sort of gray market in which U.S. companies made sales to nations with questionable motives or with less than strong allegiance to the United States and the non-Communist world.

Today, open shopping for atomic-grade materials for weapons manufacture, and even for weapons of mass destruction, is not uncommon. This is nothing new. According to news stories back in the 1970s, President Quaddafi of Libya, for one, had been trying to buy a bomb at any price. Viewed from several decades later, such quests do not seem to have been overly successful. But perseverance and unlimited funds are a powerful combination. Despite controls and intense monitoring, weapons-grade materials and—according to some sources—nuclear warheads have changed hands.

Another report from the '70s concerned a confidential memo from the Energy Research and Development Administration (ERDA) to a congressional subcommittee. It stated that at least twenty-two sales of nuclear materials and artifacts had been made to foreign countries by U.S. companies since the onset of privatization. These did not include secret aid reportedly rendered by the CIA to selected governments.

Competitive pressures on American firms with high investments in the nuclear field have been intensified by the formation of several consortiums of foreign governments and corporations. Brazil entered into an agreement with West Germany, and through the West Germans, with Holland, for reactors and plutonium reprocessing. Pakistan signed a contract with France for a reactor, postponed the agreement due to "political unrest," and after a military coup resulting in the removal of Prime Minister Zulfikar Ali Bhutto, the French attempted to stall the deal. When the Pakistanis indicated they would go to "other sources," believed to be a reference to their close ally China, the French came through. France also pursued the sale of breeder-type reactors in the United States.

One reality the United States achieved through a policy of vacillation is the end of American supremacy in many areas of nuclear technology. This, in turn, made already bad matters worse by giving everyone who wanted to make secret or hard-to-trace nuclear purchases the added anonymity that comes from a competitive market, buyer-seller relationship.

So worldwide control of atomic materials slipped from U.S. hands. While this might have happened anyway, the removal of American governmental regulations through the termination of the powers of the AEC clearly hastened the situation.

In the late 1940s, only one country had the bomb and the ability to harness the atom for peaceful uses. In the 1950s, two more nations joined the team of atomic sisters. Then, in the 1960s, several gained the necessary technology. Now those who have nuclear know-how compose a rather unruly and diverse family. Many nations, some of them surprises, have or will shortly have some form of atomic explosive device. In addition to the United States, Russia, the United Kingdom, France, China, India, Israel, South Africa, Taiwan, North Korea, and Pakistan are members of or applicants to this now not-so-exclusive club. Six more nations (Australia, Belgium, Canada, Italy, Japan, and West Germany) have a nuclear weapons capability but so far no compelling need to develop a bomb. At least twenty nations, including Iran, are capable of making a nuclear weapon within a short period of time. And more are applying daily. Over forty countries have the technology to make nuclear fuel, which is an early step in weapons development.

Sooner or later, there is a strong possibility that some not-too-disciplined, over-egoed demagogue heading a one-man dictatorship is going to have the capacity to set off a nuclear explosion. Unhindered by problems of morality and driven by the necessity of preserving power, he is going to unleash a warhead. A lot of people are going to meet an untimely death. The radiation content in milk in Minnesota is going to go up. Hens' eggs in the Ural Mountains will cause a slight but perceptible increase in clicks on a scintillation counter. We have only one earth. Even a "clean" nuclear explosion of reasonably small proportions makes a big enough mess to contaminate and pollute for a measurable period of time.

The issue of illegal nuclear proliferation is made worse by the existence of both gray and black markets. Illicit trading of radioactive elements has become almost routine.

Where do these fissionable materials that are sold for cash originate?

Good question. Especially since the manufacture of nuclear materials is an expensive, difficult process with potentially dire consequences to those who perform the work. The number of production sites is limited. It would therefore seem easy to monitor output and establish stringent standards of accountability for every ounce of material produced. Gold smelters do not have unaccountable amounts of gold lost in the extraction processing, or in smelting. Even though plutonium is a rare and valuable element, the same concerns have played only a small role in the nuclear industry.

The seriousness of lost nuclear material was revealed as early as 1976 when the United States still controlled much of the world's production. In that year, the U.S. Government Accounting Office (GAO) reported government-owned atomic installations could not account for slightly more than eleven thousand pounds of plutonium and enriched uranium. This is called "Missing or

Unaccounted for Materials," or MUF. A subsequent GAO report is said to have come up between fifteen thousand and twenty thousand pounds short in an audit of privately owned manufacturing plants. Those figures did not include weapons facilities, for national security reasons. Then-Representative John D. Dingell (D-Mich.) is said to have noted that according to an independent GAO audit, the government substantially underestimated losses. To the original missing tonnage, add even greater amounts found missing in subsequent decades. Uses for these elements are limited to fueling reactors or building weapons.

Lost materials had to go somewhere. And since risk is required in the removal of the missing uranium and plutonium, the price of this MUF on the world gray/black market could amount to millions if not billions of dollars. A portion of the unaccounted-for critical elements may have passed into the hands of the CIA for dispersal to selected overseas allies based on secret government policy. Another small amount was anticipated to be missing, as it is lost in the processing system. Inventory control procedures, record-keeping errors, and other factors may account for still more of the total. Even so, a substantial amount has disappeared without a trace.

It is difficult to determine exactly what has happened to this missing material. In the early days, many unofficial statements maintained a theory in which the major producing firms have held out certain amounts awaiting price increases in the gray or legitimate markets. Another possibility is contained within the congressional testimony of Dr. Arthur Tamplin, a man admittedly opposed to the use of nuclear power. "It's certain," quoting a statement attributed to Dr. Tamplin, "that the MUF accounting methods are not adequate to prevent the theft of strategic quantities of [plutonium]. They are not necessarily even adequate to detect the loss of that amount of material; that's why they have what's called the 'limited error of MUF!'" Outright theft of the radioactive substances appears to be possible. The NRC, however, opposed that comment and denied any great losses over and above those caused by accounting or processing. And they defend their position with logically presented evidence.

As can be seen, America's past policies have contributed to worldwide nuclear proliferation. That was not the intention of the programs or those who enacted them. And continued proliferation on an even wider scale is not the intention of the U.S. Department of Energy today. Yet the recently announced Global Nuclear Energy Partnership (GNEP), created by the United States, has an ominous familiarity.

In a quote attributed to Samuel Bodman, U.S. secretary of energy, GNEP "brings the promise of virtually limitless energy to emerging economies around the globe, in an environmentally friendly manner, while reducing the threat of nuclear proliferation." Those words apply just as well to the old, and failed, Atoms for Peace program. Despite new technologies for disposing of spent fuel, and even though the new GNEP envisions more control over atomic fuel elements, the same key problems that existed with the earlier Atoms for Peace remain. In particular—and this will certainly happen—is the limiting of U.S. "partners" to those nations friendly to America. And since the "partnership" includes "other fuel producing nations," countries with views and stances contrary to U.S. interests will benefit. This situation supports a gray or black market.

Then there is the well established fact of unaccounted for materials, or MUF. The United States was unable to maintain control of MUF during a period when this nation dominated the nuclear scene. Now with several other countries involved in the joint research and development effort, the MUF will be still more difficult to contain. So the gray/black markets should have little difficulty in finding materials to buy and sell.

This is not to imply that the GNEP effort is doomed to failure, especially if those conducting that activity can learn from the past. Commercial companies will play a huge role in developing and perfecting the technology needed for the GNEP projects. This also is an area where the past teaches strong lessons. Historically, anti-nuclear power groups have demonstrated against private contractors in this field. In some instances, protests have escalated to alarming proportions. There is also the issue of labor problems in the private enterprise sector. One such case, made famous in a major motion picture (*Silkwood*), dealt with the death of an obscure nuclear technician. Which brings us to the next example of atomic drama. It's the strange and some say still unsolved story of Ms. Karen Silkwood.

SEVEN

Karen Silkwood

By 7:30 on a chill November evening the first few stars, their brilliance not diluted by city lights, shone with sharp intensity. The narrow farm road cut a black strip across the gently rolling Oklahoma countryside.

A lone girl nervously checked the time on her Mickey Mouse wristwatch. She sat tensely behind the wheel of a white '73 Honda Hatchback. Speeding through the night, she was late for an appointment set days before with a union leader and a reporter from the *New York Times*. Beside her in the other bucket seat, a large brown manila envelope slid as she corrected the car's direction. She hoped it contained the final, much-needed evidence required to back up the statements she was soon to make about large amounts of missing plutonium.

The headlights sliced through the blackness along Highway 74, revealing compact shoulders that edged the narrow, thirty-four-foot-wide asphalt road. At 55 mph, the wind noise inside the small car blocked all other external sounds. She had been driving about ten minutes and was 7.3 miles south of Crescent, a small farming community where she lived and had friends.

Her previous home had been in a bleaker place over five hundred miles to the south. There, the brown, flat, featureless land had smelled of refined oil and petrochemical production. She was settled in Crescent now, sharing an apartment with a roommate and working in the Kerr-McGee Cimarron plutonium production facility.

The road, following the contour of the hills, turned slightly down, and without thinking, she adjusted her speed.

Suddenly, from nowhere, the blinding flash of another car's headlights reflected off her rearview mirror. Squinting, she turned her head away from the annoying illumination. She allowed her Honda to pull closer to the shoulder, giving the overtaking vehicle the maximum possible room to pass.

Unable to ignore the intrusion of the intense light, she shifted in her seat. The other car drew closer. She gave a quick glance in her mirror. The second vehicle was directly on her tail. Vexed by its closeness, she pushed down with her foot and increased speed. The second car followed. Then, without warning, she felt a sickening lurch as the second automobile slammed into her left rear bumper. The Honda's wheels broke contact with the pavement and spun madly. The nose of the small car slid to the right. She struggled to correct the skid, but the car, crossing over the narrow roadway's center stripe, was almost out of control. On the verge of the hard-packed shoulder, she slammed on the brakes. Ahead, the gray-white square of a concrete wing abutment for an under-the-road drainage pipe loomed directly in her path.

The noise inside the Honda was insane. Wind and shrieking tires, then a multi-sound crash as the car smashed into the immobile barrier. Rending metal and the tinkle of breaking glass blended into a final cacophony. Afterwards, a resonating silence was broken only by the noise of the car that had caused the wreck. It slowed to a stop some yards farther ahead. Gravel grated under the rear tires as the driver threw it into reverse and gunned the engine, backing rapidly to a position across the road from the shattered, smoking Honda.

A man emerged from the vehicle. Running lightly, he crossed to the culvert. Working by the light from the destroyed car's still-bright headlamps, he fished inside the passenger space and retrieved the manila envelope. Rummaging through it, he tossed papers into the air until he found the ones he sought. Clutching the envelope to his chest, he sprinted across the roadway and jumped into the waiting car.

The driver, hesitating only long enough to hear the door slam, came down hard on the gas pedal. Roaring into the night the rapidly accelerating vehicle crested a low hill a hundred yards down the two-lane blacktop and was gone. A final booming note of the exhaust was absorbed into the darkness, and the countryside was still again.

Nothing stirred. Less than two minutes had elapsed from the point of impact between the cars. The broken, bleeding girl at the wheel was dead. The documents she had so valiantly collected and tried to deliver, gone.

That's the version of what happened that Wednesday night, November 13, 1974, that a lot of people accept as gospel. And gospel truth it may be. We may never know for certain.

But there is another side to this story. Another reconstruction of these events—equally plausible and elegantly more simple. It goes like this.

A distraught twenty-eight-year-old woman, Karen Silkwood, completed a telephone call shortly after 6:00 PM. She reminded her boyfriend, Drew Stephens, to pick up Steve Wodka, a union official from Washington, D.C., and David Burnham, a reporter for the *New York Times*. They were to meet her at 8:00 that night at the Holiday Inn–Northwest in Oklahoma City.

Satisfied all was in order, she left the Hub Café, and driving slowly, made her way to Highway 74. The girl with the Mickey Mouse watch was in a highly emotional state. On the previous two days, Monday and Tuesday, November 11 and 12, she, along with Stephens and her roommate, Sherri Ellis, twenty-two, a fellow worker at the Kerr-McGee facility in Cimarron, had undergone stringent medical examinations. At the Los Alamos Scientific Laboratory in New Mexico, they had been studied to determine how badly they were contaminated by plutonium.

The trio returned home between 10:30 and 11:00 PM on Tuesday and spent some time consuming a number of Bloody Marys made from tomato juice and 190-proof alcohol. Liquor and methaqualone, a sedative prescribed by a doctor some weeks before, made a powerful combination. No certain testimony exists as to the time Karen went to bed, but according to her roommate, it was later than 2:00 AM.

The day had been arduous enough. First she'd been in a morning-long meeting over contract negotiations between Local 5-283 and Kerr-McGee representatives. Then she'd had a tiring session with investigators from the Atomic Energy Commission who were trying to run down the source of her contamination. According to the testimony of FBI agent Bill Fisher, an AEC inspector was interviewed by one of the official investigators after the accident. The inspector reported the girl appeared emotionally upset at times during their conference. On one occasion she had broken into tears.

A great many things must have been running through Karen's mind as she turned her car onto the farm road for the thirty-mile drive to Oklahoma City. A lingering fear of permanent injury from plutonium contamination had to vie with frustration over stymied union-management talks. Then there was her restriction from radiation work because of the contamination. And with it all, a general lassitude from a combination of drugs, lack of sleep, and aftereffects of alcohol.

Little traffic passed on the dark, silent road and her headlights bore hypnotically into the almost palpable blackness. What started as an agitated mind switching from subject to subject became, in minutes, a brain gone random, absorbing the darkness and tempo of the highway.

The first gnawing of drowsiness nibbled at the edges of her consciousness. She shifted uneasily in the narrow bucket seat. Fixing her attention, she fought to stay alert. But her eyes were involuntarily closing. The small white car, following her steering input, veered slowly to the left, over the center line, edging closer and closer to the shoulder.

Something—a natural awareness causing a return from the realm of half-sleep, or the change in the sound of the car tires as they migrated to the edge of the road—brought her around once more. But this time she was confronted with a moving emergency. Not fully alert, and working with the hyper-reflexes of an adrenaline-charged system, she started to swing the wheel. Closing at a rate of almost sixty feet a second, the white Honda shot toward the concrete abutment. What had started as a potentially serious accident had now become a deadly one. The impact threw the passenger violently forward.

Minutes later a trucker, following another car, came onto the scene and spotted the crumpled wreck. Stopping to investigate, he found the girl's battered remains inside the overturned vehicle.

Papers were scattered about, and among them there might have been a brown manila envelope. But no one is certain. There were no documents indicating massive losses of plutonium in the Cimarron plant found among her effects.

Within hours of her death, Steve Wodka notified the AEC of his union's suspicion that Karen's death might have been the result of foul play. Even though the highway patrol investigating the accident felt it was merely a case of falling asleep at the wheel, and the union could find no governmental agency to check its allegations, Wodka initiated a probe.

The accident investigator hired by the union saw the car in Oklahoma City, where Drew Stephens had it towed two days after the accident. He found damage to the left rear of the Honda, which he considered sufficient evidence Karen's car had been hit from the rear and forced off the road. But another witness, who had seen the car shortly after the accident, said there was no damage to the Honda in that area.

The death of Karen Silkwood, coming as it did after her unexplained contamination at a plant with known AEC violations, created a cause célèbre. By now, regardless of the truth, she is regarded by many as this country's first atomic martyr. The main significance of her death lies not in the mystery of the events surrounding her violent demise but in the information produced by the many lengthy inquiries into those circumstances.

Karen Silkwood was born in Longview, Texas. She grew up in the small town of Nederland, located in the center of the Gulf Coast petrochemical production area. At school, she was a member of Future Homemakers of America, a flutist in the band, and belonged to the National Honor Society. She was interested in science, especially chemistry, and took a special course on radiation.

After a year at Lamar College in Beaumont, Texas, she met a pipeline worker while on vacation. They married and for the next six years lived a nomadic life as he moved from job to job across Texas and Oklahoma. The end of their relationship came after three children.

Divorced, Karen drifted for a short time, then headed north to Oklahoma. Custody of the kids went to her ex-husband, who had remarried. After a short stint as a clerk in a hospital, she became, on August 4, 1972, a laboratory analyst in the Kerr-McGee plutonium-producing plant in Cimarron, Oklahoma. This facility was built in 1970 to fulfill a multimillion-dollar federal contract to supply 18,500 plutonium fuel pins for the Fast Flux Test Facility in Richland, Washington. Located next to another Kerr-McGee operation, an automated uranium-reprocessing plant, the Cimarron works rolled pencil-thin tubes from metal sheets, welded the seams, then filled them with plutonium.

According to company officials, Karen was, in her early days of employment, an excellent worker. She displayed a cheerful attitude and showed enough interest in her job to have considered it as a career. After about three months, things began to change. Karen, through her friends, became progressively more involved in union activities. Gaining quick recognition for her spirit and willingness to speak out, she soon managed to become one of the leaders in carrying workers' problems to management.

Why she found satisfaction in this role is unimportant. One group maintains she started to see the real plight of those who worked with radioactive materials and reacted by redoubling her activities and commitment to the union. Others say she found a gratifying outlet, peer respect, and recognition by associating herself with the leadership of a dissident group. Whatever her motives, she soon became well known. Comments about her ran from "emotionally troubled divorcee" to "a good kid."

Her devotion to the union cause was matched by her antagonism toward Kerr-McGee, and especially the plant in Cimarron. The plutonium facility was a problem to Kerr-McGee in many ways, including labor relations and operational safety. The Kerr-McGee Cimarron plutonium plant was an atomic installation of a unique nature, and at times management at the site had difficulties in their dealings with safety regulations.

An examination of the accident record of any major manufacturing facility will reveal events in which workers were injured and those in charge failed to take the immediate steps specified in their plant operating plan. Those same omissions, when coupled with the problems of dealing with dangerous radioactive materials, become more serious.

One protection against negligence is constant training. And according to union official Anthony Mazzocchi's testimony before a House of Representatives investigating committee, the Cimarron facility had no such ongoing program. In addition, several individuals who had received little or no training for their jobs were working in crucial areas.

A chronological listing of incidents and accidents at any site the size of the Cimarron plutonium facility gives the feeling of massive and consistent disregard for employee safety. While most of the items by themselves were of no great significance, collectively they indicated management controls needed strengthening.

Story after story listing plant failures have appeared since Karen Silkwood's death. Some incidents reveal management mistakes and others, worker errors. Still more would seem to be attributable simply to chance.

In October 1970, shortly after the official opening of the plant, two men were contaminated when a storage container was mistakenly left open for three days. Then, three months later, in January 1971, twenty-two individuals were exposed to radiation when a defective piece of equipment failed and allowed plutonium oxide to leak into the atmosphere of the work area. No other significant nuclear incident occurred until April 1972, when two maintenance men working on a pump were splashed with plutonium particles in liquid suspension. Not realizing their contamination, they left the plant at noon for lunch in a nearby town and did not become aware of their condition until they returned to the facility hours later. Both underwent successful decontamination processing and their car was cleaned up. But Kerr-McGee staffers reportedly failed to check the restaurant where the two had eaten, and neglected to report the matter to the AEC as required by operating regulations. The AEC learned of the incident a month later, and the affair, a violation of the federal nuclear code, was processed through channels. Mild corrective steps were reported to have been taken.

Other events during this period included the appearance of tiny holes in the gloves workers wore while handling radioactive materials inside gloveboxes. There were also drum leakages in tanks used to store plutonium and process system errors in which plutonium flowing in solution through a complex piping network was wrongly routed to areas of the plant not designed to receive it. Then there were equipment failures such as an exploding compressor that killed one man. All of these incidents are regrettable.

Union officials in testimony before the House investigating committee indicated improved training, along with closer adherence to operating rules, might have prevented some of the trouble. Not unnaturally, the accident rate at the plant contributed to poor relations between the local Oil, Chemical and Atomic Workers International Union (OCAW) and Kerr-McGee.

Oklahoma, as much of the Sunbelt, is not a strong union area when compared with many parts of the United States. Traditions of Old West independence coupled with labor practices rooted in the founding days of the oil and gas industry have made union and management relations troubled.

The OCAW, in its bargaining attempts with Kerr-McGee for a new contract at the plutonium plant, came to the conclusion a strike was their only alternative. So, in late 1972, its members walked off their jobs.

Kerr-McGee responded by bringing in others to fill vacated positions. According to the union, there was no sufficient training program for replacement employees. While no significant number of incidents was reported during the time the facility operated with these less-experienced workers, the strikebreaking attempt served to further irritate union members. So the gulf widened between the local's officers and plant management.

This is an unhealthy climate in any manufacturing facility and lends itself to the development of constant strain, which adds yet another distracting element to an unstable environment.

Karen Silkwood's death gave the union a means of forcing the AEC to examine working conditions at Kerr-McGee. The AEC, in specific answer to the allegations and rumors about safety, conducted an extensive on-site investigation. Workers and management alike were called upon to come forward and testify. Documents dealing with the operation of the Cimarron facility were stringently reviewed.

In the final analysis, thirty-nine safety grievances were investigated; twenty were found to be true or at least to have some basis in fact. Plutonium had been stored improperly—in one instance in a desk drawer instead of a locked vault provided for that purpose. Workers had labored without wearing respirators in areas not tested for contamination as required, or in places where leaks had occurred. Kerr-McGee operating management did fail to report a May 1974 incident in which a serious leak closed the plant. And written standards had not been fully followed in checking and inspecting respirators. In addition, the AEC team found improper worker training in several areas of the facility.

Granted, none of these problems should have existed. But they are far from being criminal acts. In fact, the AEC did not consider them worthy of censure. And other than including the incidents in a file on Kerr-McGee and the Cimarron plant, no punitive action was recommended or taken.

Antinuclear groups have developed an elaborate explanation for this lack of censure, based on the fact that Cimarron was the production site for plutonium fuel rods to be used in the still-under-construction Richland, Washington, breeder reactor. According to several articles, the AEC was afraid to take strong measures against Kerr-McGee's breaches of regulations because it would have spelled bad publicity for the breeder program and cast doubt on the success of the project. Others claim inordinate political influence was the source of a cover-up. Dear as this logic may be to the hearts of those seeking a national conspiracy of big business and government, another explanation suggests itself.

In the period 1973–1974, AEC investigators found 3,333 violations of regulations in various nuclear establishments in the United States. Only eight of these were judged serious enough to permit a penalty. The balance, while still considered to be noteworthy, as is any rule breakage in an atomic installation, were deemed to be of no real consequence. They were entered into the records of the plants and stations so future inspectors would be able to re-check from time to time. In short, a rule infraction sufficient to result in a penalty was rare. It is therefore not surprising that no steps were taken against the Kerr-McGee operations at Cimarron.

This is not to say that penalties shouldn't be given for less serious violations. The NRC, in fact, has pressed for this. But no evidence exists to suggest the AEC was too lenient in the Kerr-McGee case, based on its previous history.

Karen Silkwood began work in the plant in August 1972. By November the strike was called. Nine weeks later, of the original 130 union members, only 27 were left to return to their jobs. Karen was among them. In April 1974, she was elected to the union's governing committee. On September 29, 1974, she was in the Washington offices of the OCAW, along with two other Cimarron employees, to discuss "strategy" with union executives

Anthony Mazzocchi and Steve Wodka. Wodka said he and his boss, Mazzocchi, after hearing stories of alleged quality-control violations, asked "Karen to go back to the plant to find out who was falsifying the records, who was ordering it, and to document everything in specific detail."

With urging and backing by the union, it is easy to see how this request became an obsession. Karen later vowed to her boyfriend Drew Stephens that she was going to get proof that Kerr-McGee management was falsifying records in order to avoid trouble with the AEC. According to a published quote, she said, "We're really gonna get those motherf...ers this time."

Much of the information on quality control she gathered was common knowledge among both workers and supervisors in the facility. A retouched photograph of the welding on one of the fuel rods manufactured at the plant, often mentioned to show she had found evidence of falsification of records, also came to the attention of the AEC. They did more than Ms. Silkwood by finding the man who had doctored the photo to make a questionable seam appear to be passable. In an interview, this employee said he "used a feltpoint pen to dab a small amount of ink" on spots he considered "caused by defects in the emulsion [of the film], static electricity, etc." Even in this case, the welds had been visually inspected prior to taking the photograph, on a device called a metallograph, and the technician was "correcting" photos to pass a superior's inspection. Statements of individuals involved indicate they were very concerned about controlling weld quality as they knew the potential problems that could arise from a weak tube.

The combination of the climate at the plant and Ms. Silkwood's attitude explains why she was so ardent in her investigation and so adamant she would find something. In virtually every report of this case, Karen Silkwood has been shown gathering information about safety irregularities in the Cimarron facility. In fact, some of the union documents, written after her death, reinforce this idea. The reality, however, according to statements of almost everyone involved, including union officials, is that she was engaged in the collection of data that would show discrepancies in quality control.

Ms. Silkwood was known to have gone into private company files and copied documents she thought were of vital importance to the union's case. Those same files were also scrutinized by the AEC and were the basis for their validation of some of the previously mentioned regulations breaches.

The stress on Karen Silkwood during this period of her life was extreme. Yet, outwardly, she appeared to be coping with the situation. She shared a small apartment, had a number of friends, partied a little, and was considered by many to be a "good listener."

But she had two significant problems. The first was her use of drugs. In addition to marijuana, common enough in our society for her age group, she also took regular doses of methaqualone, purchased with a prescription issued by an Oklahoma City doctor and calling for one tablet a day on retiring. In a period of ninety-two days she purchased 180 tablets. A handwritten note found in her apartment shows she made a $300 expenditure for some type of "dope" during one period. Her use of chemical substances was further revealed by her attempt to commit suicide in September 1973. According to a statement by a friend, Connie Edwards, Karen called to say she had tried to kill herself by taking an overdose of drugs. Ms. Edwards stated she went to Ms. Silkwood's apartment and found her "in a stoop on the sofa."

Her second problem was she had become contaminated by plutonium.

A lot has been made of this peculiar circumstance, with one group maintaining she was deliberately exposed by a faction in the struggle between union and management. Another espoused the theory she deliberately contaminated herself. And a third

viewed it as an attempt on her life by a group interested in pre-
venting her from telling what she knew about theft of valuable but
toxic plutonium from the Cimarron plant.

According to the evidence, Karen was involved in several separate incidents, starting on Tuesday, November 5, 1974. She had
been absent from work the first four days of November. FBI documents contain a reference to a statement from Donald Gummow,
a fellow employee and Karen's close personal friend, indicating she
had spent those four nights with him at his residence. Gummow
and Silkwood had received letters of reprimand from Kerr-McGee
because of an incident on Thursday, October 31, when Karen had
taken a prescription drug without informing her supervisor, as
required by company regulations.

After reporting for work at about 1:20 PM on Tuesday, November
5, she dressed in a smock and performed routine paperwork in
Room 135, a metallography laboratory. At about 2:45, before
leaving the area for a break, she and her supervisor monitored
themselves. A hot spot was found on her superior's plastic disposable shoe cover. A health physics technician was called. He monitored the floor but found no further sign of contamination. At
about 3:15 PM, Karen left the lab after checking herself thoroughly.
She was apparently free of radioactivity at this time.

At 3:45, after returning, she dressed in a protective coverall and
donned a pair of thin plastic gloves with tape around the top of
the wrist, in preparation for working in a closed container called
a "glovebox." In this process, the technician was seated at a large
tablelike device that had a glass top so the contents inside were in
clear view. Workers inserted their hands into special gloves fixed
over holes in the side of the box allowing them to reach inside to
manipulate samples without direct skin contact.

The work could be seen through the glass top, but radioactive
material could not get into the air. Thin plastic gloves, placed over

the hands before reaching inside the box, provided a double layer of protection and served as backup if the outer, more rugged glove was damaged.

Which is exactly what seemed to have happened to Karen.

After each task was performed inside the glovebox, the workers, upon removal of their hands from the strong outer gloves and sleeves, checked for contamination using an instrument mounted on the front exterior of the box. Karen followed this procedure and, at about 6:30 PM, found radioactivity on her fingers. She called another lab analyst, and the health physics technician returned.

After following the prescribed cleanup process, Karen was again checked, and findings affirmed she was free from the earlier reported problem. According to W. J. Shelley, whose statement was included in the FBI review of the case, no leaks were found in the glovebox used by Silkwood, even though her fingers were contaminated.

As a precautionary measure, Karen was required to give urine and fecal samples for five days after exposure. Close monitoring of her body samples, as reported in a paper by the union, showed that when she gave a urine or fecal sample at home, the level of contamination was high, and when a sample was taken under controlled conditions in the plant, levels were low. The AEC investigation concluded that plutonium had been added to at least two of her specimens after they had been voided.

Wayne Norwood, Health Physics and Industrial Safety Manager of the Cimarron plant, also commented that Karen Silkwood was the only individual in his twenty years of experience who, when found to be possibly contaminated, had been uncooperative in the submission of samples.

Another unexplained incident followed the one on Tuesday, November 5. During a routine test on Thursday, November 7, a nasal smear was taken from Karen and a high radiation count was present. She claimed this was from bringing up contaminated mucus from her lungs or stomach and that the exposure had occurred on Tuesday. But on November 5, Karen had been working on plutonium pellet lot number 35. Contamination in the smear was from another pellet lot, number 29.

Karen suffered from sinus trouble. According to a statement from Drew Stephens, she was a mouth breather. Ingestion, then, of a minute amount of plutonium was possible. In any case, there was some confusion as to what actually happened on November 5, 6, and 7 in regard to her contamination.

But on Thursday, November 7, a team of health physics technicians from Kerr-McGee accompanied Karen home and made a survey of her apartment. They found significant levels of plutonium in the bathroom around the toilet and in some lunch meat and cheese in her refrigerator.

Her roommate, Sherri Ellis, was awakened and examined. She was found to have slight contamination in two areas. Drew Stephens, who had spent the night at the apartment but had left early Thursday morning, was later checked. Reports show neither he nor his own dwelling or clothes was contaminated.

In an effort to settle, once and for all, the level of Karen's exposure, she was sent to the Los Alamos Scientific Laboratory for examination. Included in these tests were Sherri Ellis and Drew Stephens.

Results, given by Dr. George L. Voelz, stated the problem of contamination was so low as not to present "a significant health hazard . . . either now or in the future." Even though the total amount of plutonium found contaminating the individuals and the apartment was small, it appeared that somehow, some way, someone removed a quantity of the material from the Cimarron plant.

A review of facts suggests these possibilities: Karen Silkwood could have contaminated herself and added plutonium to her own urine and fecal samples. Supportive of this theory were statements made by her roommate, Sherri Ellis, to the effect that Karen might have stolen a small amount of plutonium. She also thought it most likely Karen had "spiked" her specimens to lend weight to her allegations about Kerr-McGee. A motive was present. The intensity of her desire to embarrass Kerr-McGee and gain publicity for the union cause was unquestionable. There is no doubt her contamination could have been used to gain national awareness.

Against this theory, however, is Karen's well-known abhorrence of becoming contaminated. But she was aware of how to handle plutonium and could have done it. Such an act is not without similar self-sacrificial precedent in the long and tumultuous history of disagreement between American labor and management.

Another possibility is that her friend Drew Stephens, with or without her consent, managed to place plutonium in her apartment and in several of her body samples. Unfortunately, Stephens did not testify before the House subcommittee, and we do not have his first-hand version of the story. The facts involving Drew Stephens are taken from records of the hearings before the Subcommittee on Energy and Environment of the Committee on Small Business in the House of Representatives.

This theory is plausible, however. First, Stephens had access to Karen and her apartment. Second, at least one of the specimen bottles used by Karen at home, and from which a sample with a high radioactive count was taken, is said to have come from the trunk of Stephens's car. Third, Stephens had worked in the Cimarron plant and had been active in the union. He was the one who met the union representative, Wodka, at the airport the evening Karen died. Fourth, Stephens, who then had a job as an auto repairman, had the battered white Honda hauled away to Oklahoma City. And he held the vehicle there while the union located an accident investigator to look into their suspicions of foul play.

According to a statement from an individual who saw and actually touched the left rear fender of the vehicle within hours after the accident, there was no damage to the auto body in that area. Two days later, after the car had been in Stephens's hands, the investigator hired by the union examined the same body panel and found damage.

It is possible this was a series of coincidences. Or, conversely, these facts may indicate Drew Stephens, working with the union, assisted them in a campaign aimed at Kerr-McGee, and used Karen as a means to get to them.

Members of the Kerr-McGee management team at the Cimarron plant must also fall under suspicion. The facility's safety record left something to be desired. And there is a documented incident of an employee tampering with a quality-control photograph because he felt it was expected of him by his superiors, and he didn't want to make the photo over again. Added to this, there was a move to discredit and remove the union from the plant. No part of a conjecture involving this group, however, stands up after reviewing available evidence.

The AEC either knew of, or soon discovered, the safety violations and the photo-negative doctoring. And the union won its vote to remain at the plant. In short, there was no rational basis or motive for Kerr-McGee management to have become entangled in an attempt on Karen's life—unless they were involved in a plot to remove large quantities of plutonium from the Cimarron center for resale on the black or gray market.

Which brings us to the part of the story that has been given wide national publicity and has kept the Silkwood affair alive for many years. This version holds that in her research to discover violations, Ms. Silkwood came across shocking news concerning the illicit removal of plutonium from the Kerr-McGee plant. Such theft, depending on the version being told, was done either without

Kerr-McGee's knowledge or with their full aid and consent. The missing manila envelope, in this theory, contained proof positive of theft and the identity of individuals involved. If true, here indeed are grounds for killing. And drama: the alleged theft of a deadly, strategically important radioactive substance vital to the construction of atomic weapons, a lone girl struggling valiantly to get the information to the proper authorities, a vicious car chase, then finally murder. A great deal of work has been done on this thesis, and some of it bears review.

A number of spectacular accusations, such as the report attributed to David Burnham, a *New York Times* reporter, about sixty pounds of plutonium missing from the site, caused widespread comment.

Additional credence for this version of the story came from the actions of an FBI agent, Larry Olson, who at the time was a forty-four-year-old, six-feet-tall, slim, fair-haired man with fifteen years' experience on the force. He came across the rumor that there were large amounts of missing plutonium while investigating Ms. Silkwood's death. In an "official letterhead memo" seconded, according to published reports, by Ted Rosack, the acting agent in charge of the Oklahoma City FBI office, Olson requested the opening of a new investigation.

The request, and a second official petition, were both refused by FBI headquarters because a study of the AEC records showed no such loss. A full inventory of the facility had been made, and although shortages were found, they were explainable as normal MUF, missing or unaccounted-for losses.

All this sounds mysterious, especially because of the controversy surrounding Karen Silkwood's death. But an objective view of facts as presented to the House investigating subcommittee tends—regrettably for those who love mystery, collusion, and meetings in dark places—to show the incident for about what it was.

Ms. Silkwood displayed signs of emotional disturbance and had espoused a cause with more than average vehemence. During the thirty-one-month period from March 1972 to September 1974, nine inspections and one investigation were conducted of the Kerr-McGee Cimarron facility. As a result of these inspections and investigations, nineteen items of noncompliance with AEC regulatory requirements were found. And two letters from the NRC to Kerr-McGee expressed concern regarding excessive MUF rates.

In the atomic industry, loss is an expected event. In any chemical process where many thousands of pounds of a material are run through, certain amounts are missing at the far end. The material does not vanish but, rather, is accumulated in pipe bends, tiny surface irregularities on the inside of processing tanks, and in other areas where chemicals are suspended in solution.

Kerr-McGee's plutonium MUF was higher than expected, and at least some of this loss might be accounted for by the removal of tiny amounts of plutonium from the plant site by employees.

But the total loss was sufficiently small to be explained away to the AEC. In other words, amounts were not too far above loss levels predicted for the operation of the processing system.

The real refutation of this version of the story comes from another source. As noted in an earlier chapter, the GAO in September 1976 submitted a report indicating as much as eleven thousand pounds, mostly plutonium and enriched uranium, were unaccounted for at government-owned facilities around the country. Another document, not released, showed an additional fifteen thousand to twenty thousand pounds missing from privately owned facilities. These figures are interesting because an August 1977 update totaled the loss from nuclear facilities in the United States at about eight thousand pounds.

But neither figure, according to the reports also mentioned previously, is correct. Both sources deliberately left out MUF from the two major U.S. weapons facilities in Colorado and Tennessee for fear of providing classified information to unfriendly intelligence services.

Reported figures did not include additional amounts of low-grade uranium missing from the sixty-five atomic reactors operating at that time to produce electricity for various parts of the United States.

The total MUF from the Kerr-McGee facility was included, however, and no special mention was made of any astounding shortage, even though one report did cite other locations where large amounts of material were unaccounted for.

The most famous case of MUF enriched uranium, and the one that has given credence to the idea of an international black or gray market, concerns the Apollo, Pennsylvania, facility. The AEC, FBI, and CIA were called in to investigate national and international aspects of a twenty-year loss of 381.6 pounds of the valuable element. One of the facility's top executives, according to the *New York Times,* was suspected of being an agent of a foreign government, and there was widespread speculation that the lost material had been sold to or stolen by Israeli activists.

The AEC, responsible for the facility, finally concluded after much study that there was no evidence of any theft and that the missing materials were lost due to crude statistical and measuring systems working in combination with processing loss. What no one seems to have focused on in their alarm at these figures is the acceptance of loss due to processing. The Kerr-McGee Cimarron operation had, for example, an estimated allowable MUF of around 1.8 kilograms (about four pounds) in a given time period. This was increased when several months of operation showed their loss would be higher. The Kerr-McGee plant, like virtually every other nuclear installation in America handling enriched uranium or plutonium, had a minor problem of accountability with the AEC and received numerous memos on the subject. But no action was taken and no censure was imposed because everyone involved knew and understood processing-loss accountability was not a completely refined science when applied to atomic materials. No matter how hard any group of engineers might try, the amount of material remaining in the system, trapped in piping or thrown out with other low-grade waste, could not be pinpointed by pre-production-run estimates.

Sixty pounds of plutonium was not found to be missing from Cimarron, even though unaccounted-for amounts were a few pounds greater than levels set by a preoperational estimate. The implication of large losses and Karen Silkwood's involvement in the matter, either as detector or thief, is difficult to sustain in the face of the plant's lack of documented major losses beyond the limits of measurement error.

Another problem with the theory that she found evidence of large-scale theft is the fact she did not mention her findings to any of her friends. Indeed, on the night she died, just minutes before leaving the Hub Café, she made a telephone call to be certain her meeting was set. In that call, she made no reported mention of such a blockbuster fact. And earlier that same day, in a meeting with an AEC representative to discuss her contamination, she did not bring it up.

From all accounts Karen Silkwood was not one to quietly keep a secret, and she seems to have shared her innermost feelings with her friends. Conversely, if she had been engaged as one of the thieves, she would have had to have been a part of a long chain of people. Plutonium is not the easiest material in the world to sell. A letter to a foreign nation or a clandestine contact arranged by an unknown person, offering a quantity of the element at some price, would be treated with great suspicion and probably be reported to our own FBI.

The implications of a huge loss from a nuclear facility go even further than this. Such a quantity would be extremely valuable. If the loss occurred without management's involvement at the highest levels, the resulting reduction of corporate profits would have certainly brought strong investigative measures from the company itself. From this, we may deduce no large-scale theft would be possible without collusion of top management. No evidence has ever been offered to suggest this as even a remote possibility.

Actually, much of the theft theory stems from a combination of incidents. Sherri Ellis, Ms. Silkwood's roommate, is said to have been the originator of the idea that Karen might have smuggled small quantities of plutonium from the plant. Their apartment was found to be contaminated. And analysis showed the radioactive material causing the contamination had come from the Kerr-McGee facility.

These facts, supported by rumors and the odd behavior of a number of people, one of whom insisted on leaving clues for the FBI in public telephone booths and other spy-like places, became distorted. Fertilized by the desire of a few individuals to see Kerr-McGee placed in an embarrassing public light, fiction was embraced as fact.

The concept of dramatic losses and a theft-smuggling ring is interesting and exciting as speculation, but it seems to be based on imagination and wishful thinking as opposed to reality. While it is possible to build a theory of an elaborate conspiracy, it would have needed to encompass a vast number of responsible people, including several congressmen.

All this leaves one unanswered problem. What about the mysterious manila or brown envelope, sworn by a single witness to have been in Ms. Silkwood's possession shortly before the accident (or, if you will, murder)? It supposedly contained information from her hours of interviewing Kerr-McGee employees and searching through company records.

The envelope, according to most versions of the story, was missing when the wreck was found. Karen Silkwood's possession of the envelope is given by some as the motive for her death. Their contention is that a party or parties unknown ran her off the road, she died in the crash, and her assailants made off with the documentation of Kerr-McGee's wrongdoing.

A subsequent AEC investigation, in which the same files Ms. Silkwood used were reviewed and many of the people who had talked with her offered testimony, provided little new insight. Thus the evidence that she was killed to prevent information from reaching the press and the AEC seems a little thin.

Only one witness has sworn, in an affidavit, that Karen had such an envelope in her possession at the Hub Café. Numbers of other union co-workers, however, who met with her the same night and spent time in her company, are not sure, and none has stated they recall seeing such an envelope.

Papers were found in the car and around the scene of the wreck. They were boxed up and turned over to Drew Stephens, who had permission from her family to claim the effects of their deceased daughter. The envelope, according to Stephens, was not included. An FBI investigation to determine if the envelope ever really existed proved indecisive. But aside from the sole witness, neither Karen's roommate nor her friend Stephens testified under oath as to its existence. And the one person who stated the envelope did exist did not appear at any point in the hearings. In addition, the single testimony concerning the envelope was taken by the union, not the FBI. And the OCAW can hardly be described as being impartial in the matter.

Official reports from trained, experienced police officers declared the event a single-car accident. And the medical examiner's autopsy found a sedative in her body.

All this inevitably leads to a single conclusion. The only mystery in the unfortunate girl's death is why some individuals have chosen to ignore both fact and logic to develop theories based on speculations of sinister conspiracy. There is a part in all of us that loves the mysterious and longs for tales of dark-of-the-moon drama. Sometimes we let this portion of our hearts rule our heads. A lot of those responsible for the Karen Silkwood mystery have done exactly this. There is no reasoning with them, especially when their assertions of intrigue are closely joined to claims against the nuclear industry. The anti-atomic forces have taken this incident and expanded it all out of proportion to serve their needs. In short, enough people want the shadow of a conspiracy for there to be one.

Regrettable in this instance is the fact that the darkness cast by the suppositions about Ms. Silkwood serves to obliterate the deeper insight we could obtain into the inner workings of a modern nuclear manufacturing and processing site. And that insight is disturbing.

To a large extent, we see a somewhat primitive operation, in part due to the cost difference between a chemical processing plant and an installation for the handling of atomic materials. In today's marketplace a first-class chemical plant, with all necessary pollution and worker-safety equipment, costs hundreds of millions of dollars. A plutonium-processing plant can be built for a far lesser amount.

With great sums of money at stake, design factors of the chemical plant will be centered on smooth, uninterrupted operation. Automation is at a maximum, and manpower is used to service equipment, not forward the processing itself.

In a plutonium plant, the opposite is true. Manpower is the basic force in the system. A multitude of jobs are performed by humans. The difference is more than philosophical. People are allowed to come into close contact with radioactive substances instead of remaining protected from the flow. And since the dollar investment is far less, the continued throughput of the facility, which assures its maximum usage and therefore the highest possible dollar return, is not as vitally important.

The Cimarron plant was, from all reports, an installation as advanced as the state of the art at that time allowed. But the art needed to advance a great deal more for much safer handling of nuclear substances.

The upshot of the matter is clear. In those formative years, the manufacturing system was too directly related to the laboratory technology from which it sprang. Insufficient engineering thought had been given to the design of a safer method of processing radioactive materials. Techniques in other industries were far ahead of those apparently being used in working with plutonium.

If nothing else is derived from the Karen Silkwood story, an understanding of the risky production techniques in use at the time should stand out as a warning. With seventy-three people exposed to internal dosages of plutonium during the operating history of the Cimarron plant, the need for more efficient processing is made alarmingly clear.

The most important question brought out by the death of Karen Silkwood is not whether she was murdered, but how much needed to be done to make the refining of atomic materials as safe as any other major manufacturing operation. Procedures acceptable in the time of the Industrial Revolution are no longer tolerated by reasonable people. The message to the atomic processing industry was clear: They had to advance.

An update on the Silkwood situation makes an interesting point on safety in nuclear manufacturing facilities of that era. On November 5, 1976, Karen Silkwood's father filed a law suit on behalf of Karen's three children. Reportedly, that action charged officials of the Kerr-McGee corporation with conspiring to prevent Ms. Silkwood from organizing a union and reporting nuclear safety hazards to the U.S. government. The civil action further alleged that corporation officials, a former newspaper reporter who cooperated with the FBI, and three agents conspired to suppress information about the intimidation and harassment of Ms. Silkwood. Finally, the claim charged Kerr-McGee officials with failure to exercise sufficient security controls over plutonium produced in their Cimarron plant in the incident in 1974 when Ms. Silkwood and her apartment were contaminated. A jury determined Kerr-McGee had some degree of responsibility in the radioactive contamination of Ms. Silkwood and awarded a $10.5 million judgment. That judgment was settled for $1.3 million in August 1986. The issue was only on contamination.

As of 2005, the Cimarron facility was closed, and site cleanup was being done under the supervision of the Nuclear Regulatory Commission.

There is no indication that antinuclear forces have been any more inclined to accept the information and decisions from this trial than they were to accept the facts presented in the House subcommittee's report. To them, Karen Silkwood is a nuclear martyr. Her death has enveloped her work and actions in an emotional aura. Those who believe she was killed by persons unknown to prevent her delivering incriminating documents to the government, or because she knew of a massive plutonium smuggling operation, will never accept any other explanation.

Some good had risen from the ashes of this episode. If nothing else, the death of Karen Silkwood caused attention to be focused on improving all levels of safety in nuclear installations of all types.

EIGHT

Theft, MUF, and Terrorism

Plutonium and enriched uranium have been stolen from nuclear processing plants in the United States. There is no question of this fact. In the Karen Silkwood matter, for example, someone illicitly removed small amounts of plutonium from the Kerr-McGee plant, or the Silkwood apartment would never have been contaminated.

The issue is not whether there have been thefts but how much has been taken, and what materials were involved. Some of the most exciting true adventure stories of the twentieth century come out of the activities of many nations to develop their own nuclear explosive devices.

The clandestine operation by the state of Israel is an excellent case. This project involved secretly bringing two hundred tons of uranium concentrate into their country. It is a sterling example of how far a legitimate government will go to keep knowledge of its nuclear business from other nations it considers hostile.

The Israeli story is filled with ships sailing at night to deep-ocean rendezvous, machinations as governments cover their tracks, secret agents, and the trading of nuclear secrets. In brief, during 1967 and 1968, the Israelis had need for a large quantity of enriched uranium and plutonium. Their goal was to manufacture nuclear explosive devices at their French-built reactor station south of Haifa at Dimona in the Negev Desert. Fearing an open-market purchase might push the Soviets into furnishing nuclear armaments to Arab states, an elaborate scheme was developed. A huge amount of uranium concentrate, commercially called "yellowcake," was purchased through a defunct West German chemicals firm. The buy was possible after assurances were given by the coalition government of Christian Democratic Chancellor Kurt-Georg Kiesinger that the transaction would appear as a matter between two private companies. Informed sources indicate that, in exchange for their aid, the West Germans received an advanced uranium separation process developed by the Israelis and vital to the production of atomic weapons.

Once the uranium concentrate was purchased, it was loaded onto a ship, the *Scheersberg A*, headed for Italy. But the vessel never reached its declared destination of Genoa. Instead, it arrived in Iskenderun, Turkey, minus its cargo. A certain amount of attention in the European community was directed to this mystery, but it took months for active investigation to begin. By then, a cover-up was tightly in place. What likely happened was that the ship sailed from Antwerp with the cargo of uranium worth about $3.7 million. It bypassed the stated port of Genoa and went on radio silence. In the dark of night, a hundred or so miles from Haifa in the Mediterranean Sea, the *Scheersberg A* met an unnamed Israeli vessel. There, sailors worked in pitch blackness, protected by a pair of Israeli gunboats. Crews of the two vessels transferred the cargo. Once it was safely aboard the new ship, *Scheersberg A* sailed quietly away. Days later it arrived in Turkey. The secrecy of the operation was sufficient to prevent its becoming known to the Soviets, as well as to most Western nations, until several years afterward. Even today, there is some uncertainty as to the exact details.

Many nations find themselves in situations similar to the Israelis in 1968. A major movement of certain atomic materials required in the development or production of nuclear weapons is bound to cause response from other nations interested in maintaining status quo.

Little-remembered today, the efforts of the white South Africans in 1977 to convert a nuclear power station into a weapons arsenal and manufacture a bomb is another good example. Both the Soviet and U.S. governments, joined by the other nations with the capability of making nuclear explosive devices, hastened to halt this attempt with a swiftness uncharacteristic of government dealings. The notable exception to the list of participating nations was China, which stayed out partially to respect the wishes of the other countries and partly in response to the counteraction having been instigated by the Soviet Union.

With nations going so far to control access to information about their purchases, and conducting nuclear experimentation in secret, it is no wonder there is a problem in determining whether or not large amounts of enriched uranium or plutonium have been surreptitiously removed from U.S. facilities. Worse, since American controls are tighter than in other countries, how much is "missing" from foreign installations? In comparison with what is known about U.S. shortages, our knowledge of overseas MUF is limited.

It has long been known that shortages have occurred in India, and it is suspected the government or at least highly placed members of the government have been involved in the sale of radioactive raw material on the world open market. Records indicate such activity has been conducted without official Indian sanction, and profits from the sale may have gone into the pockets of a few individuals.

In 2002, ex-CIA Director George Tenet told Congress that weapons-grade nuclear material had been stolen in post-Communist Russia. Tenet further stated, "We also believe that [Osama] bin

Laden was seeking to acquire or develop a nuclear device." And "Al-Qaeda may be pursuing a radioactive dispersal device—what some call a 'dirty bomb.'" A dirty bomb is one that uses a chemical explosion to disperse radioactive material over a large area.

Taken as a whole, not much is made public today on nuclear materials theft in the world. Various intelligence agencies of many countries keep classified files on stolen or purchased weapons-grade material, but little of this is released to news media.

One reason for this secrecy lies in the fact that refining enriched fissionable material requires sizable processing and manufacturing facilities. And additional extensive plants are needed to produce the weapons. These installations demand a capital outlay most governments find daunting. So for financial reasons alone, nations produce fissionable material, not gangs or small players. And nations hold what they know about other nations close to the vest.

As differentiated from other kinds of theft, the real work of a nuclear thief starts after the radioactive substance is in hand. If the elements are not properly stored and extreme care taken in their transportation, nuclear materials will injure or kill all involved. Unless caution is used in storage, these substances will burst into flame and grow hot enough to vaporize, sending out plumes of radioactivity.

It would take a knowledgeable, well-planned effort not only to steal but to handle the contraband. And a team of experts would have to be along in order to look after the shipment. Some of the most desirable elements are the most volatile. An entire branch of science has even developed to deal with the delicate problems associated with plutonium and enriched uranium. Specially designed canisters, built to a critical geometric formula, must be kept separated by precise amounts of space and never stacked over certain heights.

The antinuclear faction has called attention to dangers inherent in the possibility of theft of atomic materials, especially by a terrorist organization. To date, no results of such activity have surfaced. This is no assurance of what may take place in the future. In fact, as more atomic facilities are built, chances for theft become greater.

To help offset such a possibility, new processes are being developed to limit the ability of reactor owners to make weapons-grade materials.

Interestingly enough, during the 1960s and '70s, there was a considerable amount of Sunday-supplement publicity about how easy it would be to build an atomic bomb. From casual reading, it would appear any individual could make one in a home workshop. Although the principles are simple, the construction, aside from theoretical considerations, is complex and time-consuming.

A news story in 1977 about a Princeton University student, John Phillips, describing a paper he had written on how to produce a nuclear explosive device by acquiring $150,000 worth of plutonium and a few thousand dollars' worth of other equipment is a case in point. Phillips received national publicity and attention for his efforts, which were ingenious. But his work did not deal with the full array of practical difficulties that come into play after all materials are in hand.

The South African attempt to secretly construct a nuclear weapon shows how well things are monitored and how difficult it is to go from paper theory to actual explosive hardware. The stages of assembly and handling of radioactive materials pose problems that do not lend themselves to easy or inexpensive solutions.

This is not to imply it would be impossible for a group of well-financed, strongly dedicated individuals to make a crude bomb using suicide labor. Workers, without protection, could handle and machine needed components. They would die horrible deaths. But sects that bring forth suicide bombers might be able to find motivated volunteers.

A weapon produced by such means, however, would most likely be of unknown performance and reliability. It might not go off at all, or it might explode with more force than anyone expected.

It is a little hard to imagine a terrorist group getting together the expertise and financing for such a project when the same amount of money might be better expended in obtaining a ready-made weapon by a sudden shock attack on an ill-defended arsenal. There are several such arsenals in the world, including some controlled by U.S. armed forces.

But is it necessary to have an atomic bomb in order to influence a particular situation? Is there a nuclear weapon easier to manufacture yet still impressive enough to be intimidating? A weapon that might strike even more fear into a society, achieving the terrorist group's aim of publicity and public awareness?

There is an entire class of such weapons. Dirty bombs do not possess the destructive force of a nuclear blast. They have an inherent fear quotient of a far higher level.

Although difficult, it is within the realm of reasonable possibility for an organization to acquire a limited amount of plutonium, radioactive cobalt, or other "hot" material. This could be achieved by theft, secret international purchase, or through a direct gift from a supportive government that possesses a reactor.

In the last example, the reactor itself might be used to irradiate, or make radioactive, some available substance. The half-life of this material, as long as it is a week or so, would be unimportant, as plans could be made to use it before it became too old to injure or kill. Other sources of noncontrolled material might be industries that use radioactive substances for quality-control measurements and other commercial activities.

Once obtained, such material could quickly and simply be made into a weapon of respectable proportions. A limited amount of common explosive—say, dynamite—would work but would be less suited to the task than one of the "plastic" concoctions. An electric or clockwork timer and primer, also easily available or quickly fashioned, is all that would be needed to complete the device.

With the radioactive material encased in a fractionable container along with the explosive, and the timing device set to a specific ignition point, the weapon—as small as a suitcase—could be left in a variety of places. It might be slipped into an air-conditioning duct, for instance, or placed in a public locker in a transportation terminal, or simply stood innocently against a wall. Great size is not a requirement for an effective bomb. A small one would, in many situations, be as efficient as a larger device.

When a timer sets off the chemical explosive, phenomenal heat is generated. The protective lead container is vaporized, as is much of the radioactive material, and the gaseous mass is forcibly dispersed over a large area. If an air-conditioning system were chosen as the site for the device, it would be possible to design a container shaped to direct the force of the blast down the duct into the heart of the unit, where fans would force radioactive vapor and particles throughout a building in a matter of minutes.

Anyone who breathed the hot material might be in trouble. Panic potential would be tremendous, as would, of course, the publicity value.

Radioactive materials have one interesting thing in common. They can be detected with a number of electrical or mechanical devices, but without special apparatus, there is no way to know of their presence. If, after the blast, an announcement of the nuclear nature of the explosion were made public and trained contamination crews were sent to analyze radioactivity levels, the anguish of people present would be enormous. The shock effect of the weapon, coupled with threat of its possible future use, would cause long-term panic and disruption, regardless of what authorities might say about its relative lack of effectiveness or danger potential.

In short, those individuals who even imagined themselves contaminated by the blast would react fearfully. But there would be no way to tell. A few, who might have received high-dosage exposure, could show symptoms. But just how serious the level of contamination might be in any given person could only be determined by extensive medical examination. Even then the gnawing fear of a developing cancer would produce anxiety.

The idea for such a weapon is not new. It was discussed by our own military and has been the subject of speculation in a number of technical articles. A little work by a small number of informed people would produce an effective prototype. Again, it could be done even more quickly if a few suicidal fanatics were recruited to handle hot materials with only minimal protection.

After 9/11, cities were required to develop emergency preparedness plans. Large metropolitan areas have programs for radiological incidents and have conducted drills. Even so, a review of capabilities in a number of major U.S. cities indicates difficulties remain when dealing with large-area contamination or sizable numbers of people exposed to radioactivity. States are better off in this regard because they have access to the National Guard and other military units that have received special training.

Doctors and emergency medical care facilities, while often not sufficiently prepared to cope with large-scale nuclear contamination, have access to a phenomenal resource. The Oak Ridge Institute for Science and Education (ORISE) manages the Department of Energy (DOE) Radiation Emergency Assistance Center/Training Site (REAC/TS). REAC/TS provides around-the-clock emergency medical services involving radiation to any location on earth. Work is also underway at Columbia University Medical Center to develop the means to quickly screen large groups of people for radiation levels in the case of a terrorist action or other event.

To date, no massive exposure has occurred in America. Fortunately, the right elements have not come together to cause such an incident. They may never do so, but the possibility does exist. And it grows as radioactive material becomes more widely distributed and available throughout the world.

NINE

Windscale

There is little doubt the worst nuclear accident to date in a Western nation happened in 1957 in England. The Windscale incident, as it has come to be known, is similar in many respects to the Soviet disaster of the same decade. Results in terms of injury, loss of life, and property damage were, however, significantly less in the English event, as no individual not directly connected with the operation of the facility was physically injured.

The Windscale No. 1 pile was a graphite-based plutonium producer. Along with its nearby neighbor, the Calder Hall nuclear facility, it composed a major portion of the United Kingdom's atomic research and development capability. The area has been likened to Oak Ridge, Tennessee.

The antinuclear energy movement has publicized the Windscale matter, pointing to it as a prime example of how close humanity has come to a major disaster. Pronuclear forces have tried to ignore it. But if anything was proved by the event, it was that we tend to function at the extreme limits of our knowledge of nuclear science. And if facility operators are presented with the choice between a full meltdown or the release of radioactivity into the environment, a release will occur. It also demonstrates how even unanticipated difficulties can be overcome by the courage and coolness of those who run the installations.

The Windscale incident polarized the press. Some papers hewed to the line of the official plant release, maintaining everything was well. Others, using boldface black type to silently scream doom, played up the event day by day for weeks afterwards as the full international implications unfolded.

In the end, after the committees had adjourned and filed their voluminous reports, things went back to normal. But the No. 1 pile at Windscale was out of service. Ten years would pass before the radioactive remains could be inspected closely by man.

Forewarning of the accident occurred in September 1952, when the unit spontaneously released a small blast of heat and radiation during a phase in which it was shut down. Temperatures rose dramatically in the graphite material that encased the uranium in the core, but radiation was mostly contained, and none of the uranium cartridges caught fire. A study of the surprising incident revealed that graphite, used to slow neutrons to give them a better chance of hitting other uranium nuclei, built up and held energy after being bombarded by neutrons. First explained by Nobel Prize–winning physicist Eugene Paul Wigner, this form of buildup bears his name and is known worldwide as "Wigner energy."

Results of the study called for a planned, controlled reduction of Wigner energy in the pile on a regular basis to prevent an unexpected and unplanned-for spontaneous release. By the end of 1956, this operation had been done on eight occasions.

The procedure was simple. The pile was shut down, a series of instruments to measure heat and radioactivity were arranged in appropriate places, and the rapid airflow, which took the place of a water cooling system in this particular reactor, was shut off. The result was an almost instantaneous increase in the temperature of the uranium and graphite that made up the pile. This added temperature started a slow release of the stored-up Wigner energy in the graphite. Once initiated, the process became self-sustaining. At a given point, when it was determined enough energy had been released, the fans were restarted and the pile was brought back into operation.

The trick, it appears in retrospect, was to obtain an even and equal release of all Wigner energy. On three occasions prior to the one in which disaster struck, in order to free all the pent-up energy and get proper instrument readings, it had been necessary to heat the pile twice. This appeared to solve the problem, so the technique became a regular part of the system operation. On the day of the accident, the procedure was instigated in the usual manner. The pile was shut down, the main fans stopped, and after checking all instrumentation and verifying that the pile was indeed off, the technicians waited. At the prescribed time, readings were taken and a decision was made to repeat the process to complete the release.

A later review of the data indicates this is where the mistake occurred. The physicist in charge decided to reheat the pile to boost the release rate. But he made his decision without sufficiently detailed instructions. The pile operating manual had no special section on how to achieve a Wigner release. It was left to the judgment of individual operators to determine how long the pile should be allowed to heat and to what temperature. The outcome was disastrous—and it spread the name Windscale around the world.

———

John Bateman was a cattle breeder, a farmer, and an early riser. He was accustomed to the cold, blustery dawn hours when darkness still covered the rolling green countryside. Outside his main house looking toward the horizon, he could see the cooling towers and spires of the Calder Hall nuclear power station and the Windscale plutonium refining installation. The manmade structures were the first changes in the landscape to have occurred in years. Bateman liked his land and his little town of Yottenfews. "Town," really, was too grand a word for the small collection of buildings and homes. Three families lived there, more than a mile off the main highway. It was quiet, on the coast of the Irish Sea, and life had gone on unchanged for generations.

Somehow, though, the atomic plants had altered more than the skyline. The government, for instance, had run a high wire fence across a meadow belonging to one of Bateman's neighbors. The neighbor, Hewitson, a dairy farmer, had filed a formal complaint. It availed him of naught. And the Ministry of Agriculture remained deaf to the man's charges that the new facility had affected the fertility of his cattle. Officials had talked to him on several occasions, but nothing was changed.

On this particular morning, Bateman ignored the vision on the horizon. He had work to do, and standing around mooning over the way things were wasn't going to get it done.

Three miles away, a handful of technicians also had work to do. Inside the Windscale enclosure, the No. 1 pile had been shut down at 1:13 AM in preparation for a routine maintenance release of the built-up Wigner energy. The men, acting as a part of a larger group, were verifying the closing of the system and replacing all defective thermocouples, necessary devices for measuring differences in temperature.

They labored with almost exaggerated care, checking each output signal against the main control panel in the command room. Their team, a part of the 11:00 to 7:00 shift, had been through the Wigner release operation before, and the work had become routine.

Finally, by 7:00 that evening, Monday, October 7, preparations were complete for the release maneuver. Graphite control rods were moved, and the pile was actually opened twenty-five minutes later. Everything seemed in order. The physicist in charge gave his okay to the procedure, and the nuclear heating of the graphite continued throughout the night. Early on the morning of Tuesday, October 8, the heat flow was stilled, and readings, taken during the process, were evaluated.

Several hours passed to allow the thermocouples to trace temperature trends in the material they were sensing. The data produced considerable disagreement. Instrument readings were conflicting. Some of the controllers on duty believed the overall pile was cooling off. Others argued only certain portions of the graphite were cooling, thus showing no sign of energy release. A lengthy debate ensued, and the final decision was to apply further nuclear heating to enhance the Wigner release process. The physicist in charge of the operation had no previous experience with the maneuver, and none of his manuals outlined the technique. But based on his judgment, the overall indication was that insufficient heat had been applied to trigger the desired result. So, at 11:05 Tuesday morning, October 8, the pile was once again heated.

Thermocouples attached to the uranium cartridges immediately showed a dramatic temperature increase. They remained borderline safe for the next fifteen minutes.

The physicist monitoring the records was diligent in taking readings but not astoundingly swift in his calculations. While the recordings of the temperature show not a single reading exceeded the specified maximum, the actual heat must have been many times higher, or else the buildup would not have been registered so quickly. Also, unknown to the physicist in charge, the thermocouples monitoring the uranium cartridge temperatures were placed to show the hottest or worst points during normal operations. During the

Wigner release maneuver, however, the areas of maximum heat and stress were elsewhere in the pile. The result was a drastic overheating of some of the uranium.

Disturbed by the rapid temperature rise, the physicist ordered the control rods pushed in to allow the fuel cartridges to cool. But the damage was already done. During the minutes of highest stress, several of the rods had burst from the strain.

The result took time to reach its maximum potential. Behind concrete and lead shields in the heart of the radioactive pile, the Wigner energy release was still taking place. The graphite control sections grew increasingly hot. The uranium, in the split containers, was exposed to this heat and began to burn and oxidize. As uranium combines with oxygen it rusts in a fashion similar to iron. The major difference is uranium continues to heat until it is too hot to exist in its present state and turns to a yellowish-brown powder. All day on Wednesday, October 9, the uranium smoldered, giving out great amounts of heat not registered on instruments in the control room because of the placement of the temperature-measuring devices. This constant energy release caused failure of other cartridges, adding more uranium fuel to the fiery mass.

During the next twenty-four hours, fire slowly spread until it was affecting a major segment of the reactor pile.

Readings taken on Wednesday, October 9, indicated a continuing, expected, slow temperature rise in the graphite, which showed the desired release was taking place on schedule. One reading, however, thought by some to be due to a faulty instrument, registered a marked increase. By 10:00 PM, it had reached a point where the physicist in charge was required, according to a specific written instruction, to take certain operational measures to cool the mass down.

Windscale No. 1 was of a unique design. Instead of water as the cooling medium, a series of chimneys was utilized to conduct airflow through and around crucial components. As long as the uranium remained sealed in its protective cartridges, the circulating air could be filtered to remove residual radioactive materials before being sent out from the towers in a reasonably safe, noncontaminated state.

The physicist in charge, following standing orders, called for the fans to be turned on. This allowed airflow through the pile to lower its temperature. At 10:15 Wednesday night, his order was carried out. Air streamed through the central chimney for minutes, drawing up uranium oxide and other radioactive particles from the pile's core. Spewing out into the open air, they formed in a long, hot, invisible plume carried by the prevailing winds. Readings showed the pile to be cooling, but the decision was made to give it another shot of air for safety. So again, at 12:01 AM, Thursday, October 10, there was an additional ten minutes of cooling. Still not enough. Two more doses were called for, and the fans pushed hot material into the air for a total of forty-three minutes during the damper openings that occurred at 2:15 and 5:10 AM.

Later testimony indicates no one in charge of the operation had any idea there was a major emission of radioactivity during the first three air flushes. But alarm bells began to ring about thirty minutes into the fourth and final cooling effort.

The single graphite temperature reading that had steadily risen and set off the secondary cooling operation remained stabilized even though the pile itself began to lose heat early in the process. Then the pile radiation meter, located near the top of the tall air chimney or stack, showed a sharp increase in radioactivity. The physicist in charge noted the high levels but thought they were only a result of air movement through the huge vent.

At 5:40 Thursday morning, readings were still high. Then they seemed to fall for a few minutes. But by 8:10 AM, they again showed steady increases. The situation was getting seriously out of hand.

The pile was shut down but was still releasing radioactivity—enough to cause instruments on the roof of the meteorological building to show very high counts.

An immediate council was convened. Tom Hughes, deputy works manager; Ron Gausden, reactor manager; and Tom Tuohy, general works manager, agreed to ask for air samples from the health and physics staff. A quick study was undertaken and the worst confirmed. Radioactivity in the air was up many times greater than normal.

The three managers called for half-hourly air testing at between ten and fifteen sites within the compound, then sat down to decide what course of action to pursue. Their meeting was of short duration, interrupted by news of another sharp increase in the graphite temperatures.

They were now faced with a difficult problem, but it had only one answer. The pile, composed of graphite shielding, could not be allowed to reach too high a temperature or a meltdown would occur. The release of nuclear radiation would multiply a thousandfold. So, after notifying their superiors, they took the only course available. They ordered the vents opened again at Thursday noon for fifteen minutes and used the fans at full blast to cool down the smoldering monster.

The radioactivity-measuring meter at the top of the stack went wild as soon as air started passing through, and everyone knew hot materials were being dumped into the atmosphere. The small group of technicians waited tensely in the main command room, scanning temperature gauges. At the first indication of a remission of the heating, they would order the flow stopped. Minutes ticked by but there was still no reliable sign of heat abatement. Then, slowly, one by one, upward progress of indicator needles on the instruments halted. The technicians immediately gave the order to halt air flow through the stack.

But it was too soon. By 1:40 PM, heat buildup was almost as bad as it had been earlier. And additional amounts of heavy radiation had streamed from the top of the tall chimney into the atmosphere.

Against their best moral judgment, but in an effort to keep the pile from melting, a final cooling flush was ordered. This called for another five-minute flow. Gauges registering radioactivity were well into their red zone areas as they measured outgoing air. Through it all, and working under conditions of almost unbelievable pressure, the management group battled to determine the cause of the malfunction. The health physics manager was given the job of finding out where and how far afield radioactivity was spreading. The remainder of the team wrestled with the technical problem. They finally decided they were faced with one or more burst cartridges. Their analysis was correct.

To prevent a major disaster, they needed to examine the insides of the core and locate the ruptured units. After determining how many there were, they could quench the fire and dump the broken canisters into a protective container. It was a difficult undertaking and had never before been carried out. The operation started going wrong from the first. Thursday at 2:30 PM, the turbo-exhaust system was switched on to clear the air in the pile so an inspection by means of a built-in radiation scanner could be made. The pile was flushed clean and then, to everyone's horror, it was discovered that intense heat had jammed the gear drive of the mobile scanning apparatus so it could not be moved. Tom Hughes and Kenneth Ross, the national operations director, worked on the large machine, but it was no use. In later testimony, the pile manager indicated loss of the instrument was normal during a Wigner release. In fact, he noted that the scanning device was in operating condition, just having been worked on the day before and left functional. But it had also become immobile at the end of the previous energy release maneuver some several weeks earlier.

It was at this time the health physics officers ordered air sampling trucks sent out into the countryside to map and quantify the amount of radiation that had been discharged from the chimneys. The vehicles, lumbering through the misty, bright green, rolling land, stopped again and again as samples were taken and readings made. An elaborate map was started, but hours would pass before there would be a full understanding of how massive an amount of radioactivity was actually involved.

Back at the plant, a special team was gathered. Tom Hughes and Ron Gausden, the reactor manager, dressed in their protective clothing in silence. Every man present knew what they had to do next was extremely dangerous.

Completely covered, wearing gloves, overshoes, helmets, and respirators, the pair was going to visually examine the inside of the pile where temperature readings were highest. In so doing, they would expose themselves to immense amounts of radiation.

The decision to risk station personnel had not been arrived at lightly. Tom Tuohy, works general manager, after being informed of the reasonable expectation of having a burst cartridge, suggested an alternative scanning method. It worked, but its reading indicated almost impossibly high levels of radiation and provided the staff with little new information.

Ready for their task, the two men hurried out of the main building to the concrete structure containing the runaway nuclear pile. No one had ever attempted the maneuver they were about to perform, but according to best available estimates, it was possible. However, the potential for death or injury was very high.

The procedure had directness in its favor. First, an air count for radioactivity would be taken to assure there was enough safety margin for the men to work in the area. Then, in addition to the usual dosimeters, extra body sensors had been affixed to their outer clothing so later analysis could determine how much radiation they had received and which parts of them had been exposed.

The men stepped on to an elevatorlike hoist and were lifted off the ground up along the side of the pile building. Once in place, they set out to remove the cover from an opening designed for passing uranium cartridges into the interior of the pile. When the hole was open, radiation would stream out. But by taking turns they could place their protected heads in line with the aperture and visually inspect the inside of a working atomic reactor. It was not something the designers had ever intended as a means for determining the extent of a problem. However, the desperation of the situation at Windscale No. 1 was apparent from the willingness of the two specialists to perform such a hazardous maneuver.

It would be hard to describe the invisible hell that composes the innermost portion of a nuclear reactor core. To eyes capable of seeing a range of radiation higher up the scale than humans can attain, the sight would resemble a surrealist painting. Precise arcs of varied hues would leap from the cartridges and curve gracefully through the shimmering air to ground themselves at another point. Auras and halos of diverse colors would hover over and encircle the tracks on which the uranium rested. The very air itself would be alive with tiny fairy motes of flying color.

To a human observer, however, the scene would take on a totally different look. In a dimness broken only by a limited amount of light filtering in from the outside, the rows of capsules, each in its own track, each with identical coloring, would present a dull spectacle. No hint of the restless, seething energy forces would be revealed by visual inspection. The vista is one of another drab, slightly incomprehensible industrial hodgepodge of containers, tracks, gray concrete, and spaced baffling.

No man or woman, however, could stand to take a long look. The damage to his or her system from radiation would be, in a matter of minutes, so intense as to be irreversible. Too long a look at the nuclear Medusa results in certain death.

The men on the lift, though apprehensive, proceeded with deliberate speed. Cautiously they removed the plug from the wall. Once the opening was clear, Hughes, standing well back from the narrow aperture, raised his eyes in line with the hole and took a long look. What he saw came as a total surprise.

The four cartridges rested securely in their assigned channels. But instead of the dull metallic color they normally had, each was cherry red. The glow from the surface of the steel container, which encased the now-active uranium, gave off a dim rosy light. Heat was so intense Tom Hughes took one long look and pulled his head out of the line of sight.

He and Gausden talked briefly, digesting the information. Then Gausden decided to inspect the mechanism used to discharge spent cartridges in the process of normal maintenance. This system refused to function.

Standing a little further back from the opening than Hughes had, Gausden studied the scene for a long minute before withdrawing. His experienced eyes covered the hot, glowing cartridges, the tracks on which they rested, and the ejection mechanism. Finally satisfied, he drew back and rejoined his companion.

Their conversation was staccato-quick from the emotional stress. According to the visual analysis, the dumping system was jammed because heat had distorted the shape of the outer metal shell of the uranium cartridges. This prevented them from sliding down the tracks into the disposal area. Several possible solutions were discussed. Finally the two agreed to attempt to dislodge the jammed units by prodding them with a long metal pole. At this point, they had been on the lift platform a little less than five minutes.

Six more men, also in protective clothing, joined them in the narrow space on top of the lift. Working with haste, they rigged a long rod. As one man directed the operation by sight, his eyes in line with the opening, the first dislodgement effort was started, only to be quickly abandoned.

The metal casings were far from fragile in their normal state. However, heated to red incandescence they were in a severely weakened condition.

The group huddled closely together again beneath the deadly opening. Another suggestion was agreed upon, and they stepped into position for a second try. Exposing themselves to varying levels of radioactivity, the men worked through the night to free the stuck cartridges so they could be removed from the pile.

As they labored, the temperatures in the affected area continued to build. Fearing the fire inside might result in an excess of heat exposure to the uranium cartridges in adjoining sets of channels, all capsules were removed from a wide space on both sides, creating an open firebreak. The equipment worked perfectly, and the normal cartridges were expelled in accordance with regular operating procedures. The problems in the system were now limited to an area of four channels. But the four distorted cartridges continued to increase in temperature at a slow but dangerously steady rate.

The efforts of the men on the outside lift, who were working directly on the containers, met with a little success. A whole cartridge, albeit one showing less tendency to temperature increases, was dislodged and came free into the disposal system. There were now only three left. But these were the hottest and therefore the most severely damaged.

Realizing the situation was becoming more serious, the management of the reactor site met in hurried council. In addition to several engineers, this quickly assembled group contained Tom Tuohy; Bill Crone, the fire chief; Tom Hughes; and Kenneth Ross. They were faced with a difficult dilemma, and hard decisions had to be made.

First, the temperature in the affected area was still rising. The fire, now contained in one section of the reactor, was showing no signs of spreading but was obviously not going to extinguish itself. There was some likelihood a new release of Wigner energy in another part of the huge pile might overheat more of the cartridges, and they would have a second, or even third, hot spot to deal with.

Then there was the matter of the fans. The men working on the hoist lift were exposed to radiation from the inside of the pile. To minimize this and lower the levels of radioactivity in their area, the blowers had been turned on to carry away some of the heat. This added a screen of moving air to the minimal protection of special clothing, but there was a possibility the fans would add to the atmospheric contamination.

All present at the meeting understood that if the constant temperature increases were not stopped, the already cherry-red cartridges would become yellow, then white-hot, and finally molten. At this point the out-of-control uranium would be released from its containment, and the resulting mess would be impossible to correct. A meltdown situation was slowly taking shape before the weary and astonished eyes of the scientific and management teams.

Action was required. But what they did had to be set off against the damage from additional air releases of radioactive gas and particles. One issue, however, was paramount in everyone's mind. The defective cartridges had to be cooled. And the cooling had to be accomplished in the next twelve hours or the chance of saving what was becoming an unthinkable situation would be drastically reduced.

After a reasonable amount of debate a number of decisions were reached, and an action plan was formulated. First came protection for the workers in the area, as well as employees of the Windscale No. 1 pile and the nearby Calder Hall facility. Respiration masks to filter out harmful particles from the air and prevent them from being sucked into their lungs were issued to all staff members. Then, a systematic program of employee activity was calculated to enable the various staffs to have adequate warning should massive amounts of contaminants be released. Next, the civilian population, much farther away from the site and therefore less susceptible to exposure, had to be notified on a preliminary basis. The chief constable of Cumberland was alerted to the possibility of an accident. He was asked to arrange for transportation of the factory and construction workers from the site on an emergency basis, if necessary. The constable quickly mobilized a motor pool by commandeering a number of vehicles from farms in the nearby area. He would prove to be quite ready when called upon.

Additional respirator masks were issued to workers and visitors at the Calder Hall facility. All personnel not directly engaged in the cooling-off effort were asked to stay indoors, and they gathered, finally, in the canteen areas of both Windscale and Calder. There they anxiously awaited further information. This preparation was in anticipation of the possible use of the ultimate, and most drastic, solution.

If the now-glowing cartridges could not be dislodged and dropped into safety, they might be cooled by the use of compressed carbon dioxide. This had been tried earlier on an experimental basis by the management staff. If that failed, then the reactor would have to be flooded with water. While there was little or no question the water bath would cool the fevered capsules, there was also no doubt this was a final, desperate act to prevent meltdown. It would not be tried until all else failed. Once water hit the hot containers, a great cloud of steam would be produced. This could cause a steam explosion, which might damage the pile container and potentially wreck the facility. In any case the hot vapor would rise up the chimney of the Windscale unit and scour millions of radioactive particles from the walls of the flue and other parts of the vent system. The result would be a massive discharge of radioactive iodine, strontium, cesium, and other elements into the atmosphere.

These particles would be carried by winds and, as they settled back to earth, would produce contaminated surfaces on grass, tree leaves, homes, cars, and farm machinery. Some effort was made at this time to analyze the discharges that had already occurred. A health physics survey van, out since 3:00 PM that afternoon, ran the more quickly performed grab-sample gamma measurements. These revealed a very high radioactivity reading at Bailey Bridge, near Sellafield station. Joined at 5:00 PM by another survey vehicle, they managed to take an air sample from the area of Calder Farm Road at 11:00 PM. The reading there was about the same as at the Windscale No. 1 pile site: 23.00 milli-R per hour, or ten times the normally accepted English standard for safe lifetime breathing. Crews in the two vans were ordered to continue their sampling work throughout the night and well into the long next day.

Acting on their new plans, the management staff sent for a second supply of compressed carbon dioxide. This gas, used in fire extinguishers, produces a dense, cold cloud that shrouds and smothers a fire. The hope was that the cold would be enough to stabilize the hot cartridges and prevent further escalations of temperature.

A team, working with desperate speed, loaded a truck with cylinders and drove to the Windscale pile. The bulky protective clothing they wore, along with the numerous radiation sensors clipped to their clothes, gave them an otherworldly appearance. It also hindered their movements as they transferred the cylinders to the site where the gas would be released into the hot chamber. Radioactivity levels in the air were high, and there was the probability they would rise even higher. A number of construction workers who normally were employed outside the buildings had no shelter of their own so were dismissed and evacuated from the area by the constable's commandeered auto brigade.

Tension was high in the main control room as the compressed CO_2 flowed into the hot area. More and more of the cold gas was delivered into the chamber, and for a while it began to appear there was a good possibility of stopping the continued heat buildup. The rate of temperature increase was slowing, but then it stabilized and dropped no further.

Additional carbon dioxide was delivered and forced in, but the result was the same: no real change in the situation. Finally, after repeated attempts to dislodge the capsules, and the addition of even more carbon dioxide, the management group gave up.

In a midnight meeting they decided to take the ultimate solution: They ordered the compartment flooded. The chief constable was put on alert should it become necessary to evacuate area residents.

At 3:44 on the morning of Friday the 11th, hoses were hooked up. All work through the window into the pile was abandoned. The men who had labored there in unselfish disregard for their personal safety were removed to an examination site where their conditions were evaluated. The facility was teeming with people, and the film badge detectors were being developed and processed on the spot to determine amounts of radiation exposure.

A final effort to dislodge the capsules was made before giving the order that would surely release a huge amount of radioactivity. But the steadily increasing temperatures in the most severely affected cartridge indicated further delays would be disastrous.

Friday, at 7:00 AM, the command was passed to Bill Crone, who gave the order to flood the area. Before it was carried out, steps were taken to ensure all workers were under cover. Then a change of shift necessitated another delay. But finally, at about 8:55 AM, the valves were turned on and everyone shuddered.

Water rushed in, and as it contacted the incandescent steel of the outer surface of the capsules, great clouds of steam hissed into existence. Vapor went billowing up the chimney, only to be followed by more as the hot portion of the reactor converted water to steam at an astonishing rate. The cooling effects of the flooding were not immediately apparent. So many hot spots had developed that much of the water was boiling before reaching the glowing cylinders.

Minutes passed. Then quarter-hours. Water flooded in until the broken cylinders were submerged. Still they gave no evidence of cooling.

Since the men had come down from the elevator platform where the outside wall had been breached, the fans that supplied a limited protection against their exposure were shut down. This slowed the drafts through the pile to a minimum. Finally, after an hour, the flooding achieved its aim. First one gauge, then another, began to indicate the heating process had been checked.

Tom Tuohy, Ron Gausden, and Ken Ross relaxed for a moment. But a major problem still lay ahead.

As predicted, the billowing steam had spewed forth from the chimney, and streams of cloudlike vapor carrying radioactive particles shot skyward. The trouble came from the breeze. During the final phases of the hookup, before water was actually flooded in, the winds, which had been blowing out to sea, changed course. Radioactive contaminants were now forced into a north-northwesterly direction at a speed of about ten knots. In addition, a slight temperature inversion, a not-too-uncommon occurrence, caused the air higher up from the ground to flow in another direction.

A nuclear rain was about to fall on a large portion of the countryside around the Windscale No. 1 pile. What its effects would be was hard to judge. Theoretical knowledge of this kind of fallout was exactly that, theoretical only. No previous instance was available to use as a basis for predictions.

Reactor flooding continued for a full twenty-four hours. After the first twelve minutes, the level of radioactive materials streaming from the flue was drastically reduced.

The health physics manager now had a multifold problem. A large portion of the countryside in a rough elliptical area had been subjected to fallout of radioactive particles. This could cause several distinct hazards for humans and animals. First was the possibility of strong gamma radiation to the whole body. Then there was the likelihood of severe, nonreversible injury due to inhalation of the various hot particles. Finally, there was risk of ingestion of radioactive materials due to contamination of the food chain. After careful analysis of the problems involved in the high release levels, and following consultations with other members of the staff, the health physics manager reached a conclusion. Materials escaping from the heavily filtered stack were normal fission products. He therefore planned an approach to handle contamination by iodine and strontium.

By Saturday morning, field workers confirmed this diagnosis. While doing routine samples of the air and radiation levels, one of the vans made a check of fresh milk. Since the area around Windscale was heavily dependent upon the production of dairy products, this was a fortuitous and wise move.

The results were shocking.

The British government had, at that time, no standards for an acceptable level of radioactive iodine in milk. Dr. Scott-Russell, in a scientific paper, had postulated 0.39 microcurie (μc) per liter as the point at which milk became unsafe for infants.

Early analysis indicated the cows in the affected area had produced milk with traces of Iodine-131, a highly radioactive substance, ranging from just the slightest amount to over 0.48μc per liter. This was 0.09μc per liter more than the theoretically arrived at maximum safe dosage. The news got worse. On a subsequent test, several hours later, the figure had risen to an astounding 0.80μc per liter, more than twice the dose considered harmful.

These results coincided with other information brought to the health physics manager. Air samples taken during the greatest emission, from locations near the spewing stack, revealed a higher level of iodine activity than would normally be present in fission products. The explanation was simple. Elaborate filters located in the bulging top of the flue vent stacks had functioned well. Particulate matter had to a great extent been trapped. But iodine, in vapor form, had passed through without much hindrance.

The health physics manager was faced with a real quandary. The milk's iodine content showed a process that was rapidly contaminating a basic food substance. As the iodine settled to earth, it coated blades of grass in pastures around the site. The cows ate the grass, and as they digested it, absorbed the iodine into their systems. Then it was passed into the milk they gave. The more grass they ate, the stronger the concentrations became. In short, the cows were giving radioactive milk, and the radioactivity was in a form that would be readily absorbed and stored in the body of all humans who consumed it.

There was no standard for defining an "acceptable lifetime level" for radioactive iodine in milk. To halt the production of the many area dairies would have a dire influence on the economy of the farmers and the region. There was no other choice. Not only was the milk contaminated, but cheese and other products made from the milk, which had even wider distribution, would be heavily laced with radioactive iodine.

The decision to cut into the livelihood of an entire region was far too big to be made by a single man. But the need to act quickly was clear. To his everlasting credit, the health physics manager did so.

His interview with Tom Tuohy, the works general manager, was brief. Upon explaining his fears, the works manager asked a few questions and acted with decisive swiftness. A group of medical experts with knowledge of radiation effects on humans was gathered together. Several of the top men could not be present so their opinions were sought by telephone. They were charged with the establishment of a limit for the presence of radioactive iodine in milk. This step was necessary if all milk produced in the area were to be pulled from circulation. Such a dramatic act was bound to provoke the question "Who says so?" and an authoritative answer had to be ready. The specialists spent several difficult hours forging a standard. While many views were expressed, they finally managed to agree a level of 0.1μc per liter of milk was the absolute maximum allowable. This content had been surpassed by 800 percent on Saturday, the second day of field testing.

The figure, while considered low by some experts, came from an analysis of probable absorption into the thyroid glands of young children. Iodine has a strong tendency to be stored in this organ, and taking into account the facility of the thyroid to build up iodine over a long period of time, all felt that any great concentrations should be avoided. These findings were quickly delivered to a higher echelon, and members of the Atomic Energy Authority and the Medical Research Council agreed with the limitation.

While the scientific work was in progress, Tuohy arranged another set of meetings. These were to discuss the political and social implications of a milk ban.

At this point, even though the specially equipped vans were out sampling additional milk supplies, no exact knowledge of the range of the radioactive fallout was available. For immediate purposes a circle about two miles in radius was drawn. That became the area under debate. A total of twelve milk producers operated in the zone and would bear the brunt of at least the first proscriptions.

Field testing took time. Still more time was required to study the data. Shortcutting unnecessary debate, the scientists, engineers, technicians, and politicians were able to combine their findings. By 11:00 PM on Saturday, October 12, they had reached a three-part decision. All milk from the dozen suppliers in the two-mile field would be declared contaminated and disposed of. Sampling vans would work outward from this immediate area and define the furthermost limits of the fallout. Their judgment would be based on iodine levels in fresh milk. If they exceeded the 0.1μc-per-liter critical level, these supplies would also be declared unfit for human consumption and confiscated. Finally, additional support would be called in to take random samples in a huge geographic area as far away as the coasts of Lancashire, North Wales, the Isle of Man, into Yorkshire, and the southernmost portions of Scotland.

At this same time, additional studies of the iodine content of such other farm produce as eggs, vegetables, and some meats were authorized. These were given a lower priority.

Shortly after group agreement, action was taken. John Bateman, the cattle breeder and farmer, was awakened at 1:30 Sunday morning. After a commotion in his front yard, motorcycle policemen knocked on his door. When he answered, they told him, with measured politeness, about the contamination problem. The Cumberland police, assisting the Milk Marketing Board, seized the milk at twelve farms. The individual dairymen were stunned though cooperative. They had no wish to place a harmful product on the market but were noticeably concerned about their livelihood. A portion of their loss would be protected by the British government, but long-term damage, which would affect both the consumer's attitude toward their milk and other livestock farmers' feelings toward their herd animals, was a problem that would trouble them for years.

As the testing vans expanded their radius of operations, the area of known contamination began to grow. In stage after successive stage, the original two-mile radius became three, then five, and finally the idea of a circular ring of fallout gave way to a clearer picture. The pattern became one of a long ellipse with the Windscale No. 1 pile at the upper end. It stretched to cover a parcel of land thirty miles long, ten miles wide to the south, and six miles broad in its northern extreme. The upper tip of the area terminated about six miles from Windscale No. 1, and the southernmost point included the Barrow Peninsula. The total was over two hundred square miles of fine farm and dairy lands placed under quarantine. All milk shipments were halted. Months later, while the radioactive levels in most areas had dropped, the milk ban still remained in effect throughout the fallout zone.

Other testing activity was underway at this same time.

The workers who had been on-site during various periods in which the radioactive materials were spewing into the air were closely studied. While several showed signs of hair and hand contamination, all responded to standard treatments, which consisted of degreasing and scrubbing the skin. Large doses of a heavy iodine drug were administered to prevent the thyroid from absorbing radioactive iodine.

Tests were also run on residents in areas near the facility to discover the extent of their exposure. Several cyclists going to work along the track near Seascale on Friday morning had fairly high counts on their outer clothes, but the levels were well into the so-called "safe" zones. Other individuals also had some low-level contamination, and all were able to clean up to normal standards.

An ongoing radiation test for iodine in the thyroid was instituted for all men, women, and children in the exposed area. When one child showed a 0.28 µc level, additional tests were planned. A new study by the Medical Research Council was also begun, and this work continued into 1977.

A great national uproar met news of the accident. What had been so long feared was now fact. Tempers, as well as emotions, ran high. Government studies and committees of examination were formed and charged with projecting probable damage to the economy. These investigations were progressing at a typical governmental pace when the real blockbuster was dropped.

Danish scientists, concerned by the news of the Windscale accident, studied the pattern of air currents in the upper atmosphere. This caused them to begin checking milk produced on the part of their peninsula closest to the disaster site.

By October 23, their results threatened to bring about an international crisis. Tests revealed levels of contamination equal to or greater than those reported in the British press. The affected area, while smaller than the two-hundred-plus square miles under ban in England, was of a considerable size—especially since it was centered on one of Denmark's most vital milk and dairy areas.

Increases in both strontium-90 and other radioactive trace materials had been found in milk before, and causes had been attributed to the test explosions of nuclear weapons. The around-the-world travel of hot debris cast upward into the atmosphere in the famous mushroom-shaped cloud had been tracked on a number of occasions. These studies had shown that wide belts across the face of the earth were contaminated for short periods of time. But the Windscale pollution was another matter entirely. In this instance, contamination rates were of sufficient magnitude to render milk unfit for human consumption. There was no guess as to how long levels would remain intolerably high.

New questions of international law were raised by the incident. Was the government of one country responsible for losses of either private citizens or the government of another nation due to the accidental release of radioactive substances? Or was the release merely an act of God? These questions were never answered. Discussions took place in parliament, and an official government policy was formulated. This acknowledged only minimal responsibility for the accident in the first place and no acceptance of liability in the second. Likewise, in Denmark, governmental councils convened, and although incensed by the incident, only the most civil and noncontroversial communiqué was drafted and sent. Judging from newspaper coverage of the time, the issue came up and then, in a matter of days, after a violent series of threats, complaints, and intense media coverage, drifted into oblivion.

Meanwhile work continued on the reactor. New designs were proposed for a second plutonium production unit on the same site—with several noticeable improvements—showing that the government's commitment to the area remained unchanged.

More than six hundred dairy farmers were affected by the ban, which continued over the entire two-hundred-mile area for longer than nine months. For part of the contamination zone nearest the Windscale site, it lasted more than a year. During the time the total area was under quarantine, an estimated $11,000 of milk was daily poured down drains and allowed to flow into the sea. Financial losses exceeded $3 million from this one product alone. And those were 1957 dollars.

Even further financial devastation awaited the farmers and landowners near the center of the contamination. Breed cattle from these farms dropped drastically in value, as did the selling prices of the land itself. Financial lending institutions, which had long considered the region prime for investment purposes, began to look with disfavor on further loans for capital construction and expansion. Fortunately, given sufficient time, things do return to normal. But years were required to reestablish confidence in the areas of maximum contamination.

Some final questions about the Windscale disaster remain:

Did the reactor protection systems work as they should? Was there a serious chance of an uncontrolled chain reaction that would progress to disaster proportions? And did the engineers, using the incident as a stimulus, improve their technology?

In answer to the last question, the process upon which the Windscale reactor was based is no longer in use. Considered to be intrinsically too dangerous, air cooling has been largely replaced by other systems. Scientists and engineers knew long in advance of the Windscale incident that the graphite pile was destined to give major troubles. A great part of the informed scientific community did not view the Windscale disaster with surprise. The majority of these knowledgeable people were relieved the consequences had not been even worse.

It is apparent that many of the components of the system were either inadequate or nonoperational. It is equally clear, from the number of instances in which workers were exposed to potentially intolerable levels of radiation, that management of the pile did foresee a developing disaster of enormous proportions. That they were finally able to contain the problem by direct human exposure and emergency measures developed on the spot says a great deal about their ability to reason in periods of duress. This also indicates too little thought went into the design in the first place. Their attempt to settle the situation by directing streams of water onto the containers was both a brave and a last-ditch solution to a difficulty that was rapidly assuming the dimensions of an ulti-mate accident. Allowed to continue, heat buildup would finally have caused the release of an almost incalculable amount of radioactive "ash." Uranium oxide is highly toxic. At the levels it was being produced by the Windscale pile, overheating it wasn't too serious a matter. Most of the particulates were trapped by the elaborate filters in the tall, bulging ventilating stacks. Further progression of the problem, however, would have resulted in a far different ending. Finally reaching overload points, the filters would have then started to bypass an ever-increasing amount of waste, and this virulent material would have been forced into the atmosphere in quantity. London, three hundred miles to the south, recorded twenty-fold increases in radioactivity during the incident and might have become too contaminated to allow for the continued residence of humans there.

Two things have to be taken into consideration when examining this scare story. First, cooling was attained, albeit by unusual means, under emergency conditions. Second, great technological strides have been made in the ensuing years. Designs of both the basic reactors and the safety equipment have improved immeasurably. But Windscale again shows us it is just possible we may not, at any given time in our technological development, be as advanced as we think we are.

Had the press questioned the reliability of the Windscale No. 1 pile before the incident, and asked specifically about safety during the Wigner release process, the answer would have been calming. Based on management's honest belief, every contingency had been analyzed, discussed, and dealt with, so safety was assured. It seems to be the nature of technicians, no matter how well intentioned, to take somewhat simplistic attitudes toward the various processes they operate. Their very familiarity with the technology produces a feeling of safe acceptance. Suggestions of potential danger or problems generally tend to be rebuffed by an increase in references to the "fail-safe" nature of the designs, and finally, an irritated "This thing is safer than a loaf of bread" kind of remark.

In other words, at any point in our development of nuclear knowledge the processes in use represent a technology that is advanced yet still under development. Safety has always been a basic criterion for design in this field. Therefore, any suggestion the system might not be sufficiently safe is bound to come up against an especially positive assertion that there is absolutely no way the device might malfunction or fail.

But such a possibility, no matter how remote, is always present. And the designers, no matter how positive, know it.

TEN

Browns Ferry

Limestone County, Alabama, is a pretty place on the northernmost border with Tennessee. The land is hilly and runs down to the backed-up waters of the Tennessee River where it flows into Morgan County, named after an early settler.

A number of towns in this area made headlines in the 1930s when the Tennessee Valley Authority (TVA) began to dam the mighty river in a multi-state project designed to stop the disastrous annual flooding and produce electric power for thousands of homes and new industries.

The countryside was partly open, partly wooded, and peopled by farmers who grew cotton and corn and raised cattle. In the war years of the 1940s, it changed a little as industry moved into Decatur and a few other hamlets, bringing jobs in manufacturing plants powered by cheap TVA electricity.

In the 1970s, things changed a lot more.

Just south of where the Elk River joins the dam-controlled waterway, close to the red clay banks of the Tennessee, a new kind of power plant was erected. The staff running this one had titles like "Reactor Operator," "Nuclear Engineer," and "Environs Director." They talked in a jargon that included words and phrases like "scram," "ECCS," and "core melt."

The TVA, long a leader in the production of electricity through hydroelectric generation, decided in the late 1950s to expand and maintain its preeminent position by designing and building the world's biggest nuclear power station. It would be ten times larger than any plant planned for the 1960s. The total facility would house three giant reactors, each capable of producing about 1,100 megawatts of energy to serve two million people in the area with inexpensive, clean electricity.

The group that tamed the mighty Tennessee had little trouble leaning on their Washington connections to help procure needed federal funds. So before long their second major dream in forty years became a reality. And Browns Ferry became a historic site.

The TVA is a branch of the federal government founded by Franklin Roosevelt in 1933. For years it cooperated with the AEC and the Defense Department in the development of nuclear facilities within its boundaries. Oak Ridge, Tennessee, far to the north of Limestone County, housed one of the greatest concentrations of atomic research and nuclear materials production facilities in the world. It must have seemed a logical step to turn to atom splitting when the demand for even cheaper electricity threatened the future growth of the TVA's protected area.

The Browns Ferry facility was celebrated at its opening in August 1974 as one of the best-constructed, state-of-the-art, safety-oriented installations of its kind. The rhetoric seemed to please a lot of people, made good press, and was right, as far as it went. But the installation, like some other operating plants, contained within its massive reinforced concrete structures a basic design flaw.

Picture a subterranean room 180 feet long, 35 feet wide, and 11 feet high. This cement-walled tunnel stretched away into the distance, cutting through the innards of the plant and passing directly beneath the main control room. Its purpose was simple. The facility required thousands of miles of wiring to operate the valves, pumps, and vital instrumentation necessary to safely run the three reactors and generating equipment. It was economically more sound, from the standpoint of both construction and maintenance, to build a single open space rather than bury separate bundles of conduit to carry the needed cables.

The long room, brightly lighted from above, was a maze. Along its dun-colored walls, and crisscrossing at random from side to side down the entire length, were shallow metal troughs made of gray galvanized iron. In these flat trays rested thousands of multi-colored wires, connected at one end to a valve or gauge and at the other to a control or readout in the main operating center. It was impossible, even with the eleven-foot ceiling, for a man to walk erect through the jumble.

Electricians labored in the area, known as the cable spreader room, for more than a year. Installation of each line required by the construction blueprints produced a puzzle of infinite complexity. Each wire was identified, numbered, and properly bundled with its brothers. Each started where it should start and ended where the plans dictated. One look at the accumulation quickly banished any thought that the business of generating electricity from atomic power was a simple process.

But the mass of wiring was relatively easy to comprehend. It was logical, and any licensed electrician could take the proper drawings and make order from the seeming chaos. People worked in the bright room year around, installing new items or modifying existing hookups to improve performance. They were so busy, in fact, that a shift was often on duty on Saturday attacking one project or another.

In a sense, those men existed in a world of their own. Fully unionized, they held periodic meetings with superiors to discuss the proper ways to perform their complex tasks. But they worked pretty much at their own speed, with breaks for coffee and a main meal. They also devised their own techniques for achieving their goals. Those techniques might or might not have been approved by the inspection and management teams who attended meetings but seldom entered the confusion of the main spreader room.

The Nuclear Regulatory Commission, assigned to monitor safety preparations and operation of the facility, only occasionally sent anyone into the work areas of the plant. Secure in their offices, its members perused papers showing the required number of fire drills had been performed. Or they analyzed reports that counted the number of days the facility had operated without mishap or worker injury.

Many employees of the NRC would be of little use in the actual functioning area of the plant anyway. Only a limited percentage were technically trained or specifically oriented to the components of nuclear power production.

As in most industries, the shift workmen and their managers were left to their own resources in operating the plant. To varying degrees these people came to know and respect the equipment they were assigned to run. They developed a possessive feel for the facility and its operation. The controls took on seemingly human traits and the idiosyncrasy of each meter, gauge, switch, or computer-operated event sequence was well known and thoroughly discussed. The plant was as familiar to the men as their own homes. They knew its every nook and cranny and were able to walk from one place to another in the widespread complex without a guide or even conscious thought. This familiarity breeds a relaxed air. Even the tension each man may have felt in the early stages of dealing with not one but three huge atomic piles faded with repetition of control sequences and a never-ending string of successful, uneventful operations.

From the lowest member of a cleanup crew to the plant operating superintendent, the job had its routine aspects. And the

Browns Ferry installation was so huge no single person could possibly monitor the daily happenings. Men came and went on their duties and assignments. Shifts changed with only short briefings, and then a new team was manning the unit. Construction went on constantly as the third reactor was brought on stream. New office space was needed as the staff grew. And the number of electrical connections and improvements in the wiring system continually increased.

Everything went along fine until March 22, 1975. It all started simply enough. Months before, when construction began on reactor No. 3, an airtight partition had been installed in the cable room between Unit 2 and the new building. This prevented any leakage of possibly contaminated air back into one of the working control rooms. All air movement in the plant was designed to flow toward the areas of highest radioactivity. This protected the workers and, in case of a leak, prevented contamination from spreading outward, as the air pressure helped keep it in.

The time had come to remove this partition between the two units, but before authorization could be granted, there had to be a series of leakage tests. The Division of Power Production was charged with that job. Tests quickly located several areas where leaks had occurred, and these would have to be corrected before the airtight partition was pulled down.

The Division of Engineering Construction, informed of the problem, issued a work plan, number 2,892, requiring that all leaks be identified, listed, sealed off, and the work verified by an engineer. It seemed like such a straightforward order—until the electricians came to the main cable spreader room.

The maze of troughs, along with many holes in the walls and ceilings where wires came into and exited the room, made for slow going. Normal leak-testing devices were unusable because the men simply could not see to read them. Smoke was tried, along with soapy water that would show bubbles. But the most favored technique utilized a candle held near a suspected airflow. The flame, if agitated by the passage of air, would flicker and follow the draft, pinpointing the precise location of a problem.

Hard as it was, working in the tight confinement between the stacks of trays, the men were successful in developing a primary list of leak points. Work started on patching these, and as one by one they were secured, air pressure in the room increased by tiny but measurable amounts. This, in turn, caused smaller holes, which had gone unnoticed or had not leaked before, to show up on repeated inspection.

The job was tedious, but its completion was vital to the start-up date for the third reactor. A maximum state of airtightness was required before the fueling-up process began.

Management was concerned both with the magnitude of the problem and the time it was taking to solve it. To hurry the process along, they assigned several engineering aides, or inspectors, to the job of working directly with electricians testing for leaks and signing them off as they were sealed.

Many of the leaking places were caused by the addition of new wiring. When it came time to install a needed line, the electricians made a hole through the sealant foam, at the point where the loom of wires passed through the wall, and simply pushed in an additional cable. Little attention was paid to sealing up these newly punched passages as things were still in the construction phase.

March 22 was a balmy Alabama Saturday. Scattered clouds spotted the deep blue of the sky, and visibility was clear across the rolling, pollution-free landscape. It was a great day to be off duty and outdoors. Six men working in the artificial light of the cable spreader room could see nothing but miles of wiring lying in their gray trays. All thoughts of recreation had vanished from their minds as they worked on what was normally a free day, trying to seal a seemingly endless number of leaks. Dealing with some of the harder-to-locate problem areas, the men worked in pairs.

An engineering aide named Larry Hargett and an electrician were at a place where ten cable trays, placed in two vertical rows of five each, entered the Unit 1 reactor building. Hargett, a twenty-year-old who had been on the job for only two days, was in a dimly lit area using a candle to detect any airflow. He had taken the candle from the electrician because he was in a better position to reach a suspect place.

Suddenly, the flame darted off to one side where several cables had been punched through after the original fireproofing had been installed. Intrigued, the aide leaned forward, bringing the candle closer. The flame was pulled horizontal, and Hargett knew he had found a relatively big hole.

Removing the candle, he checked to see if the electrician had noted the spot. Then he pulled out of the way as far as he could in the confined space to allow the second man access to the leak. The electrician, stretching, could not reach the penetration point because it was deeply recessed into the solid wall.

Seeing the other man's dilemma, Hargett asked if he could help. Nodding, the electrician tore off a couple of hunks of the two-inch-thick sheet of polyurethane foam he carried and passed them up. Working rapidly, Hargett stuffed the pliant bulk into the hole, then brought up his candle to check the result.

Bringing the flame to within about an inch of the protruding material, he watched. Then, to his surprise, the fire, following the airflow, was pulled into the leak. The foam sizzled and before Hargett could remove the candle, the material burst into flame. He was not overly alarmed. Small fires had been started in the spreader room before during similar operations. They had always been extinguished. Many of the men pinched them out with their fingers. This fire was small. Sputtering and dropping little flaming streamers, it flickered brightly.

Calling down to the waiting electrician, who could see something had happened, Hargett told him there was a small fire. The man below handed up a flashlight, and Hargett, using the blunt handle end, tried to crush out the flames. After a minute he gave up. The area was too deeply recessed to reach easily, and every time he squelched one burning area, another cropped up.

Nearby, a third man heard the commotion and quickly passed over a handful of rags. The wall where the fire burned was about thirty inches thick and the inspector stuffed rags into the four-by-five-inch opening to smother the small blaze. After a moment's wait he removed the wadding. Peering into the narrow aperture, he could see the flame still flickering. The rags in his hand were smoldering. He dropped them quickly to the electrician below, who stamped on them as he called for a fire extinguisher.

The incident had lasted only ninety seconds. Someone quickly brought the electrician a carbon dioxide unit, which he hoisted up to the waiting Hargett. The hornlike nozzle was forced into the opening and the device emptied in a single, loud, sustained blast. He passed the white-frosted canister down to the waiting men and again peered into the troublesome opening.

Inside, he could see no sign of fire, and relaxed. After a few seconds, he checked again to reassure himself everything was extinguished. To his surprise, he saw smoke, followed by the first fingers of flame.

The fire had heated the copper wiring to the point at which it could ignite its own insulation. Carbon dioxide had forced out all the oxygen in the small hole, but it had been sucked downward by the constant draft. As soon as air returned, the blaze reignited.

From his position Hargett could see the fire had managed to spread outward from the hole through the wall into the reactor room itself. He shouted down to his companions, and two crewmen hurriedly left the cable spreader room to fight the fire in the reactor building on the other side of the wall.

One, seeking additional firefighting equipment, stopped at Security Post 8D. Running up, he grabbed the available extinguisher and began to carry it away. The guard, seeing a problem and conducting a hurried, excited conversation with the man, stepped inside his station and dialed the telephone number posted on the plant's emergency procedures card. Nothing happened. It later proved to be a wrong number. Confused, the guard then dialed the shift engineer's office to report the incident. The man on the other end of the phone punched in 299, the correct fire-alarm code, and handed the telephone to the shift engineer (SE) so he could ring the reactor operator.

Luckily, at this point the SE's office was on the "inside the plant PAX" hookup. Construction was still in progress, and a totally separate telephone system, connecting work crews, was also in operation.

Action intensified in the spreader room. By this time, Hargett's electrician partner had brought him two additional fire extinguishers. Each was exhausted then tossed aside. Volumes of acrid smoke billowed from the small hole, and when the electrician passed up a third unit, the inspector could hear the hissing roar of other fire extinguishers being released on the far side of the wall in the reactor building. He fired off his bottle, and sending it down, took up a fourth. It, too, was shot into the hole, with no more effect.

In a moment of silence after the loud sound caused by the release of the fire extinguisher, the inspector could hear an ominous crackle. Burning insulation, sputtering and throwing off tiny drops of pure flame that left smoke trails in the air, was out of control.

Hearing the alarm, the SE hurried to a control box that would release the built-in Cardox fire-extinguishing material. He was astounded to find the box still had a metal plate over its glass window, installed to prevent accidental breakage during construction. It took some time to remove the protective cover with a screwdriver.

Hargett, who remained near the origin of the blaze, heard the fire alarm sound, announcing someone was about to flood the cable spreader room with CO_2 gas. He and the others quickly evacuated the area to avoid being caught in it.

The assistant shift engineer (ASE), after determining there were no men still inside the spreader room, attempted to activate the built-in system. It refused to function. The control box had, for some reason, been unwired. Thinking quickly, the ASE ran to the east door of the room, where a second box was located. He went through the same routine, and this time was rewarded by a whoosh of carbon dioxide.

It was now just after 12:40 PM. The fire had been burning for twenty minutes.

The two men who had left the cable spreader area were joined by a third worker on their way to the reactor room. They arrived carrying an extinguisher each. The smoky fire was instantly located in a set of wiring trays about twenty feet above the floor. A ladder was nearby, and one of the crew moved it into position. A second man quickly climbed up and emptied a dry chemical extinguisher onto the flames. The fire was knocked down but quickly rekindled and was soon flickering again. Burning insulation was giving off a greasy, black smoke.

The third worker alerted others in the reactor building to the problem and returned to find the man on the ladder had been forced down by noxious fumes. An ASE arrived and, aided by another worker, released both carbon dioxide and dry chemical extinguishers onto the rapidly spreading fire. Smoke and fumes were intolerable, so the ASE returned to the floor. Taking charge of the action, he sent for backpack breathing apparatuses, and for the next five minutes he and others tried to extinguish the blaze from floor level.

Once the breathing devices arrived, the men donned the masks and were able to deal more directly with the problem. But the flames had gained a strong foothold. More and far denser smoke billowed from the cable trays, obscuring vision until there was no way to maintain a further effort.

The men, thrust away from the base of the blaze by a constant outpouring of fumes from burning plastic insulation, finally reached the end of their endurance. They could no longer approach the source and were forced down the room to a position near some large heat exchangers.

At 12:35 PM, when the fire alarm sounded in the plant control room, there was no hint this shift would be anything out of the ordinary. Since the station ran on a twenty-four-hour, seven-days-a-week basis, operators of the two reactors worked staggered hours. A team of seventeen experts manned their stations on nights, Sundays, holidays, and the normal work week.

News of the fire caused no panic among technicians in the large futuristically designed, well-lighted room. One ASE turned on the manual alarm so it would ring continuously throughout the complex, alerting other personnel. Another ASE began making announcements on the internal loudspeaker system, ordering individuals who were assigned to fire suppression to go to their stations. Back in the SE's office, the time of the alarm was noted in the logbook.

Due to the way the incident was reported, no one in the control area, directly above the main cable spreader room and therefore almost right above the fire, had any idea where the blaze was or how serious it might be. An ASE was unhurriedly given the assignment of locating the problem and reporting back.

No consideration was given to shutting down the reactors, as there did not seem to be any difficulty directly related to the control system.

Two million people were relying on the power generated by the facility, and more than a hint of trouble is required to cause the operators to close down the units and deny the populace the energy it desires.

The main plant control at Browns Ferry was designed to act as a point from which the equipment for all three reactors could be operated. Looking somewhat like a TV set designer's idea of a spaceship command bridge, the room was a complex of light displays and buttons.

The operators could not only command various valves, pumps, and other electromechanical devices to start and stop, they could regulate the speed at which they performed and monitored vital pressures and temperatures as well. Since both reactor No. 1 and reactor No. 2 were on line and operational, a pair of complete teams occupied the 180-foot-long room.

Each individual system had its primary and redundant secondary controls. Men on duty were more than mere needle-watchers. They had been schooled in the complexities of the system and could make mental estimations of the probable causes of malfunctions. They were also well versed in the steps to correct difficulties as they arose.

The ASE sent to look for the location of the fire did not have far to go. As soon as he reached the lower floor, he saw several running men and went to investigate. Minutes later, he called the SE's office with the news the fire was underneath the control room and had spread into the reactor building itself.

The report was disconcerting, but no one panicked. After all, they were contained inside a massive concrete structure and unless the fire was very bad, there was no immediate danger.

Then the first of what was to become a series of unusual incidents occurred. An alarm went off. Its strident sound carried above the routine noise of the center, and the Unit 1 reactor operator moved to investigate. Before he could react to the first problem, a second, and then a third, alarm sounded.

He studied the situation. The emergency core cooling system (ECCS) had been triggered. His eyes swept the indicators. A digital clock on the panel read 12:40 PM. The water level covering the reactor registered normal. This was one of the most crucial points. As long as the depth of water completely covered the top of the pile, the ultimate danger could be averted. Steam pressures looked acceptable, too. He checked to see if someone had mistakenly turned on the standby equipment but found no sign of error.

Two men, staring at the control panels, began to discuss the possibility of "scramming" the reactor, their term for an emergency shutdown brought about by inserting control rods to stop the radioactive energy cycle. The reactor operator was scanning his instruments when a new alarm rang. He checked the source and found that another portion of the emergency core cooling system had started of its own volition. Since pressures still seemed standard in the core, he attempted to shut the cooling systems down, but as soon as he released the controls, the system would restart.

There was some confusion in the room when, to everyone's surprise, smoke started rolling out from under control panel 9-3, which contained the guts for the emergency core cooling. Green and red lights on various boards began to act erratically. They would shine brightly, apparently at random, then dim, flicker, and glow intensely again. None of the emergency equipment would stay off. Almost as if the units had minds of their own, they would stop, pause a moment, then turn on again, causing their indicator lights to glow and add to the chaos.

The seventeen-man crew was on full alert even though only reactor control Unit 1 was showing any malfunction. The second unit seemed to be operating routinely.

At 12:48 PM, an ASE noticed the power produced by No. 1 had fallen from 1,100 to 700 millivolts. Smoke from under panel 9-3 was starting to fill the room with an acrid stench of burning insulation. The next surprise came seconds later. Entire electrical boards began to flicker, then one at a time, go blank. As indicated by their appearance, they were dead. With fire burning the wiring, the room was losing its means of controlling the pile.

Another gauge showed the level of water over the core to be a few inches above normal, so the operator took corrective procedures.

The action began to accelerate. Men were moving swiftly in the background, some telephoning for additional aid, others holding quick conferences. Voices showed tension.

One by one, a number of relief valves necessary to regulate pressure in the core were lost. Fully one-half of the reactor protective systems were out of order and of no use. Alarms rang all along the control area, and smoke was reaching a point where it had become more than a nuisance. It was now making breathing hard for the men in the long room.

One of the hurried consultations broke up, and the SE came alongside the operator of Unit 1. He spoke in a loud voice to be heard above the clamor: "Let's scram the unit."

Several men heard his shout and stepped to their stations. With all the noise and growing confusion, it took a moment; then, with deft motions, the operator manually performed the scram operation, slamming home the control rods. He threw the reactor mode switch to its shutdown position and turned to nod to the SE. But the SE was already on the telephone, reporting conditions in the plant to various supervisors.

At 12:53 PM, positive signals were received. Control rods were confirmed to be fully inserted. Reactor Unit 1 was essentially down. But there were still serious problems. Even though the main energy source was shut off, residual heat would cause high temperatures for a long time to come. So cooling had to be maintained. The two hundred inches of water on top of the reactor pile, and pressure levels in the reactor vessel, had to stay at a semi-operational level—or the core, allowed to go its own way without cooling, would turn into a five-thousand-degree puddle of molten uranium.

Everyone in the control room relaxed when the unit operator announced the successful scramming of his pile. But a look at the various control boards showed growing complications. The main water system that fed coolant to the core was out. The high-pressure emergency cooling system was out. The reactor core spray was out. The low-pressure emergency core cooling system—out. The core reactor isolation cooling system—out. Most instruments indicating conditions inside the unit were also lost. In short, every one of the usual ways to feed water into and take water out of the reactor to maintain its cooling were nonfunctional.

But other crossover arrangements could be improvised. A single high-pressure pump, used to drive the control rods, was switched to deliver its flow into the crucial area. No one could estimate if it would be effective. The volume it could produce was much less than normal, but it was the best quick solution.

During this sequence of malfunctions, people were dashing back and forth between the control room and the fire. One ASE returned to the scene of the blaze in the reactor building to take charge of the crew now trying to extinguish the smoldering wiring.

Smoke in the control room was becoming intolerable. Each time the crew below in the main spreader room would activate the Cardox system to kill the flames, the extra air pressure from the carbon dioxide would force more smoke into the main control center. There was a serious question whether the men could stay there and remain on duty.

At 12:55 PM, just half an hour after the start of the fire, all ability to monitor the radioactive happenings in the pile was irrevocably lost. Reactor No. 1 was operating blind. And Unit 2 was starting to give trouble as well. The same strange flickering of panel lights had started. Worse, alarms signaling something had gone wrong in the wiring system of the diesel-powered generators sounded, quieted, then came on again. The Unit 2 operator called the SE. He didn't think the engines would start.

The SE, meanwhile, had been frantically busy. In addition to directing calls for assistance to a number of off-duty personnel, he had been asking for advice from his supervisors on dealing with the escalating emergency. Thickening smoke had reduced visibility in the long room, and several of the staff were violently coughing.

The Unit 2 operator was faced with increasing trouble. Reactor power was dropping at a phenomenal rate, and a number of alarms were calling for immediate attention. Most of the indicating lights had failed, and the few still on were starting to flicker. After a hurried call to the SE, who had to round up several other technicians, the Unit 2 operator gave orders to scram that pile and started his own shutdown procedure.

Firefighting teams were being beaten back, and the situation was nowhere near in hand. It was hard to tell how much worse the matter might become, so all personnel not directly concerned with the operation of the reactor units were evacuated. A head count was taken at 1:15 PM, and it was ascertained all were accounted for.

Breathing apparatuses were rushed to the control room, and even though the units needed frequent changes because they would run low on air, they gave the operators a chance to stay in the area. The foul stench of burning cable insulation had seeped everywhere, and it was now hard to see through the haze.

The word had been passed to the main cable spreader room about smoke in the control center, so the firefighters had stopped using the Cardox system. This helped, but upstairs the air was still only barely breathable.

More electrical boards on the Unit 1 side were going out. Then another problem began to surface. Pressures in the reactor chamber were building higher and higher. In a matter of minutes, they had increased to well over 1,000 pounds per square inch (psi), and only the control drive rod pump had the capacity to force water in against this immense force.

Trial after trial to re-rig power to crucial valves failed, so the decision was made to try to operate them manually by sending out some of the now-arriving off-duty technicians and maintaining a linkup with them by telephone. Several workers were at their stations when all electrical power for the reactor building failed, and the elevator stopped.

One operator successfully opened the proper sequence of main steam valves by hand. Pressure inside the unit dropped to about 850 psi. But the quantity of water being delivered by the single pump was insufficient to maintain the water level on top of the core. This was slowly but steadily falling.

Unit 2 was having more difficulties. Successfully shut down, it too was experiencing failures of its emergency core cooling system. Drastic steps were taken to stay ahead of the situation.

The operator of Unit 1 and the SE held another hurried conference. Both were highly concerned over the loss of water from the core. They started to work out additional possible linkups that could handle the problem, but it was a difficult balance. Heat remaining in the reactor would turn water to steam at normal atmospheric pressure. So they had to maintain a high enough pressure inside the unit to keep the water in a fluid state but low enough to permit additional pumps to force more liquid into the core.

A new emergency arose. Part of the reactor unit, called the torus, was overheating from the failures and unusually high pressures. It was mandatory that this be cooled as rapidly as possible to prevent a steam explosion large enough to damage the main containment structure. Any breach would release huge volumes of radiation into the environment. But the means of achieving torus cooling were by now severely limited.

Working in a logical sequence under growing duress, the engineers on duty determined that the pumps routinely used to scavenge water formed as condensation would be more than adequate to hold the level above the core. So they hooked up a relay to bring these units into play. But by this time, another complication had developed.

The temporary drop in pressure in the main reactor vessel reversed itself, and the meters climbed steadily to 1,080 psi, then seemed to stabilize at about 1,100 psi. This was far too much for the condensate pumps to overcome. Designed to function at about 350 psi, these units simply could not push water in against the growing force in the main reactor chamber.

This same pressure also made the problem with the torus more serious. Water was being squeezed out by the enormous pressures in the reactor, and it was growing hotter by the moment. A failure would result in a completely hopeless situation. The pile would be unprotected, and a meltdown would be imminent.

The control rod drive pump, operating at full power, offered the sole solution. Usually, there was more than one unit in this series to provide a backup, but only the primary pump controls were effective.

At about this point, the process computer, which notes each activity instigated from the control room, failed. No further records of the action were made until about 4:00 PM. The loss was not significant to the men on duty, but it meant reconstruction of the event would have to be accomplished later by memory.

Smoke in the control area had lessened, but the stench was still bad. The technical staff pinpointed the problem of pressure inside the reactor as the most serious dilemma. Even a short-term fix was better than none at all, so they agreed to try for depressurization by allowing steam and water to blow down into the torus. The valves required for this activity could no longer be operated from the control room, so the ASEs used telephones to instruct various individuals to activate the valves manually and estimate proper settings. Four main steam-line relief valves were cracked, and as hot steam gushed downward, pressure inside the unit dropped. But so did the level of vital cooling water. From its standard two-hundred-inch depth, it fell steadily to a stabilization point only forty-eight inches above the top of the still-active fuel. Lower pressures, however, allowed the condensate pumps to force water in, and there was some sign of a depth increase.

But the trouble with the torus itself still lingered. Two men were dispatched to the reactor to enter the building and work another valve by hand. Armed with breathing apparatuses, they made three attempts but were stopped each time because they had only eighteen minutes of air in their backpacks. That was not long enough to allow them to reach the valve, operate and adjust it, then make their way out of the building. The tanks, designed to contain a much longer supply, were only partially filled, due to low master tank pressure. Dejected, the pair returned and reported their failure to the SE.

In the meantime, by using the telephone to contact men at other stations, some measure of order was being restored. Operators working from relayed instructions were performing required adjustments. Things looked better than they had for some time.

Then the fire struck again. The PAX outgoing telephone system, which had operated even after power in the building had failed, now went dead. It was possible to call in, but the crew in the control room could not dial out with vital valve-adjustment instructions. Runners were dispatched to get the teams working the valves to phone in to the master control at regular intervals.

More and more staff members, sensing the seriousness of the situation, gravitated to the main area. Working technicians were harassed by newcomers eager to be assured that control would be restored.

Pressure in the giant unit was stabilizing. The new pump hookup was able to add water to the confined space. By 2:00 PM, the reactor steam pressure had moderated to about 200 psi, and the water level was its usual two hundred inches.

During this episode with Unit 1, Unit 2 was experiencing its own little difficulties. The same irregularities in the monitor panel lights had been going on for some time. The alarm system seemed to be upset, operating independently of any observable reality. Two components of the emergency core cooling system had failed almost immediately, and a single remaining set of pumps and valves began to falter on an intermittent basis. The complete low-pressure system was still available on standby. To be doubly sure of not having a replay of the No. 1 reactor, the No. 2 controller set up the same linkage of high-pressure rod operating pumps that had proved successful earlier.

During all this time, the fire was being fought erratically. It had spread, and more wiring was being consumed with every passing minute. Command of the firefighters in both the main cable spreader room and in the reactor building had changed several times. One assistant unit operator, who had directed the operation for a considerable period, was finally forced back to the main control area due to smoke inhalation.

By 1:00, thirty minutes after the first alarm, fire-suppression crews had been divided into two operating sections. One, in the spreader room, was directed by an ASE; the other, in the reactor building, by a second management assistant. Neither man was a professional firefighter, and neither had any training for this effort. The only help came from instructions received by telephone from the SE's office. A decision was quickly reached to contact the Athens (Alabama) Fire Department, and by about 1:30 PM, the fire chief and several men were at the scene.

In addition to a supply of properly filled bottles of air, the new arrivals also had definite views on how to stifle the blaze. Recognizing he and his men were under the direction of Browns Ferry personnel, the fire chief made all his knowledge and facilities available to them.

Several relays were formed to run empty air bottles back to the station in Athens for recharging. Additional backpacks were filled by using a pump in the truck. The chief's advice—to quench the fire by spraying it with water—was considered but rejected. The plant supervisor, fearing some of the wiring might still be carrying high voltages, disallowed the use of water and instructed the workers to continue using chemical extinguishers.

About 3:00 PM, an off-duty SE arrived and immediately took charge of the firefighting teams in the cable spreader room. He continued the chemical attack but was able to better direct its application. An hour and a half later, four hours after its start, the fire was reported completely out in his area.

Activity in the main reactor room, however, was not proceeding as successfully. Fire continued in trays high up along one wall, where it seemed nothing was effective in suppressing the blaze. Flames would die, give off thick, foul-smelling, oily smoke, then renew.

The Athens fire chief argued for the use of water. It was his opinion the fire was not electrical in nature, but was, instead, semi-chemical, caused by burning insulation. He theorized if they sprayed the cables with water, it would cool the wiring enough so the wires themselves would not rekindle the blaze. There was a great deal of argument, but it was again decided to continue suppression efforts by using chemical extinguishers. Twice rebuffed, the chief was highly irritated but still cooperative.

The main control room situation, although better than earlier, remained bad. Jury-rigged lighting was being used, as all power had long ago failed. Brilliant puddles of light were crossed through with streaming tendrils of black and white smoke. A team manned the telephone, relaying instructions as each station called in. Residual smoke clung to the ceiling, and the odor of burning cable insulation permeated the air. The scene was more like a battlefield than an orderly control center, but the operators were managing to cope with each development.

Still more unneeded workers had arrived in the long room to be at the heart of the action and added measurably to the overall confusion. Individuals were dashing in and out; hurried, hushed conferences were held in tight huddles of two or three; and instructions were shouted across the room.

Torus cooling remained a difficulty. The diversion of the condensate pumps to maintain water in the reactor chamber added to this problem. The torus, technically called the reactor containment suppression chamber, is one of the final defenses against radioactive leakage from the core. It is designed as a major component in the system and is a concrete and steel bottle that contains or surrounds the reactor pressure vessel. Should the pressure vessel fail, the torus is the next and final barrier to hold in radiation.

The Unit 1 operator could not tell the water level or temperature inside the reactor because all gauges were inoperable. But even with the relief valves working, the residual heat removal system (RHR), which maintained cooling to the torus, was out, so the technicians knew things were not going well. Additionally, without the RHR, final shutdown cooling was impossible.

But time had been bought through trial and error. With shrewd speculation about the extent of damage, both the water level and pressure in the reactor chamber itself were being maintained. Once assured of this, the operating technicians began sketching possible methods to apply cooling to the overheated torus.

At about 2:00 PM, radiation monitors on the Unit 1 reactor building had failed, so there was no longer any way of telling whether or not radiation was leaking into the atmosphere.

Environment control personnel began taking samples on a grab, or random, basis, as an improvised alternative to the continual sampling usually provided by installed instrumentation. Everyone was relieved when results proved to be about normal.

At 3:20 PM, the dilemma of cooling the torus had become extremely serious. The State of Alabama Emergency Plan for Browns Ferry Nuclear Plant was implemented to the extent of notifying several designated individuals. This action could hardly be called successful.

The Director for Radiological Health for the State of Alabama was not told of the fire until 3:20 PM, some two hours after its start. He was called by the Tennessee Valley Authority Environs Emergency Center Director from his office in Muscle Shoals, and given sketchy information. Aside from a statement that there had been a fire and both reactors were scrammed, no details were offered.

At 3:40 PM, an unsuccessful effort was made to contact the state health offices. One call went unanswered, but no further attempts were made. At 3:45 PM, the Director for Radiological Health managed to get through to the Alabama Civil Defense Department and advised them that, according to available data, radiation was not above permissible levels. A request for Civil Defense to initiate all emergency plan notification procedures was also made. The on-duty Civil Defense staff member made a desultory effort to do so, reaching only a limited number of the specified individuals. After trying for only an hour, he discontinued the task.

A central emergency control center was established by the TVA, and wider-scale grab-sampling of the atmosphere for readings on radioactivity was instituted by TVA personnel.

While all this was taking place, several additional events had occurred in the Unit 1 command center. Although instruments were still out, some switchovers had been made. These, along with additional repairs, returned a few instrument panels to operation. No control was available over the residual heat removal system, however, so things in the torus seemed to be getting worse.

Constant pumping had completely restored the water level over the fuel core. Various units were able to hold the standard two-hundred-inch level without strain. Realignment of one of the systems for torus cooling was, however, impossible. Several calls were made for the assembly of all available off-duty electricians and operators, and a preliminary plan was completed that called for major on-the-spot rewiring, even though the fire was still burning and additional circuits might fail at any moment.

By 2:00 PM that Saturday afternoon, many people were at work in the big control room, adding to the tumult, but reestablishing necessary links. They would work for hours, patching where they were able, before improvements of a substantial nature could be discerned.

The furious fire was still burning, causing more and more havoc. By about 4:00 PM, though additional yards of cables and wires would be lost in the blaze, the serious damage to major control devices had already been done.

About five minutes after 5:00 PM, the director of the Environs Emergency Center on the Browns Ferry site gave an order for more air samples to be obtained. Smoke pouring from the reactor building looked alarming, and the threat of some atmospheric pollution from the earlier high pressures in the core container caused everyone to proceed with extra caution. Samples showed no trace of unusual radioactivity, but as a general precaution, the meteorological tower was ordered to be evacuated.

Around 3:00 PM, the operator in control room No. 1 had instituted a simple procedure to bring one of the residual heat-removal systems, not used in the water-pumping operation, up to on-line status. Voltage was still being progressively lost to more control boards, and the telephone system remained inoperable for outgoing calls, but the work from newly arrived electricians and other personnel gave the maneuver some hope of success. To carry it off, one or more men, wearing air tanks for breathing, had to enter the fire zone, pass through it, and manually align the necessary valves. Then, since there was no direct communication with the master control, they might have to go back for minor adjustments.

The difficulty was getting there in the first place. Backpacks contained just enough air to last about eighteen minutes, not long enough to cross through the smoky darkness, locate the valves, adjust them, and return. Although a similar operation had been successfully achieved earlier, the distance from the door to the valves this time was too great. Two teams of two men each made separate tries, but neither was successful.

They returned to the control room to face growing concern. There was no question the torus was operating at or near its basic design limit. Something had to be done.

The fire in the reactor building had to be quelled to allow passage of the crew to the valves. There was no other solution. Several intermediate actions could be taken but were mere stopgaps. Without the valves being set, there was no way to avert disaster.

Additional work on the control boards proved effective in aligning the RHR system, but since there was no way to ensure that the pipes were full of water, the decision to start the operation of the pumps was delayed.

Then, around 4:30 PM, four hours after the candle first set the fire, power was restored to about half the monitoring equipment.

A request to start the reactor building exhaust fan, to help clear the air of the smoke and stench, was approved at about 4:40 PM, and the operators tripped the switch. The effect was immediately noticeable in two areas. The air in the control room became almost breathable. But the air draft created by the system spurred the fire into new action. After twenty minutes, the SE judged the improvement of the airflow to be less important than the difficulty it was causing, so the fan was shut down again.

By 6:00 PM, the situation concerning torus cooling had become crucial. Immediate action was now imperative. Control of the last four relief valves was completely gone, despite the activity of the repair crew, and there was a limit to how much longer the entire system could be maintained by the use of the rod drive and condensate pumps. The fire had to be stopped so workers could reach the controls, or heat and pressure would destroy the torus container.

Through all the earlier hours, the Athens fire chief had spoken to one person after another about using water on the blaze. He could understand their caution due to concern about electric shock. But it was clear to him the chemical extinguishing methods, which had worked in the cable spreader room, would not be effective on the conflagration in the reactor building.

Again and again, his suggestions were rebuffed. The desperate need to pass a man through the fire area, however, finally brought a positive answer. The risk of damage and injury from water being sprayed on live electrical lines was far less than the major disaster that would occur if the torus ruptured.

An operator, equipped with breathing equipment, was stationed at the door of the reactor building. He would need the
approval of an SE before entering the blaze area, so a telephone
line was kept open.

Firefighters unreeled a hose and turned on the water. A thin,
disappointing stream dribbled out, and in the confusion, it was
decided to replace the nozzle, which was thought to be defective. One was obtained from the Athens fire company. In reality,
the hose was only partially unwound from its reel. The slow
flow was caused by the tightly wound portion still on the
storage rack.

The borrowed nozzle had threads that did not match the end
of the fire hose, and although an attempt was made to fasten it in
place, results were less than satisfactory. It popped off as soon as
water pressure became strong enough to direct a cooling spray
onto the trays of cable running high along the wall.

The problem was finally resolved, and the SE, along with two
other men, could enter the area of the main blaze. Climbing to
within four feet of the flames with the assistance of two other
workers, the SE sprayed the cable tray for only ten seconds. The
fire was out. After descending to ground level, he left the hose
stuck in a position where it would continue to wash the troughs,
then the three retreated.

Meanwhile, another team had climbed onto the second level.
Use of water on the fire again proved successful. Once the fire
chief's suggestion was followed, the blaze was completely extinguished in less than fifteen minutes. An hour later, after long-term
cooling by water sprays, the fire was officially declared out.

The operator stationed at the door of the reactor room left as
soon as it became apparent there was no further threat from the
flames. Running, he made his way through debris to the critical
valves and operated them by hand. Joined by others bringing

instructions, he soon had the adjustments right, allowing the residual heat-removal system to be operational.

There was still more drama in the control room because the gauges monitoring the water level in the system were faulty. So there was no way to tell if the feed pipes were full or empty. To start the pumps and have them suck air could cause cavitation and stop water flow for hours.

By 8:00 PM Saturday night, electricians had managed to bring the largest number of boards back into service. Another crew of technicians restored the telephone system so outgoing calls could be made. A third team was well into the job of flushing the RHR system.

The problem of pressure in the reactor chamber still lingered. Residual heat in the uranium core was causing water above it to boil, and the constant addition of steam increased the pressure to more than 300 psi. Periodically, to relieve the strain, the operator would order certain valves opened so the vapor would force itself out into the torus. This "blow-down" maneuver was thought up as an emergency measure, and it was effective because it bypassed many inoperable systems that would normally have accomplished the necessary relief process in a more orderly manner.

Each time the reactor was blown down, the temperature in the torus increased. Finally, at about 8:30 PM, the area called the dry well began to be affected by the unplanned-for heat. Pressure built up in this relatively cool zone until there was fear it might rupture or burst. A release was achieved by an unorthodox measure of venting through standby gas treatment lines. Steam fitters manually operated valves routing steam into the plant stack, where it passed into the atmosphere. Monitoring at the time showed only slight increases in radioactivity, and the level was far below any criteria of danger.

The technical staff, working rapidly, was hooking various switches into newly laid lines. By using a trial-and-error setting technique, control was being regained.

But a problem still lingered. There was no way, without the RHR and the final shutdown cooling systems in operating order, to completely close the pile. They were holding a monster on a leash but could not make it lie down. For the moment, there was no immediate danger; things were in a state of abeyance. There was, however, no final solution either. They couldn't turn it loose, but if they hung on too long, something might happen. That something wasn't very pleasant to contemplate.

The control room remained in a state of chaos. Non-essential staff members were wandering about aimlessly, getting in the way of the workers and operators. According to later testimony, supervisory personnel stood next to men who were vitally employed, continually asking for reassurances that no one in good faith could give.

One demonstration of the confusion comes from the actions taken to report an inoperable red light that served as a hazard warning to aircraft. Located on the top of the plant stack, it went out as a result of the fire. As darkness fell, its absence was noticed by a member of the environmental staff. He decided to report it rather than risk an accident.

Instead of calling the FAA directly, he found a public telephone and dialed the guardhouse. When no one answered, he was even more determined to call attention to the problem so he phoned the Environs Emergency Center, which finally phoned the FAA. It took more than a half hour to report a missing light.

Working through the night, weary men in the reactor control center made progress. One team monitored the state of the core and ran necessary blow-down pressure reductions when required. The rest aimed at restoring power and cleaning the RHR system so it could be used in a final reactor shutdown. The control rod pump and condensate pumps still labored to provide water in the core chamber, but the level was holding well.

Finally, around 2:00 AM on Sunday, the torus instrumentation hookup was completed, allowing a measurement of the water level inside. It was within its limits, and one more worry was quelled.

Work continued through the long night. The RHR system was flushed but could not be put back into use until several additional connections were made. One final period of strain occurred during the closing phases, but enough standard controls had been installed to prevent another full-scale call to action. Finally, at 10:40 PM, an entire day later, shutdown cooling was attained by the normal flow path, and the reactor was in its closed state. Reactor pressures dropped to less than 10 psi, and the monster on the leash had been laid to rest.

Air samples taken by the Environs Radiological Emergency crews, who remained in action until 5:00 AM the day after the fire started, showed no significant radioactive release. Dosimeters and film badges worn by workmen to measure their exposure had similar negative readings.

A total of seven employees reported to the hospital with varying levels of discomfort from smoke inhalation. Follow-up medical reports indicated none of the men lost time from work, and each arrived for his next regular shift.

It had been a close call. How close is guesswork. With system after system failing, operators and engineers were nevertheless able to maintain a level of safety. The game of "what if" has been played by numerous individuals who write for the antinuclear press, but none of them, apparently, took the time to review actual reports of the proceedings.

The Browns Ferry fire showed us many things about our nuclear power–generating facilities. Not all of them were good.

The people who work in the plants performing maintenance and repairs are often not sufficiently informed about the problems they can cause. And management may be too lax. On Thursday before the disastrous blaze—and it certainly was disastrous financially because in the end it cost over $10 million—there was not one but two minor fires caused by the same flickering-candle-leak-detection technique. Both occurred in cable penetrations similar to the one that got out of hand. The first little incendiary incident was put out by an electrician with his fingers. The second lasted only about thirty seconds before being snuffed out by a CO_2 extinguisher. One event was reported to construction supervisory workers. The other was entered in the SE's log. So there was certain knowledge of the possibility of a fire from the technique in use. But no one did anything about it.

A second problem lay in the design of Browns Ferry and some other plants. There were supposed to be two totally separate, completely redundant control systems. But this proven space-age technique was defeated when the cables for all the controls passed through a single space. Why was this allowed to happen? From a construction standpoint it was easier and far less expensive to design a plant with just one cable-carrying area. But the simplest solution may not always be best. If a design flaw like this defeats the redundant backup system, no amount of financial savings can possibly justify allowing such potential for disaster.

The cable trays themselves, which provided no effective fire barrier, had been the subject of several NRC memos. These same documents revealed the NRC was concerned with the commonality of wiring for both primary and backup systems. But no action was taken.

Even though operations and engineering staffs performed brilliantly under stress, they were not perfect. There was a completely different hookup, joining the No. 1 and No. 2 control rod pumps, that escaped everyone's notice. The men on duty could have breathed easier had they known of this backup. And if the single high-pressure pump had failed, their lack of this knowledge would have resulted in a disaster of uncertain, but undoubtedly great, magnitude.

Another difficulty lay in the general lack of preparedness on the part of those assigned to the various functions of the emergency plan. There was a visible deficiency in training and planning. Proof lies in the use of unskilled firefighters and state officials charged with conducting certain citizen-protection operations. In the volumes of documents produced by the NRC during its investigations of the fire, and in the records of Congressional hearings touching on the matter, one point was repeated many times. According to testimony of individuals responsible for conducting emergency programs, the plans were poorly implemented—so poorly those responsible for directing them did not even know, at times, the extent of the blaze.

The TVA's Central Emergency Control Center (CECC), charged with executing the emergency plan, was cited in the NRC report as "not being well coordinated." CECC communications with the Browns Ferry site were characterized as "not effective in keeping the CECC currently informed," and "communications with other agencies (Alabama State Civil Defense and groups responsible for emergency action) led to misunderstanding of plant status by those agencies."

The individual who would routinely have functioned as director of the CECC was unavailable when needed. His replacement did not know this and worked at the CECC for half an hour before finding out he was the man in charge. As late as 5:00 PM, the CECC was informing other agencies the fire was confined to the cable spreader room. And the CECC director did not know the fire was out until an hour after the fact.

The TVA people were not alone in their ineptitude. According to the NRC report, Alabama's emergency plan was not available to certain participants, and individual responsibilities were not clearly assigned. The plan was actually out of date. Worse, attempts by state authorities to contact city and county officials were minimal.

From the very start, safety procedures and precautions were not followed by the TVA. A one-page document dated February 11, 1972, and used by Browns Ferry personnel to learn how to report a fire, contained a gross error. Instructions read: "Dialing 299 automatically activates a plant-wide fire alarm and rings the telephone in the Unit 1 control room." Among the contact numbers in bold print at the bottom of this same training document, however, 299 does not appear as the correct fire number. Instead, it is listed as 235. This poster was displayed in a number of areas inside the facility as an emergency quick-reference guide, confusing the guard who first tried to report the fire. A plant Standard Practice Manual also agreed with the 235 number but made no mention of the plant fire-alarm number 299, or the need to inform operating personnel.

Further references to the NRC report show the sheriff of Morgan County was notified, but "had not been briefed in the State of Alabama Emergency Plan," nor did he have a copy of the document. But he fared better than the sheriff of Limestone County, who was never officially notified at all.

The problem of insufficient attention to emergency aspects of an accident, combined with a general lack of knowledge of necessary procedures, was documented by pages of testimony and reports. One defense was offered, centering on the idea that the situation was not sufficiently serious to merit full implementation of disaster procedures. According to this viewpoint, had the problem been truly serious, better action would have been taken.

This stance is hard to reconcile with the facts. Individuals in the control room considered their problems to be very real. More, they were recognized to be of a magnitude capable of producing a disaster if personnel were unable to cope with the loss of equipment. The supervisor who asked continually if things were going to be all right was a worried man. There were a lot of other worried men in the room on that long afternoon.

There is a vast difference between the cool historical reporting to be found in the records of the Browns Ferry fire and the atmosphere of emotional upset, trauma, suspense, tension, and confusion in the main control area during the incident. Laid out with precision, the events tell a logical story. Mistakes are merely recorded among the other facts. Even the style of writing in the reports is, as it should be, unemotional and formal. But it is not hard to read through the maze of material and see an underlying human drama taking place. There was no shortage of fear at Browns Ferry on the day of the accident.

On the afternoon of March 22, 1975, a real nuclear disaster was in the making. Just how narrowly it was avoided no one can really say. Some of those involved performed well. Others acted poorly. Postmortems rarely produce more than a factual outline of what happened. They offer information for technical improvement but do little to ensure improvements are actually implemented to be better prepared for the next round. Because if any system can go wrong, it will go wrong. Remember, Murphy was an optimist.

Browns Ferry Unit 1 remained shut down after the fire but was repaired and operated from 1976 through 1985. Efforts costing a reported $1.8 billion were instigated in 2006 to bring the unit back on line in 2007.

ELEVEN

Federal Assistance

In December 1951, in Arco, Idaho, an experimental breeder reactor (EBR-1) was used to generate enough electricity to make four light bulbs glow. This was the first time the atom had been harnessed to produce electric energy.

In 1954, at Obninsk, Russia, the nuclear power plant APS-1 came on line and was the world's first atomic plant to generate electricity for commercial use. Two years later, in August 1956, Calder Hall 1 began delivering power to the English commercial grid.

In July 2006, half a century later, there are 442 nuclear power plants around the globe producing energy on a daily basis. Some 103 of those are in the United States. Altogether they generate about 16 percent of the world's electricity. These numbers don't count the many small reactors used for research, education, and military applications. There are also several hundred more powering ships and submarines of various nations. As a note of interest, the pressurized water reactor—the most common type— was originally engineered as a power plant for submarines.

In short, there are a lot of reactors in operation. And there are about to be many more. As of late 2006, there were "expressions of intent" for license applications for almost thirty U.S. plants. Worldwide, 140 more are planned or under construction.

To go from one to over four hundred in fifty years averages out to be just over eight new reactors per year. The problem is, averages don't count in this game. Many of those reactors were built in the period between 1950 and the late 1960s. These units are now forty to fifty years old.

For convenience, reactors may be divided into four broad "generations." A few first generation units are still in operation. Second generation units were a marked improvement, and many of these remain in use. Japan has a trio of third generation reactors in operation, and others are under construction. Generation 3 offers further developments over Generation 2 designs, with modifications to enhance safety. The fourth generation will come on line during the decade beginning in 2020.

Today's nuclear plant designers are uneasy with the "totally safe" attitude that was the rule in the halcyon days of the 1950s, '60s, and '70s. During that period, paid teams of young college graduates armed with reams of positive nuclear facts called on media across the country. They were hired by various corporations wishing to polish the image of their industry. Their goal was to reassure the public that nuclear power was not dangerous in the least.

Behind this positive point of view was a single disturbing legal issue. It was called "liability." The threat of liability had a stranglehold on commercial development of nuclear power in the United States. In the case of the manufacturers of nuclear power plants, liability made finding buyers for those plants difficult.

Existing utilities had the necessary control stations, grids, transformers, relay stations, and cross-country power transmission systems in place. Electricity fed into these networks had to be generated at a cost that would allow it to be sold without huge price increases. The atom was the reasonable answer. But utility companies were afraid of the enormous liability on two counts.

First was the projection made by antinuclear experts about the eventual expense associated with decommissioning a nuclear power station at the end of its useful life. Future costs for deactivation were difficult to predict. So an expenditure for atomic power could not be precisely allocated to the millions upon millions of kilowatt hours of electricity the plant would produce. This objection was met by a different set of projections that provided the utilities with a means of dealing with closing down a facility.

Second, and far more serious, was the liability resulting from a major accident at one of the installations.

In the early 1950s, the Atomic Energy Commission initiated a report called WASH-740. This paper presented estimates of damage from a "worst-case" reactor incident. The idea of 3,400 deaths, forty-three thousand people injured, and property damage that would reach $7 billion was mind-boggling. Few insurance companies of that day were even interested in trying to calculate a premium for such a disaster. The utilities could easily see bankruptcy as the only recourse if such an unthinkable event occurred.

Clearly, nuclear generation of electricity was not going to come of age in America until a means was found to limit the liability of both manufacturers and utilities. That solution was the Price-Anderson Nuclear Industries Indemnity Act, which began in 1957.

Price-Anderson was intended to assure compensation to those injured in a nuclear accident and to limit liability in the event of such an incident. Those two goals were clearly in opposition. They were brought to balance by the federal government's insuring claims coverage of $500 million. This was done by establishing an annual contribution from every operating nuclear power station. These monies went into an account that would in essence help fund the federal government's guarantee.

The Price-Anderson Act has created bitter controversy from its very start. Challenged on a legal basis, the case was heard by the U.S. Supreme Court, and in 1978 the act was upheld. The lawsuit made several cogent arguments. These included the fact that all monies collected came from the utilities with no contributions made by suppliers or plant designers; the act was a subsidy only for the nuclear industry; and limiting liability encouraged less-than-safe operation of the plants.

Price-Anderson was originally to remain in effect for a period of ten years. Now, a half-century after its passage, it has been modified a few times but is still viable. Price-Anderson was extended in 2005 for an additional twenty years. Limits of liability now exceed many billions of dollars. The only claims paid under this legislation have been in association with the Three Mile Island accident, discussed later in this book.

Those against the proliferation of nuclear energy see the Price-Anderson Act as the single most important spur to the expansion of nuclear power generation in American history. Through the first half decade of the twenty-first century, this was undoubtedly correct. Added to that support was a U.S. program, the Energy Policy Act of 2005 (EPACT 2005). This called for expanding nuclear power and allocating federal funds to the Nuclear Power 2010 Program. The 2010 effort is to identify sites for new reactors, to bring advanced plant designs to market, and to ease regulations relating to new facilities. EPACT 2005 also has production tax credits for advanced facilities and loan guarantees for technology. Additionally, it protects new reactor designs from litigation and provides insurance for the first of many new reactors to be built. This amounts to $2 billion in federal insurance for constructing six plants.

In addition to the above incentives, there is the U.S. Global Nuclear Energy Partnership, which seeks to expand use of nuclear energy on a global basis by using federal funds for research, development, and construction of electricity-generating reactors.

Taken together, these acts and programs represent a huge change in governmental attitude toward atomic power. A quandary arises from all this that is difficult to answer. In a country based on private enterprise, the business sector of the community is expected to develop the power sources. The government, in turn, is cast in the role of public watchdog. It is charged with protecting the public by establishing controls, regulations, and checking procedures to assure compliance. The government cannot ignore the needs of businesses to realize a reasonable return on an investment. Yet in its larger role, the government is responsible for maintenance of society's standard of living. It must be alert to changes that could adversely affect the economy. Energy supply is one of the greatest of these possible alterations. These factors result in a circumstance in which the government is forced to set standards allowing private investment groups to develop and build atomic processing and power facilities to meet the nation's growing energy needs. At the same time, the government must exert controls on these facilities that can be attainable by industry and business at cost levels allowing some reasonable return on their investment. It is a hard task, and those who are charged with its accomplishment walk a narrow line between safety and practical need.

Government-owned and -operated nuclear facilities are subject to their own problems. While nationally developed atomic power plants are not as subject to the pressure of producing profits, other difficulties enter the picture. Historically, one governmental office has difficulty enforcing regulations on another. Results can be chaotic.

A true sea-change in attitudes toward nuclear energy is taking place. Past incidents and accidents have provided a mass of data that has been taken to heart by both plant designers and operators.

That additional knowledge has, in many cases, brought forth a better understanding of what was thought to be already known. Newer information has led to a questioning of what had been accepted as safe standards.

Plants designed in a time when computers were the size of a baseball field cannot be as reliable as those developed today. Advances in science and technology have been made. So there is little question that tomorrow's reactors will be far safer. Still, there will be many more facilities, which means more possibilities of human error or equipment malfunction.

If the examples of atomic troubles reviewed so far tell us nothing else, they point inescapably to the fact that nuclear accidents can and will occur. It is not a question of *if* another one will happen, but rather when, where, and how bad?

TWELVE

Transportation

One of the most unique things about the United States, since almost its earliest days, is the nation's preoccupation with roads. From colonial times, all-weather highways have linked important population centers. Our country is large, and as it grew westward, the need for more and more miles of roadway became pronounced. Names like Cumberland Gap, El Camino Real, Wilderness Road, and the Overland Trail are a part of our history.

The real impetus for the development of a superior network of well-surfaced roads came with the advent of the automobile. In a fifty-year period, from 1910 to 1960, this country constructed more miles of new highway than any other nation in the entire history of man. Some think this may not have been for the better. But sociological arguments aside, the development of the freeway and perfecting the internal-combustion engine gave rise to a new transportation industry.

During World War II, the "Red Ball Express" operated in Europe. Charged with supplying General Patton's armored forces with fuel, food, and ammunition, this operation proved the efficiency of rapid motor-vehicle transport on a scale never before attempted. By the close of 1945, companies in the United States were eager for the opportunity to duplicate portions of the Red Ball system on our own concrete thruways. Special truck bodies were developed to haul everything from furniture and oranges to gasoline, toxic chemicals, and hazardous waste.

Industrial and other activities, including nuclear power production, currently create more than forty million tons of hazardous materials annually. Used fuel rods account for nearly two thousand tons of the above forty million. Around eight million tons of that material is transported by trucks.

From these numbers and the added tons of raw materials, fuel replacements, and other radioactive cargos, it is easy to see the nuclear industry has great need for surface transportation. It is far better to move a dangerous substance cross-country at ground level than to add to the risk by flying it.

Surface transportation, however, has its own unique problems. Even though there are rules governing interstate commerce, individual states, and in some cases counties, have their own unique regulations. Standards and criteria for safe transfer of radioactive waste are good examples. Much has been done to develop and use improved containers. But many shipping companies called upon to carry these nuclear cargoes are not aware of the possible consequences of even a minor accident.

This next story is not atypical. Incidents like it have occurred many times. To date, no one appears to have been injured. But it is one more example of a casual attitude toward the byproducts of our nuclear time. Any accident of this type could have a tragic ending.

———

Highway 287 leaves the town of Limon in eastern Colorado paralleling the twisting banks of the Big Sandy River through the settlements of Wild Horse and Kit Carson. Then it turns straight south and, with a few jig-jogs, runs through several Indian reservations, crosses the mighty Arkansas River, then drops into Oklahoma.

The country bisected by this blacktop road is some of the most fertile in the United States. Rolling in parts, it lies north of the highest point in Texas but far east of the towering snow-peaked Rockies.

Trucks travel this stretch in great numbers. Distances between the small cities and the lack of rail freight facilities make motor transport the standard means of commercial communication. Most of this road is easy driving unless the weather is bad. Then, blinding blizzards of blowing snow can stop traffic for days, despite the best efforts of state and county crews.

September 27, 1977, arrived during one of the good-weather times. There was no sign of rain, sleet, snow, fog, or dust. The wind was even down, which is a rarity thereabouts.

Traffic was light, due more to the hour than anything else. A lone truck thundered its way along the two-lane blacktop. The driver, Donald Atwood, stretched in his seat to relax stiffening muscles. The cab-over-chassis he was pushing to tow the rest of the eighteen-wheel rig was a late model. Even at top speed, it rode well. Wind noise, although present, was sealed outside, so conversation inside the cab was easy. Don turned slightly in his seat and, in the reflected glow from the dash instruments, he could see the profile of his companion and relief driver, Willima Pipher. Trucking had changed in the last few years. The presence of women who rode as both lead and backup jockeys had somehow softened what had by tradition been an all-male industry.

Don scanned the night. His huge headlamps punched holes in the dense darkness of the early morning, sweeping the roadway ahead with an intense brilliance. The clock on the dash read 1:00 AM on the nose. They'd stop soon, for a stretch and a cup of coffee. Might be a good idea to let Willima take over for a while and sack out until just before dawn. Daybreak was the time driving was the most dangerous, with more people starting on the road and visibility at its worst in the not-quite-night, not-quite-day. Don's thoughts wandered slightly, then came back to match his attention, which had never varied from scanning the road unwinding endlessly ahead.

The early hour of the morning, that desolate time before dawn, had been selected as a safety measure by the manufacturers of the cargo stored in the big van. Fifty-five-gallon steel drums were stacked from floor to ceiling, front to back, filling all available space. Inside the round metal containers was a fine, yellowish powder. In all, the truck contained forty thousand pounds of material known as "yellowcake." Produced from uranium, the radioactive substance was fodder for the nuclear industry. Further processing would develop it into a more refined fuel, much of which would finally end up inside the reactor of an atomic power station.

Shifting again in his seat, Don Atwood watched the night roll by. Nothing seemed out of the ordinary. Then, without warning, what appeared to be an entire herd of horses, manes and tails flying, erupted into the white flame of his headlights. Startled, they ran diagonally across the road, directly into the path of the oncoming truck.

Atwood swung the big steering wheel sharply, cutting to avoid the inevitable collision. Later, he explained his shock at the appearance of the ghostly animals: "All of a sudden there was a whole herd of horses crossing. One minute they weren't there and the next minute they were."

The truck, wrenched from its straight path, resisted the turn with several hundred tons of inertial energy. Then, tires screaming, it veered across the road. Reacting coolly, Atwood compensated for the skid, steering quickly into the new direction of travel. Suddenly, the huge vehicle had run out of roadway. Coming back to the center-line, the front edge of the multi-ton truck struck three madly running horses, gave a lurch from the force of the impact, and swerved sharply to the right. The edge of the narrow highway was graveled, and the now out-of-control eighteen-wheeler flashed over this verge and banged into a narrow ditch, plowing dirt and sending a spray of gravel high into the pre-dawn air. The big truck bumped and banged its way forward. All control lost, it overturned with metal tearing from the chassis in irregular slashes. The top of the cab was crushed down on the two occupants.

In the van, the heavy barrels of yellowcake erupted. Bursting through the aluminum walls of the vehicle, some containers flew through the air for yards before smashing to earth and splitting open, spilling their contents onto the barren ground.

Finally, after a seemingly interminable period of screaming noise, what was left of the big truck came to a final stop. Ripped apart by the impact, the remains of the vehicle lay in the middle of a field of spilled yellow powder.

The silence after the crescendo of sound seemed almost as loud as the noises of the crash itself. Dazed, Atwood, squashed into one corner of the cabin, looked around.

Everything had been forced into crazy angles, so it took him a minute to get his bearings. Willima was there, moaning softly, injured from having been thrown around inside the cabin.

Insect noises resumed, and night sounds filtered through the broken glass of the battered vehicle. Softly on the wind, the smell of fall and a promise of coming cold wafted through.

Atwood tried to move. He was pinned into a small area. The crumpled steel around his head formed a prison. A moment of panic ran through his mind as he thought of the possibility of fire from spilling fuel. He calmed himself by trying to devise some way to free Willima.

The highway remained deserted. Quiet, broken only by an occasional tinkle as a shard of glass freed itself and fell onto the rest of the wreckage, was a presence over the land.

Up the road, another trucker sat humming to himself. The lateness of the hour lulled his mind, forcing him to continually pull his attention back to approaching vehicles. Then, suddenly coming totally alert, the man started. Eyes widening, he watched as the scene of a wreck grew closer. The mangled truck, one headlamp pointing across the field adjoining the highway, was outlined in his approaching lights. There was a squeal of brakes as the semi came to a stop, then a revving of the engine as it backed and turned to allow its many lights to illuminate the scene. The driver sat stunned for a moment. Then, switching off his engine, he climbed down and started for the wreckage. Walking was difficult, as there was ankle-deep yellow powder around the demolished trailer.

Stepping in close to what appeared to be the front window, he used his flashlight. The jumble inside took him a minute to sort out. Then he caught sight of Atwood's staring eyes. Realizing there was nothing he could do alone, he spoke a few words of encouragement and then ran for the radio inside his cab.

Don Atwood and Willima Pipher had been inside the broken wreckage for almost fifteen minutes.

Alerted by the driver's single sideband announcement, truckers farther back on the highway relayed news of the accident to a local base station, where a call was placed to the highway patrol. By the time officers arrived, forty minutes after the crash, several additional trucks, other automobile drivers, and a wrecker were on the scene.

In all, according to police estimates, over sixty people stopped to see if they could render assistance. And most of them marched through the yellow radioactive dust as work progressed on the project to free Atwood and Pipher.

The investigating troopers followed usual accident procedure. Required medical and mechanical assistance were summoned. A report was made up, but would not be completed until the driver could be questioned. No one, moving in the floodlit darkness from areas of dazzling brilliance to black shadow, took much notice of the spilled material.

Yellowcake is not a highly toxic substance but is dangerous if inhaled. Even though some containers remained intact, about ten thousand pounds had spilled onto the cold ground. Another five thousand pounds were loose inside the twisted van. All told, there was an ample amount of the fine powder available for inhalation.

Working as rapidly as the conditions of darkness would allow, various assistance groups managed to right the truck and free the two captives. This operation took the better part of three hours, during which time more people came and went along the still-open road. Finally, with Willima Pipher safe in medical care, officers were able to ascertain the nature of the spillage.

With no one particularly alarmed, a routine report was filed. None of the people at the accident site wore respirators to filter the dust out of the air they were breathing. But the officers were sufficiently concerned to get the names of the twenty-six persons who had assisted during the long hours required to release the two drivers.

In the meantime, cars continued to pass. As night slipped into early dawn, it brought lower temperatures. Most of the passersby had their heaters on. The slight wind that stirred the dust could easily have blown particles into the air intakes of the moving vehicles.

At first light, the eerie-looking yellow powder was seen to completely cover an area about thirty by fifty yards. Footprints through the material, as well as places where it had been tramped to bare ground, showed the passage of many people. Cars still passed as dawn became bright morning. Split, broken drums littered the area, and the battered truck cab, wheels hanging at odd angles and the name "LEE" still readable, tilted toward the ground. The scene resembled the aftermath of a bombing.

Twelve hours later, state health officials would order everyone in the area to wear air filters, and the police would set up road-blocks to detour motorists from the spillage.

During this time, a number of people were contacted: the trucking line; Exxon, which owned the cargo and was having it shipped to Oklahoma for further processing; state health per-sonnel; state police; and others. A conflict arose over attempts to assign responsibility for the accident and decide who should be charged with the job of cleaning up the scattered mess. Some finger-pointing went on as each party stated its limits of liability. A full day was to elapse before Exxon agreed to undertake the decontam-ination process and restore the yellowcake to its containers.

On September 28, the day after the accident, an Exxon indus-trial hygienist arrived on the scene. According to reports, even though the wind had increased its intensity slightly, no air samples were taken to determine if some of the yellowcake was being blown away. After a survey of the site, the hygienist called for various forms of assistance. Exxon sent Geiger counters, expecting to use them to determine levels of radioactivity present.

Shortly before this, Colorado state officials had already run tests of their own. The normal background level of radiation for the area was about 15 to 20 microroentgens per hour. In the heart of the spill, the count had increased 4,000 percent to more than 800 microroentgens. While this level is not directly injurious, it is a quantum leap upward, and there is controversy about the pro-longed effect such levels of exposure might have on an individual, even if he or she did not breathe the material.

After the reported arrival of Geiger counters for use in detecting radiation levels, state health authorities had to explain that these instruments were virtually useless for measuring yellowcake radioactivity. More sophisticated gamma scintillometers and alpha survey devices would be required to take any meaningful readings. Other hassles occurred when Exxon stated its desire to hire ordinary day labor to perform the cleanup task, instead of trained health environment workers. In the initial stages, shovels were used to scoop up the powder, even though the wind had increased in force, and, according to reports, none of the crew was issued respirators. Again Colorado health authorities intervened, and Exxon obtained protective equipment.

Working long hours, the men slowly managed to scrape up the yellow powder from the ground. Using black industrial plastic to wrap and cover newly delivered fifty-five-gallon drums, they filled them one by one.

But not all of the material would ever be recovered. Blown away in the wind, and perhaps sucked up by passing cars, a measurable amount was lost into the environment forever.

Seven days passed before the public was made aware of the mishap. Even then it was revealed only because a hard-working reporter for a Boulder, Colorado, newspaper, Robert Ruby, did the necessary investigation and put facts together. In his story, health officials merely urged any people who had stopped at the accident site or had driven by the scene to "wash their clothes and shower to wash out any contamination."

The matter did not end with cleanup, however. Two members of Congress reportedly joined with several groups to file petitions with the NRC calling for all licensees that transport radioactive materials to have emergency units for use in case of accidents.

Several groups have claimed this incident, and the reaction to it, was another example of how antinuclear forces will develop any situation into a major catastrophe. They point out, and rightly, that yellowcake, although radioactive, is not generally a material that might be considered a health hazard—not nearly so much as, say, liquid ammonia or other caustic or potentially explosive chemicals shipped through heavily trafficked cities on a daily basis.

But certain things are clear. More care is needed in the transport of a number of substances. Nuclear materials are included in this group. Use of ordinary fifty-five-gallon drums, which clearly cannot withstand the rigors of a wreck, is not sensible. Members of the Department of Transportation and the National Transportation Safety Board reportedly did not arrive on the scene at any time during the accident investigation or decontamination process. And NRC inspectors were not present until seven days after the incident.

Robert D. Siek, then–Associate Director of Environmental Programs for the Colorado Office of Health Protection, best summed up the matter in a strong letter to the NRC dated October 3, 1977. "If," he wrote, the accident "had occurred near a watercourse, in a metropolitan area, or in a mountain area, the problems would be compounded manyfold."

Additional nuclear power plants equate to even more shipments of atomic materials in coming years.

Fortunately, because of accidents like the one just recounted or the crash near Collins, Colorado, in 1980 of a Department of Energy trailer carrying plutonium, rigorous rules have been set. The NRC has established certification of containers for nuclear fuel, specified authorized transportation routes, designated specialized trucking companies, set standards for drivers, and required electronic devices that show truck location at all times.

Additionally, the Department of Transportation (DOT) and the NRC have established strong emergency response measures, including training and the use of specialized equipment.

Transportation accidents involving critical nuclear materials are not uncommon. There have been hundreds in past years.

Some, like the Rocky Mount, North Carolina, incident in which a truck carrying low-level wastes from a nuclear power station collided with another vehicle, are more serious than others. In that instance, the radioactive substance was in the form of a glasslike resin, inside special shipping containers. The truck had driven all the way from the Vermont Yankee nuclear plant to a temporary disposal site in Barnwell, South Carolina. That was a long trip and the wreck was the second suffered by a vehicle from the Vermont location.

A spokesperson from the Yankee facility was quoted as saying, "Traffic accidents" are an "inevitable result of the transportation of nuclear material."

That statement sums up all that needs to be said on the subject.

THIRTEEN

Civil Rights

From the earliest days of nuclear power, controversies arose over the issue of civil rights. Did plant management have the authority to subject employees or visitors to even a cursory search? What about a thorough shakedown that might involve probing body cavities? Should the operator of a facility be allowed to enter a home and scan for radiation? Or have a worker followed, or require a detailed itinerary of an individual's whereabouts so a number of places might be monitored for radiation? To what extent may a plant use armed force to defend itself against an attack? And finally, has the nuclear industry been involved with law enforcement officers in an effort to maintain surveillance over vociferous opponents of further nuclear power development?

These are tough questions in the United States, where a strongly developed sense of the right to privacy and freedom from infringement of individual liberties is ingrained in the population.

The relationship between state government and large-area suppliers of electric energy is well documented. Lobby activity for the utilities is commonplace at every level, and political contributions have been made to selected candidates, from city councilmen to members of the U.S. Senate. Nothing is inherently wrong with this.

But it illustrates the closeness that exists between the nuclear power industry and the structure of our government. Realistically, a certain amount of involvement is a good thing.

Is it possible to misuse this relationship? Could a vocal adversary to a new atomic installation be selected for special investigation and attack? Or would it be possible for a company to have a union figure unduly hassled by using existing laws and regulations? These are interesting questions—and hard ones to answer definitively, especially now that security measures at nuclear facilities are in a state of continuous intensification.

But there has already been an instance of harassment of a nuclear adversary by police at the state level. The individual involved could hardly be described as a radical or even as an avid enemy of atomic power generation. He participated in no protests or demonstrations. Instead, he was singled out for special attention after he availed himself of his constitutional rights and appeared before a local city council to give his opinion of a proposed new plant site.

It is a strange story, revealed only through a quirk of fate. Under different circumstances a great deal of damage might have been done to the career of a respectable citizen. Worse, the individual who had been attacked would never have known the role played by state police in his misfortune.

One example can't embody all the issues or answer all the questions of civil rights and nuclear power. But it does show what can happen when overzealous people are prodded by a series of circumstances to take actions that seem to them to be reasonable and responsible—even though those actions infringe on our constitutional rights.

It will be a long time before the civil liberties aspects of the nuclear age are fully revealed. What appear now to be dangerous conflicts may be paper tigers that fade away with experience. Or the threat that many people keenly feel exists may turn out to be more than just a vague fear. We might be confronted with a harsh new reality.

The story of Robert Pomeroy isn't as impressive, in some ways, as others in this book. No bombs fall, nothing blows up, no technicians go wild trying to stop a disastrous core melt. No one is even threatened with exposure to a radioactive substance. It is distressingly simple. One man chooses to speak out and is attacked by part of a massive state government.

———

January is a cold month in Dallas, Texas. Situated on the edge of the Great Plains, the city is unprotected by natural terrain from bitter, cold blasts of icy air referred to locally as "blue northers." As one Texan put it, "The only thing between Dallas and the North Pole is one lone barbed-wire fence. So the wind blows right down with nothin' to stop it."

The morning of January 14, 1974, found the city in the grip of freezing temperatures. The stifling atmosphere of city council chambers was a welcome relief from the chill, windy streets. The meeting had been convened as usual, but there was an air of expectancy in the crowd. Every indication showed this session was going to be far removed from the usual humdrum ritual.

The chambers filled early. People found seats and watched as, one by one, the mayor and council members took appropriate chairs on the dais. Then another group, clearly together, entered. It was composed of several well-dressed men armed with briefcases. Some bore themselves as if they were in a court of law, speaking with careful formality. Mixed in with the attorneys were a few more relaxed individuals who were along as observers and expected to take no part in the proceedings. A third bunch of men and women congregated on the other side of the room. They talked among themselves and laughed lightly to dissolve their obvious tension. A final councilman, rising from where he had been seated talking to a constituent, made his way to the podium-type desk. When he settled into place, the meeting was called to order.

Early business moved swiftly and the audience followed the various debates with only moderate interest. Finally, the agenda called for a statement to the council by a concerned group. CASE, Citizens Association for Sound Energy, had few members. About forty people banded together to oppose construction, by a combination of electric utilities, of a nuclear power station near the Texas town of Glen Rose. The facility, tentatively named Comanche Peak, was in its final planning stages. The AEC construction permit appeared certain and only a few public and private hearings remained to be held.

The CASE spokesperson, selected as leader, was Robert Pomeroy, one of the founding members. Of medium height, he dressed conservatively with his hair in a neat razor cut. Bob Pomeroy was a reasonable man. Not interested in rabble-rousing, he used CASE as a platform to publicly introduce a number of arguments against construction of the Comanche Peak plant. His appearance before council had been publicized, and a small number of people were interested in hearing his arguments. Pomeroy was known to have deep concern about atomic energy, as well as a strong opposition to the need for a plant in his area of the state.

A resident of a small suburban community, Farmers Branch, he worked for Continental Airlines as a flight officer aboard 727 aircraft. Pomeroy had been a pilot for several years. He'd completed a tour of duty in the marines where he had attained the rank of captain flying single-engine jets. After his service, he became a third officer aboard Continental's larger planes. His advancement with the company had been on schedule, and now, as copilot, even though he had some years to go before becoming a first officer and earning his fourth stripe, he was happy in his work. Flying was his life. He could imagine no other employment half so satisfactory or one for which he was better suited by a combination of sanguine temperament and relaxed style during otherwise tense situations.

When recognized by the council, Pomeroy began to speak in an evenly modulated voice. Dealing with what he felt were the facts, he introduced telegrams from individuals he described as experts in atomic physics: Drs. David Inglis and Henry Kendall, of the University of Massachusetts and the widely renowned Massachusetts Institute of Technology respectively. With council's permission, he read the messages, and they were included in the minutes of the meeting. The underlying tone of the comments dealt with the damage that might be caused to the environment by radioactivity and other releases from a nuclear power plant.

Debate ensued, but the meeting proceeded on an orderly basis. As the discussion grew heated, Pomeroy became more intense, but he conducted himself in a professional and direct fashion. At one point, shortly after the crowd had laughed at one of the council members' remarks, Pomeroy offered to debate W. W. Aston, vice president of Dallas Power and Light. He suggested a meeting place, the First Unitarian Church, but received no acceptance of his challenge.

After his speech, several people came up to Pomeroy and expressed their support of his views. A few dissident voices were also heard, but discussions remained calm. The CASE people, aware of the public interest they had generated, were reasonably happy with the outcome. But they knew, as Pomeroy had said, there was really little they could do about the plant due to their lack of membership and funds.

The meeting continued after the pro and con groups had

completed their presentations. A large portion of the audience, though, wandered off rather than sitting through the droning dullness of further considerations of new street-paving and sewer-repair projects.

As far as Bob Pomeroy was concerned, the affair with city council had come out about as expected. CASE arguments had been courteously heard, but little had been achieved. Resolved to continue their fight, the members began making plans for the next big showdown. A public hearing by the AEC was scheduled for late July in the Glen Rose High School auditorium. The outcome of this open session would decide whether or not a limited permit would be issued allowing the Texas utilities to start construction and site work for the proposed Squaw Creek reservoir. This was a vital component of the new plant's cooling system. Hearings of this nature had been held in other parts of the country for other plants under consideration. In some cases, local activist groups had managed to drag the sessions into year-long meetings, thus delaying the actual start of work. Robert T. Martin, a vice president of Texas Electric Service Company (TESCO), one of the three utilities involved in the Comanche Peak plant, said he thought the Glen Rose session would take about two days. Pomeroy and his fellow CASE members were trying to develop a clear objection to present to AEC representatives.

Miles away, in Austin, the Texas state capital, other work was started on Pomeroy.

Due to his appearance at the Dallas city council meeting, Robert Pomeroy's name was included in a list of possibly suspect people. Collected on a routine basis by the Texas Department of Public Safety (DPS), the persons named on this list were subjected to a thorough investigation. A special unit of the DPS had been formed for that purpose.

An intelligence agent, David A. Dimick, was assigned the task of making a report on Pomeroy's background, friends, and present activities. The work took some time and utilized at least two "informants." Their comments and testimony were included in the document, which was signed by David A. Dimick, agent #2449, Texas Department of Public Safety. Before being appointed to the intelligence division on July 15, 1971, Dimick had served with the DPS as a highway patrolman. Neither his job experience nor his formal education had prepared him for the role of intelligence investigator.

The report was explosive. It stated that in addition to Pomeroy's having been present at the city meeting to speak out against the plant, he had also been seen talking to a person who had "been a long-time Socialist party organizer in Dallas." Worse, one of the two PhDs who had sent telegrams, Dr. David Inglis, was said to have been mentioned in a 1961 House Un-American Activities Committee study on "possible Communist infiltration into anti-nuclear energy front groups."

Other comments included specific mention of the First Unitarian Church in Dallas, the place Pomeroy had suggested the debate be held, as having sponsored a number of radical groups, including the Dallas Peace Committee, United Farm Workers, and Gay Liberation. The report singled the church out for having been host to a "social" workshop in January 1974, where all major subversive groups in North Texas had set up information booths.

The report is said to have read, in part: "The subject came to the attention of this service on 1-14-74 when he spoke at length to the Dallas City Council in an attempt to block the building of a nuclear power station at Glen Rose, Texas, by the Texas Utilities Co. The subject alleged that he had formed a group that would file suits and attempt to stop the building of a nuclear power station."

The two PhDs Pomeroy had used as references were labeled "alleged experts," and the overall tone of the document could be taken to imply the "subject" had close connections with Communists, Socialists, far-leftists, or all three.

A code was used after each item of information to note the relative "reliability" of the data. Some was rated as being highly trustworthy, some of dubious or questionable origin.

Once the report was complete and distributed internally through the Texas DPS system, the matter should have been closed. But Dimick, acting on his own, according to reported comments made by then-director of the DPS, Colonel Wilson E. Speir, made one last distribution. He sent a copy to the security department of Continental Airlines.

The Continental security staff was dismayed to receive the document. First of all, they felt what Pomeroy did in his spare time was his own business, as were his political views. He had a proven record of stability as a flight officer and there was no indication in any of his files he might be irrational enough to fly a plane into a nuclear reactor. After brief discussion, the security staff transmitted the memorandum to Robert Pomeroy's immediate superior in Dallas. No action was specified.

The whole affair would probably have ended there as an aborted attempt by an official state agency to cause trouble between an individual and his employer. But an extra twist was added. The superior to whom the document had been sent was a close personal friend of Pomeroy's. He decided to show his friend the report and allow him to make and retain copies.

Pomeroy's response varied. He is quoted as saying, "The first time I saw it I got mad. Then I got scared, and finally I started thinking it was funny. Now I think there is a bigger principle involved."

Pomeroy realized he was the target of a specific investigation solely because he had taken advantage of his constitutional rights. He had cared enough to speak out on an issue that disturbed him, to take sides in a controversy, and to make his name publicly known.

The full impact of the situation took time to develop. Pomeroy went from reaction to reaction. He talked with other friends, and they in turn spoke with their acquaintances. Weeks later, one of the original members of CASE, after hearing of the matter, checked it out. Convinced the story was true, the unnamed individual called Jim Marrs, a reporter for the *Fort Worth Star-Telegram*. Marrs's advice was: "Tell him to come forward and go public with the evidence. When he does that, everything else will fall into line."

More weeks passed. Marrs spoke several times with his contact, but Pomeroy was considering the impact such a disclosure might have on his life in Farmers Branch and in the Dallas area. Then he made a decision. The evidence of the investigation should be made public. But the opportune time was the day prior to the formal AEC hearing on the advisability of TESCO's breaking ground for the new plant's reservoir. He waited patiently. All the while, rumors of the report spread through the city's news circles.

On July 30, 1974, Pomeroy and other CASE members announced there would be a press conference the next day to release information about the alleged investigation. Jim Marrs was informed by telephone and met with the city editor, who reminded him of an assignment already in progress. Another reporter, Rowland Stiteler, was selected to attend the conference.

Stiteler arrived at the assigned meeting place and was surprised at the lack of newsmen present. Aside from another reporter from a local limited-circulation paper, the *Iconoclast*, the meeting was largely ignored. Two individuals came from the Dallas public-service TV station, and another man represented a radio news station.

In his statement, Pomeroy told of the investigation and the report that had been sent to his superiors. Copies were shown to those present. He stated he felt the dossier indicated he was a Communist or Socialist, but he did not personally know anyone of either persuasion. Further, if he had talked to a Socialist at the city council meeting, he didn't know it. He'd spoken to a number of people. He also said he felt the report had backfired, because he had received no comments from his employer, Continental Airlines. He reiterated his stand on nuclear energy, and said he intended to protest the construction permit for the Glen Rose nuclear facility at the upcoming meeting.

His revelations, backed by copies of the document, failed to make shockwaves. The *Iconoclast* ran a story later in the week, and the *Fort Worth Star-Telegram,* on the morning of July 31, printed a two-column account of the press conference.

Then the matter seemed to die. But not for long. The Dallas public-service TV station did a presentation on Pomeroy, and this seemed to wake the rest of the electronic news media. Features followed, and the two other major dailies, the *Dallas Morning Herald* and the *Times,* finally joined the fray.

Reporters on the *Fort Worth Star-Telegram* expanded the range of their investigation by locating David Dimick, who refused to talk for publication. The issue was then taken to Col. Speir, head of the DPS, who promised to "look into it."

Pomeroy's timing was excellent. Just the day before his press conference, he was the subject of a newspaper story on the upcoming hearings. It had proven to be a good platform for him to cite his views, so he'd gone on record as saying the proposed Comanche Peak power plant was unnecessary, too dangerous, expensive to build, and the federal licensing process under which it was to be constructed was "a farce."

His comments met with instant rebuttal, both from the Texas

Electric Service Company and the AEC. Company officials stated the facility was vital to future electrical needs of the area, was safe, and had been well researched to provide minimal environmental impact. Senior Project Manager for the AEC, C. J. Hale, a native of Fort Worth who was working with the project-licensing division in Bethesda, Maryland, made a quick but limited denial by telephone. Hale said since the meeting was scheduled for the next day, it would be improper for him to respond to specific points, but he insisted the AEC was thorough, professional, and impartial. Both the commission and the utilities had conducted extensive research, and the AEC was an advocate of the site because of the many hours of questioning prior to the actual public hearing. He was careful to say the AEC's position was derived without influence by the utility and as a result of its own investigations. He stated that by the time a hearing was convened, countless facts had been brought out and discussed with the owners involved in the construction of the plant. As he put it, "all of the battles and the bloodletting between the AEC and the utility are already resolved by then."

TESCO officials shared his feelings. "From our point of view, it's no farce," Robert Martin said. "It is comprehensive, it is thorough, it's a well-thought-out plan for licensing. It's tough, they don't fool around."

Martin also said research for the environmental statement required by the AEC showed that impact would be minimal and the plant should be built. He maintained the study had been done in a professional, scientific manner, fully checked by the AEC. The data had been sent to other agencies of the state and federal governments, and "anyone in the United States" could inspect it for accuracy.

"The implication is that we are doing all this as a snow job." Martin went on. "Well, that's not true. We are doing this to design a safe plant."

Pomeroy's rebuttal, printed almost in its entirety, made good press. "They [the studies] are subject to bias from the utilities and they are subject to bias from the AEC standpoint," he maintained. "If there was some flagrant violation, I guarantee you the AEC would catch it. But it might be something that they didn't catch. A lot of things are happening [at currently operating plants] that they didn't expect to happen. For them to arrogantly assume that they know everything that could happen in those sophisticated plants is ridiculous. It is dangerous. And they have done it."

The furor caused by both the confrontation in print between Pomeroy, the AEC, and TESCO, and the revelation of the unusual intelligence investigation and report began to capture public attention. Where before CASE had little influence, there was suddenly new interest in the small organization.

On a state level, the press was making difficulties for the Department of Public Safety. Continued probing finally resulted in a statement from Col. Speir. He cited a "tip" as being the cause of the investigation, and said little else.

Robert Martin, speaking for TESCO, declared, "None of us had anything to do with this."

Finally, details of the incident were shown to Governor Dolph Briscoe and several members of the Texas legislature, resulting in an immediate call for a subcommittee investigation of DPS intelligence activities. From the start, it looked as if the motion would pass both houses quickly.

Col. Speir maintained the DPS did not investigate people solely because they had spoken out against atomic power. "We have no desire and do not compile data on persons just because of their political beliefs. . . . We have no quarrels with legitimate protest groups." He added, "We are not perfect. . . . Somewhere along the line, they are human beings . . . someone will make a mistake. But this would be extremely rare." He also stated Dimick's sending the report to Continental Airlines was "an error on the part of a young officer who gave it out without permission or authority and in violation of department policy and procedure." Speir issued a public apology to Pomeroy for the mistake and agreed to take disciplinary action against Dimick under advisement.

On August 2, 1974, Gov. Briscoe asked for a copy of the report. Shortly after, the Texas state senate scheduled subcommittee hearings for September.

The Reverend Dwight Brown of the First Unitarian Church of Dallas emerged as a spokesman for his congregation. Incensed by the fact the DPS had listed the church as a leftist support group, he began pondering legal action. Pomeroy announced the filing of a suit against Speir and Dimick, requesting $10,000 in damages. Quickly after, the church also brought action. Pomeroy's suit called for an order prohibiting DPS investigation of politically active individuals.

Hearings were not held until the summer of 1975 and had only one noteworthy incident. Dimick, who was asked by Judge Jack Roberts of the U.S. District Court to produce the identity of the two informants he had relied on in his investigation, at first refused to comply. Then, after a few days, he capitulated and provided the information.

While all of this was going on, a construction permit for the Comanche Peak station was issued, and development work for the reservoir commenced. In a way, publicity generated by the Pomeroy incident served to take some public attention away from the project.

Undocumented reports, along with the Rev. Mr. Brown's testimony, indicate the Department of Public Safety began a thorough review of its files. Acting with great haste, it had all dossiers on individuals with no criminal record pulled, sorted, and shredded. Col. Speir later said all but criminal-activity intelligence reports were being purged from the system.

By late September 1974, the matter had reached its zenith. The state senate subcommittee, chaired by Oscar Mauzy, a Democrat from Dallas, convened in special session. One of its first witnesses was David Dimick. He reiterated his story about first having become interested in Pomeroy after a "confidential informant" reported he had seen the pilot passing out literature against a proposed nuclear power plant and had also seen him talking with a known Socialist. Dimick admitted later he had given an "unofficial" copy of his report to the security staff at Continental Airlines. The officer said he had concluded Pomeroy was not inclined to violence against nuclear power stations but "anything's possible."

"Specifically, what did you think it was possible that Mr. Pomeroy might do?" asked Senator Mauzy.

"It had been discussed, I think, and I am not sure, I am not positive, but I believe that the Continental people [wondered] could this guy have the capacity, to be so violently opposed to nuclear energy, to crash his airplane into a nuclear power site," Dimick replied.

It was a dark flight of speculation to imagine a reliable veteran copilot of a 727 seizing control of the huge aircraft and then diving, passengers and all, into a preselected power station in a last, futile, dramatic protest.

"This man," queried Senator Mauzy, "while flying a plane loaded with passengers, might crash it into a nuclear power plant . . . because he made a peaceful demonstration against the construction of this [plant] before the Dallas city council?" His question brought a murmur of positive response from people in the hearing room.

"That was discussed," Dimick replied.

Pomeroy responded to the exchange by calling Dimick's testimony "ludicrous." He pointed out that crashing into a working plant would cause radiation to escape, and "this is exactly the kind of thing we are worried about." He also made a point of the fact Continental Airlines had not removed him from his job as copilot and had in no way troubled him about the report.

Dimick, in wrapping up his testimony, noted he had "never been involved in any unwarranted invasion of anyone's right to protest." But, he concluded, "vigilance is necessary to try to prevent unlawful conduct."

Col. Speir's statement included the information that since the Pomeroy investigation had been noted, the DPS had tightened its policy to limit intelligence investigations generally to criminal activities. Agents had been forbidden to make probes on their own.

Pomeroy's testimony before the committee, which also included Senators Bill Bracklein of Dallas and Tati Santiesteban of El Paso, indicated he had never experienced mental problems and his family had no medical history of mental aberrations.

"Did the thought ever occur to you," asked Mauzy, "to crash an airplane [into a nuclear power plant site]?"

"No, the other members of the crew would probably take a dim view of it." Pomeroy's response brought laughter from the assembly.

"I, as a passenger, would object," responded Mauzy. The room laughed again.

Pomeroy stated he had not known of the investigation and probably would have continued with his protest even if he had been aware of the probe. Mauzy asked if he would have continued if it had meant the loss of his job.

Pomeroy pondered his answer. "If I thought I was going to lose my job, I would have to think long and hard. I like my job. An airline pilot is pretty useless once he leaves one airline."

Several interesting points came out during the hearings. Dimick testified he was, at the time, justified in making a report on Pomeroy according to then-existing DPS policies. He was not certain if the conversation about the possibility of Pomeroy's flying an airplane into a nuclear power plant had been with the Continental security staff or with an unnamed informant. He also maintained the report, due to coding used to indicate reliability of information, had served to clear Pomeroy. No explanation of how or why the document was then forwarded to the pilot's employer was presented.

Col. Speir expressed his hope that the senators would be careful in their considerations of new laws concerning police intelligence. "To over-restrict the proper use of the intelligence function in law enforcement will not only result in the loss of police effectiveness, but the real loser would be the law-abiding citizens. . . ."

The Rev. Mr. Brown, commenting on the seriousness of the situation, charged the DPS with having purged their intelligence files by shredding the documents involved. This action, he stated, made it difficult for the committee to determine the extent to which past DPS activities had "unjustifiably invaded rights of citizens in their pursuit of lawful political activity." He also noted a temptation to conclude DPS leadership "preferred to live with the suspicion of past wrongdoing rather than submit its files to the kind of scrutiny by this committee" that might uncover misdeeds.

Brown concluded with some comments about Dimick. After pointing out that the man was not a college graduate, the minister said it is "unrealistic to expect partially educated agents to comprehend the complexities of political protest and to be able to distinguish between legitimate protest and unlawful protest. We are forced to wonder," he went on, "how many other David Dimicks there are in the DPS, men who lack the qualifications for doing the job they are being asked to do."

The outcome of the hearings was the development of several new statutes to limit the activity of the DPS in selected areas. It is likely if Pomeroy's friend and superior with Continental Airlines had not given his fellow pilot the benefit of the doubt—and a copy of the report—none of the intelligence activities of the DPS would have come to the public's attention. Likewise, the ability to cite a specific incident provided extra impetus to the hearings, making the committee's job of selling its new regulations to the other senators and legislators a far easier one.

Inquiries by reporters, including Jim Marrs, about the disciplining of David Dimick brought little in the way of response. Finally, weeks later, it was noted Mr. Dimick had been "transferred" from Intelligence to Narcotics, his $11,616 salary remaining unchanged.

On January 1, 1975, Robert Pomeroy left Dallas, Texas, and moved to California.

The matter was ended. But there are still several questions remaining. Was Dimick following DPS policy in 1974? Did that policy allow an investigator to focus on an individual for making public statements against nuclear power? Was it DPS policy for reports, supposedly confidential, to be forwarded to protestors' employers?

No one will ever know the full details. The time in which it happened, 1974, was a strange period in America. Many things previously considered to be acceptable behavior for law-enforcement agencies came under fire. The nation was in a turmoil of debate over questions of illegal or quasi-legal activities of the Central Intelligence Agency and Federal Bureau of Investigation. Civil rights was a concept, rather than a working reality, to many police officers. The feeling that laws were protecting the criminal by tying the hands of those charged with protecting the public was rampant. And to some degree, it was true.

Changing times called for new methods and an end to a number of old ones.

Col. Wilson E. Speir was a capable man, charged with a tough job. It was his duty to bring the DPS through this period of revision and into a newer era of law enforcement. In many ways he succeeded. David Dimick, who somehow emerges as the villain of the piece, acted in a fashion he considered to be in keeping with what was then DPS policy. There seems to be an undertone of surprise in his testimony, and it is easy to see why he might have been startled by the barrage of publicity and subsequent notoriety.

Over time, almost all these issues have been resolved. And the matter of facility defense has created plant security forces with capabilities that often approach those of an elite military unit. As more reactors come on line, greater interface between nuclear plant security forces and local police will occur. Will this increased familiarity lead to new levels of cooperation? The answer is probably affirmative. Will this closer relationship between private and public forces bring on new excesses? The potential is there. Responsible management of both groups will prevent this. It is not a problem of unmanageable proportions yet. But it is something we should be aware of—and watch.

FOURTEEN

Cosmos 954

The advent of Sputnik marked the start of a whole new era of technology. After the first few fledgling attempts, the masters of space began to look for ways to increase the efficiency of their orbital vehicles.

Additional electrical power provided one gateway to the improvement of this new astral breed, and the surest, easiest way to gain large amounts of electricity was by the development of lightly shielded nuclear reactors for use in instrument packages.

In a way, then, the initiation of the space age was also the instigator of a new problem—that of orbital masses of highly radioactive materials.

No orbit is permanent. All—because of the delicate balance between gravity and velocity—decay, sending the suspended object closer and closer to the point when equilibrium fails and the vehicle falls slowly, then faster and faster, on a reentry course to destruction.

The return of one of these nuclear power piles is not like the homecoming of an ordinary space vehicle. As it disintegrates, it leaves a high-altitude trail of burning dust behind. Each mote is as radioactive as its partner, and each will finally settle to some point on old mother earth.

Larger component pieces of the vehicle will also survive the intense heat of reentry, allowing an estimated 5 to 10 percent of the total satellite to arrive back on our planet in various-sized hunks.

If a portion of the remaining material is from the reactor unit, there will be an extremely hot piece of debris traveling at enormous speed toward its specific point of impact.

If this predestined, almost-preordained spot is a center of population—New York City, for instance—an inestimable amount of damage will result.

Although it is not generally known—or wasn't at least until the coming of Cosmos 954, which gained headline prominence in newspapers throughout the world—several satellites have made the reentry journey complete with their nuclear hearts.

Cosmos 954, however, is the one to remember. As a story it has almost everything: suspense; international intrigue; special operations with code names; flights in search of vital intelligence materials; treks across the hostile, frozen tundra; and more.

A look at the behind-the-scenes story will reveal many things, and will possibly remind us, the next time we gaze upward on a star-bright night, of a new kind of proliferation. This increase shows every sign of becoming another rather unpleasant facet of our already complex atomic age.

———

Silence. Blackness. Even though the forty-six-foot-long Cosmos 954 was sailing at over a thousand miles an hour, there was no sound, no rush of air. On board, a specially designed nuclear reactor, fueled by about a hundred pounds of uranium 235, generated more than enough kilowatts to provide power for the sophisticated electronic equipment the Soviets had painstakingly installed.

Launched on September 18, 1977, into a 150-mile orbit around the earth, the eight-thousand-pound vehicle was ill-fated from the first. Ground tracking stations began to notice uneasy signs in its flight stability and responsiveness from the fifth orbit.

According to SATCAT Boxscore (satellite catalog), as of October 2006, about 5,800 payloads are on orbit or in a decayed orbit. These perform a variety of tasks ranging from television transmission for civilian reception to military spying. In addition to weather and navigation control, designs have been launched to scan the seas to keep track of shipping, to guide ballistic missiles to targets, to monitor launchings of other rockets, and to perform innumerable intelligence functions.

No official information was released on the purpose of this particular satellite, but that was hardly a departure from the norm. Speculation on the actual role of Cosmos 954 ranged from reports that the craft was equipped with a unique radar system to monitor U.S. missile-firing submarines, to a science fiction–style scenario in which it was designed to be a "killer," using a laser beam or a kind of death ray to destroy other space vehicles or possibly even ground targets. The Soviets did at that time possess killer satellites, but these were simple, surface-directable proximity bombs, not flying ray guns.

Best estimates today hold that Cosmos 954 was a RORSAT, or Soviet Radar Ocean Reconnaissance satellite. It had a large atomic pile on board. The relatively large amounts of electricity produced by the one-meter-square reactor from fifty kilos of fissionable uranium must have had some end use.

The United States began a study of Cosmos shortly after it reached orbit. A visual analysis of its exterior was made from photos obtained by both ground and space installations, and several arm's-length tests were undertaken through the use of electromagnetic spectrum analysis, radio reflection, and other advanced methods.

Some aspects of the satellite were familiar to our scientists. The first of the Soviet ocean surveillance series was Cosmos 198, launched in 1966. Preceding Cosmos 954, sixteen others had been fired into orbit. Each behaved in an unusual fashion. After attaining an orbital plane about 260 kilometers high, with an inclination to the equator of sixty-five degrees, they would stabilize. Then, a few days later, at a command from ground control, on-board booster rockets would fire and shift the vehicle outward to a distance of nine hundred kilometers. The very low initial orbit for this series was a result of a limited resolving power of the spy equipment on board. One revolution took 89.65 minutes, which is dangerously close to the critical time of 87 minutes, at which point the object loses stability and will fall back to earth. The push outward to the higher parking orbit was designed to keep the on-board atomic reactor from plunging back into the atmosphere.

The first six Cosmos shots were experimental. But by 1973, the device was considered perfect enough for military use. Several were boosted into orbit. All but two worked in pairs to provide ground stations with the speed and the direction of moving ships. It appears they were used to monitor special events, rather than for continuous surveillance. In 1974, a set was orbited to keep track of NATO naval exercises held in May. U.S. familiarity with the series was limited, so the opportunity to study another one while it was studying us received top intelligence attention.

The newly launched satellite was tracked in a small green room buried over half a mile deep in the solid granite of Cheyenne Mountain. Located in the state of Colorado, this unique installation was the functioning heart and headquarters of what was then called the North American Air Defense Command (NORAD). Atomic-bomb-proof, and protected by one of the most elaborate security systems in history, this nerve center processed phenomenal amounts of information each hour of the day, ordering data into meaningful displays and readouts so the officers, scientists, and technicians could assist in regulating the retaliatory strike force of the United States.

One of its least-known duties was the maintenance of the "junk catalogue" of orbiting objects. Accurate tracking and position reports, along with information about times and places of anticipated reentry, were furnished at U.S. expense to the Soviets and the rest of the world. The goal was to prevent a nervous radar monitor from setting off World War III by mistaking the blips on a screen caused by the return of space junk for the final homing path of a multiple-warhead intercontinental ballistic missile. The number of times NORAD's junk catalog prevented a serious misunderstanding is unknown. Many say it saved us on more than one occasion.

Blue-uniformed technicians and officers analyzed the data on Cosmos 954 for forty-four days, expecting the Soviets to fire the on-board rockets to push it into higher orbit. During this time, the craft made several small random maneuvers. On November 1, these stopped. Something had gone wrong. The vehicle showed every indication of returning to earth. Where the multi-ton radioactive hulk might fall was open to a number of guesses, but there was little question it was coming down.

Official notice was passed on a routine basis to the National Security Council (NSC), and a message came back to NORAD requesting a tighter fix on the date. By mid-December of 1977, the situation had progressed to the point at which reentry was certain and a number of possible sites were listed. Even at this early stage, a North American impact point seemed likely.

The Soviets, aware of their failure to raise the vehicle into its parking orbit, tried other techniques. Utilizing a built-in remote-control rocket engine, they attempted to split the satellite into three separate portions. Two, not containing the atomic reactor and

236 Nuclear Afternoon

therefore only slightly contaminated with radioactivity, would be allowed to fall back. The third, with the pile inside, would be shot outward, where it would remain for a thousand years. This appeared safe enough to Soviet scientists, because by the year 3000 mankind would either be able to retrieve the hulk and send it on a collision course with the sun, or might be decimated to the point at which one more radioactive device falling from the sky would make little or no difference.

Two separate attempts were made by Russian technicians, but in both cases the rocket refused to function. It is likely they managed to disconnect parts of the soaring satellite but were unable to achieve a successful re-orbiting of the pile.

Alarmed by the problem, the Soviet team arrived at the same probable reentry sites listed by NORAD. Knowing for certain we had complete knowledge of the coming event, they did not make the fact of reentry public. Nor did they bother to mention it to the United States or Canada.

NSC officials had kept themselves current on the matter. When NORAD estimates improved in late December, and the North American continent had become the number-one impact site, President Jimmy Carter's National Security Advisor, Zbigniew Brzezinski, set up an appointment with Soviet Ambassador Anatoly Dobrynin.

Dobrynin's background as an aeronautical engineer gave him a good basis for understanding the erratic nature of the reentry path and the potential danger of the situation.

During the meeting between the two on January 12, several impact points were contemplated based on latest data. According to Brzezinski, there was a "serious hazard to the public" if Cosmos 954 were to fall into a densely populated area. While touchdown predictions did not specify it, one orbit occurring in the final unstable minutes could cause it to strike near New York City.

The main subject of conversation, however, was the nature of the radioactive material on board and the probability of its attaining critical mass from either heat generated by reentry into the atmosphere or impact upon landing. Brzezinski sought information from the Soviets on points of design as well as their safety features, and after the meeting he said Dobrynin's replies had been "somewhat reassuring but not fully satisfactory."

Projections based on the amount of atomic material thought to be on board the spacecraft indicated it could potentially have the explosive power of about five times the force of the bomb dropped on Hiroshima. The chances of an explosion, however, were slim by everyone's estimate. Nonetheless, radioactivity that might be released was a matter of vital concern, especially with the possibility that the object might fall into a large city.

A second meeting between Brzezinski and Dobrynin was held on January 17, and at least two telephone calls were exchanged in the next few days.

White House staff decided to prod the Soviets for more information and to alert the leaders of selected countries that could help with tracking. Later, information was extended to all our North Atlantic Treaty Organization (NATO) allies and to Japan, Australia, and New Zealand. No public announcement was made because, in the words of a spokesman, "We were trying to head off a re-creation of Mercury Theatre." The reference was to the famous 1938 Orson Welles–produced radio drama, *War of the Worlds*, which caused widespread panic among its listening audience.

During this same time, other related events were taking place. Intelligence teams from the CIA, NSC, and the air force began playing with the idea of trying to recover Cosmos 954 to see what might be learned from it. The more they developed the idea, the more inviting it became. Later, after its reentry, there was speculation the United States might have had some role in downing the erratic satellite, but there is no available evidence even pointing to such an act.

NORAD's reports pinpointed the impact site in Northern Canada, but due to a skipping effect that occurs as a reentering vehicle first touches our dense atmosphere, no entirely accurate touchdown location could be given. Unless there was a sudden change in the stability of the satellite, though, it seemed probable it would not enter U.S. territory.

On January 19, in reply to diplomatic pressures, Dobrynin contacted Brzezinski and informed him of the nature of the radioactive material on board Cosmos: It was uranium 235, in about a 100-to-110-pound quantity. The Soviet ambassador made it very clear the core was designed to prevent its going critical during descent or impact. He also gave all possible assurances it would not explode, citing the excellence of Russian engineering and stability of the type of nuclear power plant on board. "He wanted it understood that the Russians were not orbiting a nuclear bomb," one State Department official was later quoted as saying. The use of the word "bomb" was interesting, because this possibility must have been given consideration.

Even though there were treaties and agreements concerning the orbiting of nuclear weapons, there was no formal or forceful policing procedure to see that participating nations were in compliance with their words. Brzezinski wasted no time after the meeting. He issued a National Security Council directive alerting NASA, the CIA, and the Departments of Defense and State.

Response was quick. Special air force teams trained in radioactive detection and decontamination were placed on standby so they could be flown to any given spot in a matter of hours. U-2 aircraft were fitted with high-altitude sensors, and portable detectors were readied for use in low-flying ground reconnaissance transports.

By the third week in January, NORAD placed reentry over the Queen Charlotte Islands off the coast of British Columbia, the Canadian province bordering on the Pacific Ocean. The impact date was estimated to be January 24. All branches of intelligence gave their plans a final once-over, and the teams of specialists drew issues of arctic clothing to protect them from the anticipated twenty-below-zero temperatures common to the Canadian tundra. On the evening of January 23, Operation Morning Light was like a cocked pistol. The first sighting of flaming wreckage would pull the trigger.

It was cold in the early dawn of the 24th, and in the far northern area near Great Slave Lake there was a lingering semi-twilight. The habitual gray cloud cover was high, and the fierceness of the cold prevented any but the most necessary excursion from the row of houses lining the main street of Yellowknife. The town, with a population of about ten thousand, was located nearly a thousand miles north of the border between Montana and Canada. It lay in the heart of the Northwest Territories, the immense, chill Canadian outback. Yellowknife existed because of gold mined in the area, but it was a settlement with two distinct personalities. In the summer, when the days were long and light, the people moved about outside. Since mining could be conducted only while the ground was soft enough to work, labor started early and ended late. In the winter, intense cold, with temperatures dropping to more than forty degrees below zero Farenheit, forced the residents inside. Blinding blizzards of snow blew through on a regular basis, adding to the problems of the settlers. Only the rugged remained.

Marie Ruman, a pleasant woman, was standing in the office building where she worked, looking out at the gray, dim overcast when something caught her eye. She glanced away, then back again, giving a little cry of surprise. "I looked through the window and saw this object coming toward me," she later said. "The main part was like a bright fluorescent light. There were lots of small parts trailing behind it. The pieces were bigger than shooting stars and each had a long bright tail. None of it made a sound." Startled, she called others. Cosmos 954 had returned to earth.

Dale McLeod of the Royal Canadian Mounted Police steered his patrol vehicle carefully on the frozen rough road. The country seemed quieter than usual and the bleakness of the snow-covered, pine tree–spotted landscape presented a serene presence to McLeod and his patrol partner as they drove through it. Suddenly, a fiery trail shot across the sky, and McLeod slammed on his brakes. The brightness of the fireball tingled his eyes as he watched the mysterious sight. "It was like something out of *Superman*. You know, it's a bird, it's a plane, no, it's . . . it's . . . it's whatever." Astounded, he used his radio as the two men watched the glowing object sail toward the horizon.

One hundred twenty-five miles south of Yellowknife, in Hay River, another Mountie saw the light. Corporal Phil Pitts had gone up onto the roof of one of the RCMP Detachment's buildings in the compound and spotted a "bright white and incandescent" glowing object tracing a path through the dim sky. He immediately reported the incident and was informed it probably was the Cosmos reentry. Later, after learning of the high levels of radioactivity associated with the returning space vehicle, he was quoted as saying, "My gosh! I was standing on the roof watching it go by. Maybe I'm sterile."

During the night of January 23, emergency teams remained on full standby alert. They were ready to go. NORAD had set up a communications link and passed the word to the White House as their computers refined rapidly developing data. Later in the evening, they gave a landing time of about 6:53 AM on January 24. This was duly relayed to all concerned parties.

Brzezinski was on top of the situation in the early hours of the 24th, personally telephoning President Carter, whom he woke with news of the reentry. The NORAD tracking system, aided by other ground station radar, had followed Cosmos during its descent until it finally lost sufficient altitude and disappeared off the screens. Its last known height and position were noted, as were its ballistic characteristics. The general impact area was near Great Slave Lake, and since radar had indicated some fragmentation during later stages of the fall, a corridor about 1,500 miles long was plotted. All debris would, or should, be within that long, narrow zone.

After informing the president, Brzezinski called Ambassador Dobrynin to tell him Cosmos 954 was down. Then, at 7:15 AM EST, he called Canadian Prime Minister Pierre Trudeau with position estimates. Twenty-two minutes after the final fix from NORAD, leaders of the concerned nations knew of the averted disaster. Trudeau, who had been briefed earlier in the project, had known since the previous weekend the object would fall inside Canadian boundaries. He too had agreed not to alert the public to the potential menace.

Once the final impact zone was delineated, Operation Morning Light shot into action. A KC-135 and a U-2 high-altitude reconnaissance aircraft were given sampling locations and commenced an aerial patrol along the satellite's path. Checking for radiation, those vanguard planes made several sorties but returned each time with negative results. There were only limited signs of upper-level contamination. At the same time, over a hundred U.S. scientists, technicians, and soldiers embarked into the freezing winter wilderness aboard four C-130 Hercules cargo planes. A twenty-two-person Canadian nuclear-accident response team, equipped with various kinds of radiation sensors, was dispatched to Yellowknife. They patrolled the streets and surrounding countryside, moving through deep snow, but found no unusual signs of radioactivity.

A forty-four-person U.S. Air Force task force made up of trained and selected specialists was sent to the Morning Light control center in Edmonton from Andrews and Nellis Air Force Bases.

U.S. intelligence teams were also on the move. There was a good chance the satellite's remains could be found by seeking out the puddle of radioactivity that had to be formed around any remaining pieces of the reactor segment of the vehicle. Every chunk that could be located would serve the intelligence engineering staff well. From even small fragments, they would be able to deduce the state of Soviet reactor design, something about the electronics package the unit carried, the latest thinking in Russian metallurgy, and hundreds of other technical facts.

Within hours of touchdown, men wearing "man from Mars suits" that covered the head, face, hands, and feet were in Canada to search out debris. Around-the-clock flight plans were instituted for the large cargo planes, and as soon as engineers had installed the gamma-ray spectrometry equipment that would serve as their bird dog by pointing out hot spots as the aircraft flew by, they were off.

Pilots, crews, scientists, U.S. Air Force nuclear specialists, technicians, and others all gathered at Edmonton headquarters, awaiting the need for their skills. Additional increases in service manpower to provide meals and quarters for the new arrivals almost doubled the total number of people involved.

Flights were long and tiring. An eyewitness aboard special flight 6763 provided details of the mission. It was mid-morning by the time the ground crew had refueled and checked the Hercules C-130 and released it to pilot John Oliver. He, along with Serge Cothe, his copilot, did a careful preflight. Both men knew they would be flying at low altitudes over some of the most bleak and desolate country in the world. The strange terrain was an endless field of snow and ice, broken only by an occasional outcropping of black rock or a scattered grove of wind-blown pine trees. Even with the latest radio and ground-search techniques, a crashed aircraft was hard to locate there. A downed crew had only a limited amount of time because survival in the intense cold was difficult.

Satisfied with his walk-around inspection, the pilot clambered aboard the plane where technicians had completed the checkout of two 1,300-pound spectrometers. The large, square instruments in dented green containers would be the heart of the search system. Oliver spoke briefly with Peter Holman, the geophysicist who would evaluate readings from the units, then headed to the cockpit, where he checked his maps. Working with Cothe, he reviewed their navigation preparations. Then, settling back, the two men went through the elaborate before-takeoff checklist. Once airborne, they flew directly to the assigned search zone to begin a seemingly endless crisscrossing of icy terrain.

Holding flying altitude to under a few hundred feet gave the green boxes in the belly of the ship a better opportunity to pick up any signs of radiation. But because of the low altitude, each search leg was narrowed. Oliver and Cothe took turns at the controls, each man concentrating on holding a constant airspeed, altitude, and course. Occasionally their radio would crackle into life, and they would exchange brief words with a ground station or another aircraft. Only a cup of coffee from a thermos interrupted the monotony.

On the seventeenth pass, instruments registered some sign of radioactivity on the frozen tundra below. Notes were made on the maps, and an electronic fix of the plane's position was attempted. Asked later if the indicators on the green boxes had shown a piece of the fallen Soviet spaceship, Holman shrugged and responded, "I don't know, but it's worth looking at."

The search continued while other crews, responsible for taking a closer look at the spot indicated by Holman, moved into action. These specialists, trained to deal with radioactive materials and equipped with smaller radiation detectors, were maintained on standby to be dispatched for on-site ground examination. Airlifted by helicopter, they could cover a number of possible spots in a given day. Their routine was arduous.

Based on the map location of the suspected site, along with any electronic navigational information, fixes, and visual marks reported by the C-130 survey crews, the men would fly to the general vicinity of the position established by the gamma-ray spectrometers. Using this point as center, they would then conduct a low altitude hunt, following a spiral pattern, to see if any equipment in the helicopter would give them a closer indication. If so, they would land and begin an even finer search, utilizing hand-held instruments and making their way across the hostile wastes on foot. They would stay in the selected area until every square inch had been covered by both visual inspection and radiation counter. If pieces of Cosmos were present, they would find them.

The search effort continued for several days. Then, an unusual series of events occurred. Barney Danson, Canadian Defense Minister, publicly said the field efforts had turned up "either a piece of debris or the greatest uranium mine in the world." His statement resulted in increased interest in the project by the press, and his announcement was carried on American television.

The next day, though, official Canadian spokesmen countered that Danson's report had been a false alarm. In explaining the discrepancy, some vague "equipment failure" was cited as the cause.

Apparently this caught the American contingent involved in Morning Light off-guard. The crew chief in charge of the green boxes was a highly respected USAF nuclear physicist. His reputation for efficiency was impeccable, and the idea there had been an equipment malfunction that was wrongly read as a ground source of radioactivity didn't fit with the team's past performance. After twenty-four hours, the United States replied in a terse statement affirming that the instrumentation had performed as expected and "Something hit the ground that was radioactive." William Nelson, a U.S. Department of Energy scientist, stated in part, "Pieces of that satellite did impact the earth."

What caused these strange comments is still not clear. The Soviets, while admitting no liability, had on several occasions asked the Canadians if they could join in the hunt so as to be allowed to clean up their own mess. Washington, naturally, was against Russian assistance since intelligence experts wanted to examine all retrieved pieces. And both the U.S. and Canadian governments were concerned about leaving radioactive debris scattered about the countryside. In the end, the United States allowed the Canadians to deal with the Soviets, which they effectively did by ignoring their requests to participate and subsequently billing them about $15 million in search costs.

The admission of success, followed by the denial and a final acknowledgment, might be related in some way to political maneuvering that went on during this period. Or it may be only the visible aspect of an entirely different manipulation. It also could have been the result of an honest series of mistakes caused by a confusion of communications during a tense and hurried time.

In any case, even though there were signs from the overflight portion of Morning Light, as of January 27 no one had actually seen a single component of the crashed Cosmos. The search area encompassed fifteen thousand square miles of wilderness in a long northeasterly corridor from Canada's Pacific Coast to Great Slave Lake. In the grip of winter, daily temperatures of thirty to forty degrees F below zero was the norm. With the chill factor, caused by the unceasing wind, the temperature would be experienced as eighty or ninety degrees F below zero.

This land has defeated even seasoned outdoorsmen. John Hornby, leader of an expedition in 1926, had attempted to cross the Northwest Territory from the Yukon to Hudson Bay. He tried to winter in the region, but it proved too much for him. He died there.

The story of Operation Morning Light then took a strange turn. An expedition put together by a young Canadian and five American companions set out in the spring of 1977, months before Cosmos reentry to retrace the steps of the original Hornby group. Finding themselves well into the wilderness by first snowfall, the team decided to winter in the area. For headquarters, they selected a fifty-year-old log cabin near an almost unpopulated settlement called Wardens Grove. It seemed odd that a group composed of five Americans and a single Canadian was in the area of the Cosmos disintegration path. While it is possible there was more to this than happenstance, the parents of the Canadian, Robert Common, knew of his plans for at least a year before the Soviets launched their sky spy.

From their base camp, the six young adventurers planned to carry out a number of activities. The Canadian government had given them a winter wildlife study, and they were also charged with conducting a number of different meteorological surveys. In addition, for their own satisfaction, they wanted to travel cross-country about twenty miles to the site of Hornby's last camp. Since some of the team would be needed to man the base, they divided into three sets of two. John Mordhorst of Rock Island, Illinois, accompanied by Mike Mobley of Mesa, Arizona, set out by dogsled to the Hornby site. They made good time, and after a night out, completed their visit and started back to the log cabin at Wardens Grove.

About 3:00 PM on January 28, the two men were traveling along the frozen mass of the Thelon River when something caught their eye. It would have to have been something pretty unusual—with the temperature in the forty-degree-F-below-zero range, their attention was totally on their own cross-country path. They did not know of the satellite's fall. Interested, they changed course. In a matter of minutes, the dog team had drawn alongside a wide "crater about ten to twelve inches deep in the snow." They discussed the unusual array before them and one of the two ran his mittened hand over a metal spar jutting out of the white ground. They later described what they found: "There were prongs, struts, a tripod shape with the apex in the ice." Curiosity satisfied, the two refigured their direction to compensate for the brief detour and returned to the relative warmth and security of the cabin.

They arrived to find their friends excitedly discussing the reentry, and a few minutes of conversation convinced them they had stumbled onto pieces of the wreckage. They radioed authorities.

Hours later, the two who had actually seen the debris were the subjects of medical examinations to determine the degree of contamination they had suffered. A special team arrived by Chinook helicopter from Baker Lake consisting of thirteen Canadians led by Lieutenant-Colonel Donald Davidson. Backed by a U.S. crew headed by Paul Murda, they airlifted the two explorers out, to be followed by their friends and even the dogs, so whole body counts could be performed to assay their condition. Fortunately, neither Mordhorst nor Mobley had severe dosages. Their exposure was about equal to two chest X-rays. The others in the group, as well as the dogs, fared better still. Concerned about the possibility of radioactive beryllium, which is hazardous because it can be picked up through skin contact and then swallowed or inhaled, the nuclear experts earmarked a piece of the metal at the site for analysis. After exhaustive physicals, all six men were returned to their Wardens Grove camp within a few days with clean health reports.

Davidson, with his Canadian team and part of the American contingent, followed directions given them by Mordhorst and Mobley. They flew their helicopter to an outcropping of black rock near the site, then made their way through snow to the spot.

According to Lt. Col. Davidson's comment at the scene, "Something has really gone through that ice at high speed. This is all that's left sticking out."

Instruments confirmed the materials still showing were radioactive, but not sufficiently to be classified as a part of the reactor unit. The two teams set up camp and began working on ways to remove the broken pieces while maintaining a safe level of exposure.

The Thelon River discovery was only the first of the finds. Two days later another ground party discovered debris on the snow-covered ice of Great Slave Lake. The hunks were smaller, on first examination, but thinking there might be more under the water, the team established a field outpost at Fort Reliance.

The Slave Lake material was far more dangerous than anything previously found. One chunk, ten inches by three inches by about a half inch in thickness, gave off more radiation in a single hour than forty times the annual allowable limit for an employee in an atomic power station. To get in close enough to work, the men had to shelter behind a 1,600-pound lead shield, and all pieces were handled by long tongs. The effort was further hampered by a thirty-five-mile-per-hour wind that took the chill factor down to more than one hundred degrees F below zero.

The Cosmos incident is important because it calls attention to a seldom-considered aspect of proliferation. While there is little chance of a satellite exploding like a bomb, the possibility exists that a large-population area could be exposed to high levels of radiation. In any case, the upper atmosphere might be contaminated over a wide area. Most of this material would eventually reach the earth. It is another price of living in the nuclear age.

FIFTEEN

Three Mile Island

A serious question associated with the use of nuclear energy to generate electricity is the location of the plant itself. There are currently sixty-five sites in thirty-one states. Not all of these seem well advised.

In the western parts of the United States, there is more than ample territory to site an atomic station so that prevailing winds would probably not carry radioactive materials, released because of a malfunction in the system, into a population center of any size. Similar geographic isolation can be found in Canada and parts of the southern United States as well. However, long-distance transmission of electricity through elaborate linkages of grids, made up of adjacent wiring networks and transformers, is both costly and wasteful. No matter how well designed the linkups are, there is a measurable power loss all along the way. This leads to a desire to locate nuclear-powered generating plants near densely populated areas. There is one, Indian Point, within thirty-five miles of Times Square in New York City. The South Texas Project is only forty miles from Houston, Texas.

Facility proximity to hundreds of thousands of people must look reasonable and rational to the utilities. Or at least expeditious.

The NRC, which inspects and approves locations, does not seem to be troubled by this. And those engineering firms that design and build these massive installations appear to have no problem about facility siteing.

Since the basic designs of nuclear systems used in plants are "right" and the installations are "safe," why not situate nuclear power plants anywhere efficiency dictates? For believers in "right" and "safe," the question is almost foolish. That said, it would seem even the most ardent pronuclear power supporters should agree there are some pieces of real estate unsuitable as plant locations. A proven fault line, for example, which might cause damage to the facility during an earthquake, would obviously be less than ideal. Yet, in California, construction of a plant was started on a site many experts maintained was susceptible to earthquake damage. Worse, the U.S. government had to order the closing of five plants because they were at locations with some potential for seismic activity. Earthquakes are unpredictable phenomena. They happen when they happen, and, even though we are building a better picture of mechanisms that cause quakes, we remain unable to stop or moderate their effects. Both examples show that often too little thought has gone into site selection.

No one has yet built a reactor in an area that habitually floods even though reactors need huge amounts of water for cooling. So possibly there is agreement that it would be better to put the installation in an area above the hundred-year flood plain.

Far more certain to cause problems in our society than building an atomic plant in a zone suspected of seismic disturbance is continuation of the previously mentioned practice of locating a facility near large concentrations of people. If there is a release of radioactive materials into the air, individuals living inside a ten, twenty, thirty, forty, or even fifty-mile radius, depending upon the severity of the discharge and atmospheric conditions at the time of emission, will be exposed to higher-than-normal radiation levels. Obviously, the fewer people inside these release zones the better.

The problem of mislocation is a serious one. Too many plants costing hundreds of millions of dollars are already operating in populous areas. To shut them down and move them elsewhere would cost billions. As callous as it may sound, what's done is done. It is unwise to further our early mistakes. Attention must focus now on where we site new facilities.

A horrendous incident that occurred in March 1979 shows the inadvisability of improper location. It also provides even stronger insight into unforeseen difficulties that arise when engineering designs are not subjected to full-scale testing before being accepted as adequate for the tasks they are planned to perform.

———

The Susquehanna is the longest river in the eastern half of the United States. It begins in Lake Otsego in New York, meanders its way through the mountains, bisects several states, and finally drains into Chesapeake Bay, near Havre de Grace, Maryland. It was an important river to the Indians, to the early settlers, and, finally, to the people who live in Pennsylvania today. This moving body of water holds the greatest potential for the generation of hydroelectric power on the eastern seaboard.

In 1718, John Harris, seeking a place to conduct trade with the natives, established a post that became known as Harris's Ferry. It was sited at the head of the Cumberland and Lebanon valleys. This likeable Yorkshireman found a spot the Iroquois and Conestoga tribes had used for generations to cross the river. It was the best ford on the Susquehanna for a hundred miles in any direction. Harris's original venture prospered. The outpost grew to become a major center of communications. During the Civil War, in June 1863, General Robert E. Lee marked the city, by then called Harrisburg, as a key objective for his armies as they invaded Pennsylvania.

South of Harrisburg, the Susquehanna passes Middletown. It makes a gentle curve, widening to flow around three large islands that form a group opposite Goldsboro, a community on the western bank. One of the river islands, called "Three Mile" by the people in the area, was composed of about six hundred acres of bottom land.

Until the early 1970s, the island was inhabited by a farmer, who worked a small holding, and an occasional fisherman or two who would stay over in one of the shore-side cabins. Then things began to change. Metropolitan Edison Company, working with Babcock & Wilcox, began construction of a $700 million nuclear power station, designed to provide electricity to a number of utility companies around Harrisburg. The land was cleared, two bridges were built, and construction begun on a twin unit installation that would eventually contain 36,816 fuel rods filled with tons of uranium pellets, designed to heat the water to drive giant turbines and produce 880,000 kilowatts of electricity.

Reaction to the project was generally favorable, especially from an economic standpoint. Olmstead Air Force Base, one of the area's largest employers, had been closed. The new atomic power station would take up much of the slack while being built and provide high-paying jobs for years afterwards.

Over in Goldsboro, at the Wining Wench tavern, talk turned to construction work available and the long-term prospects for employees in the Three Mile Island facility. In many ways, this little hamlet was to become a tangible paradox of the atomic age.

It is a nice town, Goldsboro. Two-story, northern-style clapboard houses have small windows that look out onto hilly streets. Trees, bare for many months of the year, still have a bleak appearance in March and April, shining blackly against a hazy blue sky. Highway 262 runs through the community. The posted speed limit is 35 miles an hour. From almost any place in the hamlet, the giant forty-story cooling towers on Three Mile Island are visible. The people of Goldsboro live within the shadow of the installation that helped their prosperity.

While the four towers are the largest and most notable constructions on the site, another building, 190 feet tall and 140 feet across, also stands out. Its walls are specially layered carbon steel and concrete, four feet thick. This containment dome houses another chamber forty-one feet high with eight-inch-thick sides, designed as the reactor chamber. In this container, the uranium-filled zirconium fuel rods would produce the energy needed to boil millions of gallons of water, converting it into steam to propel the turbines that would produce electricity.

Unit No. 1 came into action with few difficulties. None of the start-up problems seemed more than new-equipment nuisance. But Unit No. 2, which plugged into the northeastern power grid on December 30, 1978, was a different matter. After operating for a short period, it was called off line for a two-week shutdown in January 1979. A pair of safety valves had failed. Malfunctions of this nature are not unusual, but with a new unit, there was some concern, and a thorough check was made of all systems. Then, in a week, three more incidents occurred. On February 1st, a throttle valve developed a leak. Next, on the 2nd, a heater pump blew out a seal. Then, on the 6th, a feed-water pump tripped off.

To completely understand the operation of the reactor and power-generating equipment would take a hundred hours of special instruction. But, in short, the facility uses two separate water systems. One is designed to flow into and out of the reactor chamber where the uranium core is housed. This is the cooling cycle, which keeps temperatures in the core at a level approved by the engineers and operators. Water in this system is highly radioactive because it comes into direct contact with fuel rods. Fuel rods heat the water, which is under pressure, and it is pumped through a heat exchanger, where it is cooled, and then sent back to the core.

The second water circulation system turns the turbines. Water is pumped into the heat exchanger where it is heated to the boiling point by the hot water in the other system. There is no contact between the water in the two separate systems. Heat from one boils the other, which produces steam. Steam spins the blades of a turbine that drives a generator that produces electricity. After turning the turbine, the steam jets into a cooling tower, where it becomes liquid water again. Then the water is pumped through the cycle once more. Called feed water, it is fed to the steam generator by an elaborate network of pumps. Water coming back in from the cooling towers becomes feed water, then steam, then out to the towers again for recycling. It's a closed system, using the same water over and over.

At one point, where steam billows upward inside the more than three-hundred-foot-high cooling tower to condense into water again, it is exposed to open air. This is normally not a problem, as the water in this cycle, which never comes into direct contact with the highly radioactive water from the cooling cycle, has very low levels of radiation. And the towers themselves are fitted with filters and scrubbers to remove even the slightest traces of active elements.

The concept of a contaminated system running alongside a clean system is good engineering, as long as the two never mix and become one. Then, the radioactive waters would have access, through the cooling towers, to our world, where they would become deadly poisons.

About 3:00 AM on March 28, 1979, the third shift crew, which had been on duty for a few hours, ran through their usual routine.

All systems were within their operating ranges. The team was scattered through the complex, performing assigned tasks. Some were drinking coffee, talking in the animated way late-hour workers do when they are up and most people are asleep. In the main control room, Craig Faust and Ed Frederick were tending their duties. Everything seemed normal. The nerve center of the two-unit plant, where they were stationed, was a large open space. White fluorescent fixtures, mounted in egg-crate frames in the ceiling and covered with light-diffusing plastic, provided an even, secure illumination.

Just away from the center of the space, a series of desks and tables, some equipped with telephones, occupied almost the entire width of the room. Seated in one of the comfortable office chairs, a person could see across the gray-tiled floor to the banks of controls. On the walls, at a height starting above a man's head and running down to about four feet from the floor, was an array of indicator lights and meters. Each turbine unit was tied in to these devices, which showed green or gave no glow at all. Below these, jutting out from the wall itself at a forty-five-degree angle, were the actual controls and switches, intruding into the work area. These units were in sets. Twenty, thirty, or even forty buttons, some as large as two inches across, interspaced by black, red, and green-handled rheostat adjusters, were fitted to a console. Then the next set was placed at a twenty-degree angle to the first, and so on in a horseshoe shape around the room. Each control was electronic, connected by miles of wiring to innumerable valves, sensors, and slave relays. It was one of the simplest, yet most complex, industrial systems in the world.

At 3:53 AM, things seemed to be operating routinely. Then, at 3:54, all hell broke loose. The harsh, strident burp of an electronic warning horn interrupted the otherwise chill quiet of pre-dawn. The men in the room, jolted for a second by the suddenness of the sound, focused their eyes on display after display of warning lights, seeking the source. Unit 1 was fine. Unit 2, producing 97 percent of its capacity, showed a malfunction light. That single red warning started a chain of events that would take months to complete.

One valve, located in a filtering device that removed minerals that might clog the system from water, failed. Most evidence today indicates the malfunction was due to moisture in an air line that had not had time, since start-up of the plant, to completely dry out. Opening this valve automatically stopped all flow of water to the massive steam generator. This, in turn, created a drop in suction pressure to pumps feeding water into the steam generator. They worked perfectly, and shut themselves off. Relay after relay reacted to the sudden change in pressure. Light after light, corresponding to the electro-mechanical sequence of events being carried out in the huge dome, winked red on the control board.

At the sharp blast of the horn, Faust and Frederick jumped into action, responding to feedback information being provided by their panel indicators. Having run numerous faults on a simulator, they began a deliberate but rapid shutdown. Fifteen or so seconds later, they completed their chore. Now things were just starting to happen. The gigantic turbine, driven by its own controls, noted the stoppage of feed water to the steam generator, and closed itself off, starting to wind down with a dying hum.

Sensing trouble, the fission-quenching boron control rods slammed home in the pile, stopping the wayward dance of random uranium atoms. Even with this done, it would still take time to right the problem because of intense amounts of residual heat in the system and lingering radioactive decay.

Pressures began to build in certain lines and, in a few minutes, had attained forces greater than their normal operating ranges. Soon, there were over 2,350 pounds per square inch (psi) in some of the piping.

An emergency backup system, designed to kick in at first sign of an unusual occurrence, failed to do so, primarily because two more valves refused to snap open and allow access to the auxiliary feed-water line.

Up to this point, all malfunctions had been confined to the secondary coolant system, which carried non-radioactive water. Less than ten minutes had passed. There was an immense amount of action in the main control room and in other areas of the facility where the staff of sixty people was galvanized into action.

Robbed of its usual outlet lines because of the shutdown of the secondary heat removal system, the primary heat removal system, filled with highly radioactive steam and water, had no place to dump its building heat. As a direct result, pressure began to increase. It climbed to two thousand pounds. Meters in the main control room followed the course, indicating 2,300, then 2,350, which snapped open a safety valve on the pressurizer, allowing a spray of hot steam to flood into a quench or cooling tank inside the containment building.

A computer in the main control room started by itself, printing "????????"—an endless line of question marks showing something unknown was happening to core temperatures.

When the relief valve popped, pressure inside the reactor began an immediate drop. The valve, set to open and close at 2,300 pounds per square inch, waited until that point was reached, then tried to shut. It failed to do so.

Up in the gray tile–floored control room, operators watched their boards with intense concern. Finally a light, indicating the nonfunctioning valve had closed at the 2,300-pound point, came on. There was a momentary relaxation before the next shock hit. Pressure in the reactor continued to come down. Either the meter reading was in error or the indicator showing that the relief valve had worked as planned was faulty. One of the operators, moments before, had scanned the control consoles again, and noticed for the first time that red tags, marking valves out of service for maintenance, were on two key controls. He quickly opened them, adding to the problem. Coolant continued to escape at a rapid rate through the open valve, lowering gauge readings even more.

Then the real trouble started. Working under tension in the control room, an operator saw that the emergency feed-water valves had not cycled open. So he used a backup system and opened them manually.

This action dumped cold water into the steam generator, which, having been without a water supply for some time, had boiled dry. Cool water rushed through the pipeline and sprayed its way into the red-hot generator, violently hissing into live steam as it contacted superheated metal. The result resembled an explosion. As the shockwave spread through the container, it broke off or ruptured several lines carrying contaminated water from the reactor, so now the previously clean feed water was rendered highly radioactive.

With the steam generator drawing heat from the reactor again, pressures inside the container began a rapid descent. Meters and gauges in the main control room slid downward from 2,000 psi, first to 1,800 then to 1,600, which was the magic number. At 1,600 psi, the emergency core cooling system (ECCS) began forcing water under high pressure into the reactor. Leaks from broken pipes in the pressurizer continued to pour this same radioactive water out almost as fast as it flowed in, until a disc, placed in the side of the quench tank and designed to rupture before the tank itself broke, finally gave way. Thousands of gallons of contaminated water gushed from the system onto the floor of the containment building.

By 6:10 in the morning, a chilly dawn outlined the tall cooling towers against a steel-gray sky. Two hours and sixteen minutes had passed, and the core damage had been done. Steam, made radioactive by its contamination in the generator, rushed down the lines to a cooling tower, then, as it condensed, released large quantities of atomic gas into the quiet dawn air.

Inside the control room, one of the four operators completed an inspection of the system. Something didn't look right, so he double-checked. Then it came to him. Contrary to his first thoughts, the valve in the feed-water system was stuck open. Reacting quickly now, he took steps necessary to close it. A regrettable case of too little, too late.

When the temperatures and pressures inside the reactor chamber had shot up, the zirconium alloy tubes, which keep pellets of uranium in an orderly array, had reached the limits of design tolerance. Gradually, they began to react to the unending stress. At some point, cooling water in the system probably dropped below the tops of the upper ends of the rods, adding to the problem. Some of the fuel rods, no one is certain how many, bent and twisted. Others split open, dumping their uranium into the remaining water.

The floor of the gigantic containment building was now covered with tens of thousands of gallons of radioactive water. In response, as it was designed to do, a sump pump cut in and started to suck up spillage, transferring it to a special container located in a remote building. This tank, for some reason, was unable to hold all the water it received, and dripped it to the floor.

Dawn's light was met by a gentle early spring breeze along the banks of the Susquehanna. As it blew over Three Mile Island, the air changed from benign to radioactive. Water, which had come from the containment building and spilled onto the floor of the catch tank facility, had begun to evaporate, releasing radioactive gases. These were picked up by the air-conditioning equipment and, after a short cycle, released into the air.

Few people had any knowledge of early-morning difficulties at the plant. The men in the control room had asked for assistance from their company, Metropolitan Edison (Met Ed), and a handful of technicians, executives, and scientists had arrived. The company's customers had no warning. As soon as the plant had shut down its generators, other sources of electricity had been called into the system. Service was uninterrupted. The large belch of radioactive gas from the cooling tower sounded normal and alarmed no one.

At almost 7:00 in the morning, a decision was made to call the Nuclear Regulatory Commission and civil defense personnel at city, county, and state levels. Monitors on the island were reading levels of 20 millirems per hour (about as strong as a chest X-ray). Worse, eight miles away, there were readings of 7 millirems. In a short period, these levels rose appreciably.

A sensor at the plant gate showed 30 millirems per hour. Across the river in Goldsboro, readings varied from the normal 5 to 7 millirems per month all the way up to 35 millirems per hour. It was a serious situation—but no one could determine exactly how serious it was likely to become.

Pennsylvania Governor Richard Thornburgh was notified by his staff at 7:50 AM. His response showed his executive ability. "I can't make much sense out of what Met Ed is reporting," he is said to have told his assistants. "You can't make decisions about people's lives without solid facts. See if we can't get more information."

Met Ed telephone calls notifying specified agencies were, according to later reports, somewhat vague, referring to an "incident" and discussing the fact that small amounts of radiation had been released into the environment.

Actual amounts of radiation in various places were still a matter of confusion. One monitor, hit by steam inside the containment building, showed a level of 6,000 rems (full rems, not 1/1000th rem, called a millirem) per hour. A Pennsylvania Department of

Environmental Resources helicopter flew over the facility, taking air sample readings. A statement later attributed to William Dornsife, a nuclear engineer on board the chopper, put the reading downwind from the plant at 1 millirem per hour, an almost unnoticeable dosage.

The governor's staff immediately went to work developing a more accurate picture of the extent of the threat posed by the incident. At the same time, civil defense teams in Harrisburg began to map out a contingency plan. This included possible evacuation for the nearly one million people living within twenty miles of Three Mile Island.

The program they developed did not inspire confidence in many hearts. Interstate routes looked like the best bets. By blocking off lanes going the other direction fifty miles up and down stream from the plant, they could have access to both sides of the freeway. Two are better than one, but virtually every analyst saw the flaw. A few wrecks would halt traffic flow entirely. Cars running out of gasoline would have the same effect. In short, there was no way to be certain of removing a large population from even a scattered metro area on short notice. Their plans were better than no contingency program at all, but not much. That was a difficult fact to accept.

Met Ed, in response to a growing swell of concern, issued a statement designed to relieve the public and place the situation in perspective. "There have been no recordings of any significant levels of radiation and none are expected outside the plant." The release continued: "The reactor is being cooled according to design by the reactor cooling system, and should be cooled by the end of the day. There is no danger of a meltdown. There were no injuries, either to plant workers or to the public." Don Curry, Met Ed's leading public relations figure, also stated, "Everything worked. The shutdown was automatic."

The statement is not atypical of those made by other industries during time of crisis. But it is hardly in keeping with the personal experiences of Ron Fountain, an auxiliary operator of Unit 2. He knew something was amiss when he arrived at the plant site early Wednesday morning. Police had not yet closed the two bridges connecting the island with each bank of the river, but he said, ". . . on Wednesday, it was kind of scary. No one was around."

Fountain reported to work only to find a control room operator and about a dozen other men dressed in emergency clothing, consisting of yellow rubber suits, respirators, and disposable tie-on plastic overshoes. The group, one after the other, was entering an off-limits area, where exposures up to 100 rems were possible, to manually operate a series of valves. In minutes, Fountain had suited up. He took his turn in line.

"I had to get up to the second level to open my valve, but the elevator was broken. I should have walked, but I started running. I started hyperventilating. My instinct was to rip off my mask, but I knew the air was heavy with particulates. I said a prayer. I had to gather my wits. I saw I was sweating and breathing heavy. I made myself walk to the valve. I opened it. Then I walked towards the door. My air pack's two-minute warning bell was tingling. I burst through the door, kicking it open. I ripped the mask off and put on another. Usually we've got personnel to help us, but not that day."

Dosimeters on Fountain, as well as on others, indicated they had received more than three times their allowable weekly intake, or 1,000 millirems. This is equal to, depending upon whom you trust, between thirty and thirty-five full-body X-rays.

After the incident, Fountain told his story to the press. He was later quoted as saying he was sorry he had done so, but had spoken out because he wanted people to realize the matter was not as serious as they might have believed. His attitude was typical of many of the plant employees, who at any given time saw the situation as being abnormal, but did not feel a sense of imminent danger or disaster.

By 9:00 Wednesday morning, the NRC had dispatched a team to Three Mile Island. At the same time, President Jimmy Carter, who had worked on a damaged reactor during his naval career and who was familiar with nuclear power generation, assigned aides to watch over the developing situation.

To this time, there had been no public notification of problems at the plant. Reporters, making routine checks of police, public safety, and public defense sources, were alerted by the Met Ed emergency telephone calls. Their early reports reflect the Met Ed release. There was little or no cry of doom. The closest any of the public came to being made aware of a problem had been by hearing roaring noises issuing from the mighty cooling towers on the island. Residents nearby were awakened by a sudden steam release shortly after 4:00 in the morning, but they were accustomed to similar sounds and ignored the disturbance.

Back at the plant, more people were becoming involved. Met Ed continued throughout the day to issue bulletins minimizing the seriousness of the incident. At 11:00 one spokesperson announced there was no danger of a meltdown. This point was later disputed by the NRC. At 2:00 in the afternoon, Jack Herbein, a Met Ed vice president, was quoted by the *New York Times* as saying, "I wouldn't call it a very serious accident at this point."

It was serious enough to those on-site. More men were called upon to expose themselves to dangerous levels of radiation in order to operate valves or take samples of water. Other things were happening too. A sudden spike appeared on the pressure-reading graph paper, indicating that some kind of explosion had occurred inside the containment building. What had caused it or what damage had resulted was unknown. The main effort was to bring the various flows of cooling water back to a level of normalcy, thus preserving the already-damaged pile.

Early Wednesday afternoon, officials of Met Ed, in answer to queries from the governor's office, met with Lt. Gov. William Scranton III. Their report, while more detailed than their bulletins to the public, was still optimistic. Yes, they said, there was damage, or they believed there was damage, to the core of uranium rods. Analysis of samples of coolant water, obtained by workers at the plant who had exposed themselves to radiation to acquire them, confirmed this. No, there was no danger of a meltdown. Operators were keeping the core covered with water, and it was in a scrammed, shutdown mode. But yes, there was more than a remote possibility additional radioactivity might escape.

While this conference was taking place, NRC specialists were having a hard time of their own determining conditions at Three Mile Island. On-site for several hours, they had reviewed the operating records and log, talked with supervisors, and discussed the incident with several of the work staff. That a leak had already seriously contaminated parts of the system was apparent. Several gauges had gone off-scale trying to keep up with the amount of radioactive material present. Leakage into the atmosphere continued, and air counts revealed noticeable, but still low, increases up to eighteen miles away. It took until 10:00 PM that evening, hours after Scranton had made his initial statement, to issue an opinion.

That afternoon, Scranton had been direct. He said, "This situation is more complex than the company first led us to believe. Metropolitan Edison has given you, and us, conflicting information."

The NRC statement, delivered at their press conference, was more optimistic, but, as it turned out, somewhat more misleading. Charles Gallina, an NRC investigator, answered the question as to whether or not the reactor was under control by saying, "The reactor is stable. They are now bringing it down to a cold shut-down condition. It is in a safe condition."

For all the positive nature of reports, the main control room was still a center of tense activity. The cracking open of fuel rods early in the accident had released "burned" materials, which are by-products of radioactive decay. Ten or twelve steam-laden "burps" given off by the plant through the cooling towers had resulted in a significant release of radiation into the atmosphere. That was bad enough, but the spike-like excursion on the pressure graph recording an explosion inside the containment structure was cause for further worry. Hydrogen could be released by a combination of intense heat, high pressures affecting the zircaloy rod-covering material, and water. If the blast had been caused by a hydrogen explosion, more still might be building.

Hydrogen alone is inert. In the presence of small amounts of oxygen, it is a terrifically powerful explosive—powerful enough in large quantities to possibly rupture the container itself. Or, almost equally as bad, an explosion could wipe out remaining water systems and allow the core to progress into a meltdown state.

Smelling breaking news despite the issued statements, reporters began arriving in the area. Concerned parents kept their children home from school. If they were going to have to make a run for it, they wanted to do so quickly, without having to stop and pick up the kids.

Antinuclear forces, on hearing of the situation as it was reported in the news media, began worldwide antinuclear demonstrations. The House and Senate, both without full information but with enough knowledge to realize something was wrong, had selected members to come forward to speak. Others went to view the situation for themselves.

Accurate information was still, into late Thursday, the real problem. Phone lines were jammed. Even the NRC had difficulty contacting their representatives on the site. Gov. Thornburgh was having as much trouble getting a story and was less than fifteen miles away. Midafternoon Thursday, he dispatched Lt. Gov. Scranton to the facility for a first-hand report. Once there, he met with assurances from Met Ed staffers, then reported back. Thornburgh, relaying the results of the visit and briefing, said, "There is no cause for alarm."

Later in the afternoon, however, faced with an increasing buildup of spilled water and the need for more coolant water, plant personnel were forced to dump tens of thousands of gallons of slightly contaminated water into the Susquehanna. This was apparently an emergency effort, as there was no notice given to municipalities downstream.

Gov. Thornburgh, angry over the lack of warning, then spent the next several hours talking with anyone in authority he or his staff could locate. At bedtime, he was quoted as saying to his aide, "I'm not sure anybody really knows what's going on inside that reactor." Subsequent events showed the painful accuracy of his comments.

All night Thursday, reactor staff teams labored at Three Mile Island, trying to bring the unit under control and allow for a cold shutdown. First one thing then another prevented their success. Valves were operated manually, and pumps were switched into unusual combinations. But a little after 6:30 Friday morning, an unusually strong burst of radiation was allowed to escape from the plant. Instantly, monitors scattered about the area picked up the radioactive trace. Then, one after another, monitoring stations, which had been established throughout the countryside, began to report increasing levels of radiation. Civil defense workers were warned about the release but could only stand by.

Information, or lack of it, was still the chief worry. Gov. Thornburgh had grown weary of not having clear data, so he called NRC

Chairman Joseph M. Hendrie, who likewise could offer little accurate intelligence. The two men discussed the possibility of evacuation, but because no reliable information was available, no decision was made. Hendrie, in reaction to the call, complained to other commission members. For two very tense days, there had been scant solid knowledge, which had caused him and the governor to reach conclusions "almost totally in the blind. His information is ambiguous, mine is nonexistent, and . . . I don't know. It's like a couple of blind men staggering around making decisions."

Gov. Thornburgh decided to wait no longer. The need for action in response to a growing question of public safety caused him to issue a statement. He asked people in affected areas to remain indoors with their houses closed up until an analysis of the latest emissions could be completed. Reporters were requested to stay calm and help the population through the ordeal. But no one could foresee what was ahead.

Shortly after the governor's comments and requests, a series of unusual events took place. Singly, they might be funny. Viewed as a whole, they were alarming.

In Harrisburg, a siren went off, setting up a nerve-wracking wail over the town. Residents, already jumpy, over-responded. Diners in a downtown restaurant left their meals and headed for home. Prisoners in the jail, afraid of being trapped and abandoned, started a noisy demonstration. People crowded the streets with cars, making the usually light traffic hour look more like a heavy holiday weekend. Through it all, the mournful shrieking siren continued until someone finally had sense enough to shut it off. The after-silence was almost as bad.

In Middletown, a loudspeaker truck cruised the streets, barking out the governor's message. It was garbled because of its amplification, but the truck's presence was a catalyst to action. Cars raced to filled roadways and lined up at gasoline stations.

The telephone system, already overloaded, completely jammed. Still, no one outside a possible few at the Three Mile Island plant knew the seriousness of the problem.

Newspapers and television news programs, supported by hourly radio reports, began to cover the story from coast to coast. Relatives and friends of those in the area added to the impossible load of phone calls. Overall, many reacted as if there were an impending disaster. Others took the affair in apparent calm, by doing exactly what the governor had asked. They went inside and stayed there.

Less than a hundred miles away, in Washington, D.C., President Carter, knowledgeable in matters of nuclear engineering, was undergoing another type of crisis. Despite his best efforts, he did not feel he was receiving consistent, adequate information. Harold R. Denton, NRC reactor regulations chief, was dispatched to Three Mile Island to resolve problems and alleviate confusion. To establish an open line of communications, an Army Signal Corps team was sent to set up a private telephone link to the White House. Then, fearing the worst because of the scarcity of reliable data, the president authorized shipment of a considerable quantity of anti-radiation medicine and medical gear.

Finally, by mid-morning, Carter was delivered a summary of the situation. Reacting to this, he called Gov. Thornburgh at about 11:15 AM. The conversation lasted several minutes. The governor updated the president on the latest his office had received from the site and was in turn told of activities at the federal level.

Thornburgh, still worried but satisfied with the talk, turned to his press secretary, Paul Critchlow, who was waiting for a briefing. "He thinks we've done the right thing, so far. He says it's best to err on the side of caution and safety." All through the morning, environmentalists had been gathering in Harrisburg, congregating around the Friends' Meeting House, where they demanded clearer information about the potential seriousness of the incident.

They were met with more differences of opinion and conflicting stories. Dr. Ernest J. Sternglass, professor of Radiology at the University of Pittsburgh, declared that radiation samples from earlier that same day showed levels up to a full fifteen times higher than normal. He compared his readings to "a major fallout pattern from a nuclear bomb test."

Sternglass was answered by Jack Herbein, Met Ed's vice president. "There is presently no danger to the public health or safety. We didn't injure anybody, we didn't overexpose anybody, and we certainly didn't kill a single soul. The radiation off-site is absolutely minuscule."

Antinuclear groups immediately jumped on Herbein for his "no-danger" position. A war of words only added to the general confusion and the public's growing lack of faith in what they were reading, seeing, and hearing.

In the first twenty-four hours of the incident, about ten thousand people had, of their own volition, evacuated the area, heading north to Hershey or to other points of relative safety. This exodus, combined with growing uncertainty created by a lack of official information and conflicting reports of the degree of danger, produced rumors. The latest word spread from person to person by telephone and small gatherings. Slowly, without apparent panic, the evacuation urge began to gain ground. A nuclear threat was unlike, for example, fear of flooding from a rising Susquehanna River. In a flood situation, all anyone had to do was stay tuned to the radio and leave when officials announced it was wise to do so. Somehow more vague, the fear caused by an invisible threat of radioactive emissions was more terrifying.

Antinuclear agitators, venting their frustrations with the situation, began to speak out loudly against how Met Ed and the government were handling the matter. Their arguments, more excited than logical, matched the mood of the populace, who were also beginning to react emotionally. The number of families leaving the area increased dramatically in the next few hours.

Inside the main control room of the plant, where only a few experts knew the whole story, tension had again grown. The release of radioactive xenon-133 gas, a by-product of nuclear fission, which had occurred earlier that morning, had been reported to the press and waiting officials. Readings at the site were as high as 1,200 millirems. The governor's reaction to the plant's having released forty thousand gallons of low-level waste water into the Susquehanna had everyone on edge. They'd had no choice. In order to make room for the highly radioactive primary coolant water, which had been spilled and was now being pumped into holding tanks, a release was a necessity.

Those issues, however, were overshadowed by another difficulty. A huge bubble of potentially explosive hydrogen gas had formed at the top of the reactor containment chamber. How serious this was, no one could tell. But even pronuclear expert opinion worried that this abnormal event could have grave portent.

Hydrogen gas, produced by a chemical reaction of zirconium with water, is lighter than air. Early dirigibles used it to generate lifting force. The Hindenburg disaster, in which thousands of cubic feet of hydrogen had burst into flames, showed how easily the gas might become ignited. In the presence of sufficient oxygen, ignition of this gas, enclosed in a space made of steel and concrete, could produce an explosion of extremely high magnitude. An eruption might even burst open the containment building and release its radioactive contents into the atmosphere. Such a force could certainly damage or break more fuel rods, destroy the water piping and pump system needed to keep the core underwater and cool, and thus create a meltdown.

The bubble came as a surprise to some but apparently not to others. At least their statements made at the time claimed they had previous suspicions about the possibility of such an occurrence.

Communications were improving, since the president had taken steps and Gov. Thornburgh had applied pressure for clearer, more precise information. Just before noon, Thornburgh received a call from Hendrie with the NRC. His update, while still not as exact as Thornburgh would have liked, showed the definite possibility of more radioactive discharges. His advice was for the governor to advise and urge pregnant women and children of preschool age who resided within five miles of the plant to leave the immediate area. After a brief discussion, the governor, at a noon press conference, made the announcement. Its effect was instantaneous. In the next six hours, more than one hundred thousand people fled the vicinity of Three Mile Island, leaving block after block in Middletown vacant. In tiny Goldsboro, a few football-field lengths away from the hulking towers of the facility, a few stayed, but most packed up and left. Many never returned, selling out for what they could get, seeking a new life farther from radioactive threat. Ken Myers, mayor of the little city, called it a ghost town and speculated on the loss caused by diminished property values.

The need for a definitive public statement of conditions inside the facility, and the probability of the situation becoming worse before it got better, was, by now, apparent. Fortunately, Harold Denton, as directed by the president, arrived with his team of experts at 1:00 PM. This was an hour after the governor's announcement concerning the advisability of evacuation for part of the population. The group went directly to work acquiring accurate information by undertaking a complete inspection of the facilities and records.

What they discovered did little to assure the public of the eventual outcome of the accident. Complications were greater than anyone outside the facility imagined.

After meeting initial resistance from the officials of Met Ed, Denton, director of the NRC office that dealt with regulating reactors, proved his true value. He quickly realized his staff would be a necessary addition to the technicians and specialists from Met Ed. Working together, they could achieve more in a shorter period of time.

In a few hours under Denton's direction, the teams began delivering definitive reports. Yes, there was damage to several of the flow systems. Yes, fuel rod cladding had split, releasing an unknown amount of radioactive uranium into the heart of the pile. No, there was no immediate (meaning within the next ten or twelve hours) risk of a great radioactive release. Yes, there was a hydrogen bubble. It was not something previously envisioned in any theoretical reviews of reactor problem areas. And yes, presence of the bubble was more than serious, because it could explode. Worse still, it could create so much pressure on the vessel that none of the available remaining pump systems could force water in to be certain the top of the core remained covered.

Denton, finally feeling he had a complete story, placed two calls. In the first to President Carter, he outlined his findings and discussed possible resources that might help avert disaster. In the second, the director summarized the situation to Gov. Thornburgh in a straight, succinct way. Now, everyone but the public knew the size of the problem.

Citizens were informed through a late-evening news conference. Terse and direct, Denton laid out the situation in clear layman's terms. He called the possibility of a meltdown "very remote" and cited a need for calm, as there was no "imminent" danger. He went on to say there would probably be no change for some days, and that great caution was needed to bring the reactor into a completely cold shutdown condition.

The announcement of the presence of a hydrogen bubble set off arguments in the scientific community. How and why did it form? Was it still developing, or was the present state the maximum hydrogen release that would build in the confines of the reactor? The bubble occupied a large part of reactor space, and if it grew only a little, problems would be magnified by a factor of ten. It was acting like a lid on a pressure cooker, keeping temperatures and pressures high.

Theories were propounded and rejected. One thing became clear. Regardless of comments from individuals who stated they had conceived of the problem, no anticipation of the hydrogen bubble's formation had occurred in plans dealing with potential mishaps.

The focus of attention by scientists led to a two-fold solution. First, in order to be able to release some of the hydrogen into the reactor containment area, which would lower pressure in the reactor chamber itself, it would be necessary to change or alter the atmosphere and its oxygen content in the reactor containment chamber. Failure to do this made the risk of an explosion too great. A pair of catalytic recombiners were rushed into place and installed in the huge room. They would combine available oxygen and released hydrogen back into water vapor. As these units worked, the hydrogen level in the chamber would decrease, thus allowing operators to let some of the bubble's hydrogen flow from the reactor container to the main protective containment chamber.

Another tack was also selected. The bubble, where it pressed against the surface of the water cooling the pile, was in some form of chemical balance. As the gas dissolved into the water, hydrogen was released, so as some went out, about the same amount came back in. If there were some quick way to reduce the hydrogen content of the coolant water, the exchange would be more one way. Hydrogen would pass from the gas bubble into solution in the water, but less would replace it. Slowly, under these conditions, the bubble would shrink.

They began the procedure with some hesitation, but it became apparent in a few hours the plan could work. Given time, it would reduce the size of the hydrogen bubble and the pressure.

Since the operation was in its early stages, it was impossible to be sure how effective it might be. The lack of highly positive assurances—even though the information was presented fairly and the statement of danger, or lack of it, honestly made—resulted in an increase of volunteer evacuees. Many, with no place to go, stayed in public shelters. Others called upon relations or vacation cabins for their relocation. There are only estimates of how many left their homes. Civil defense emergency evacuation plans called for relocating hundreds of thousands, but there was no provision for measuring traffic in and out of an area within twenty-five miles of Three Mile Island.

Tens of thousands of families, in cars packed with stuffed animals, sleeping gear, clothes, and favorite possessions, clogged service roads and area freeways. Yet some residents, motivated by a sense of homestead, ignorance of potential danger, or security in their knowledge the plant would not emit sufficient radiation to harm them, stayed on, to see what the new day would bring.

What came was still more controversy.

Trucks hauling heavy equipment to dehydrogenize the air and water were rolling into the plant site over the police-guarded twin bridges. Dr. Melvin M. Levine, director of the thermal reactor safety division of the Brookhaven National Laboratory, said, in an interview with an English scientific publication, "The bubble is a surprise." It was also a surprise for the public to learn, from an NRC release, of the small hydrogen explosion inside the reactor chamber.

Walter Creitz, president of Met Ed, started the official day by announcing there had been "no surprises throughout the night." Denton, confronted with the need for more expertise, called upon the scientific community, and a wide range of experts were airlifted to the facility. It's a tribute to these men that they came with full and certain knowledge of the danger in which they were placing themselves.

By mid–Saturday morning, the evacuation rate slowed. Those who felt an immediate need to depart had done so. Those who had elected to stand fast were settling in. The number of undecideds dwindled.

In the main control room, orders were passed regarding the installation and operation of the hydrogen-oxygen combining equipment. The bubble was still a serious threat, because its force, pressing on the top of the coolant water, required pumps that could deliver 900 pounds per square inch of pressure to keep the water circulating. If outside electrical sources had failed, the only pumping facilities left would have been driven by diesel standby power units. These were capable of giving out less than 700 psi on a sustained basis.

At a mid-afternoon press conference, Denton sounded optimistic. While deriding a previous claim that all danger was over, he said he could see "things moving in a positive direction."

But after 8:00 that same evening, a blow to the morale of area residents came by way of the news media. A report based on faulty data was given wide circulation. It said, in part, the bubble was growing and there was a possibility of an explosion in the next forty-eight hours. Hearing this after a day of relative calm, many remaining people decided to depart. By 10:00 PM, roads were once again jammed.

The report was accurate to a certain extent. It reviewed the situation as it had existed for days. Forty-eight hours was the length of time it would take for the hydrogen to build to a danger point if nothing were done in the meantime. But something was being accomplished. As Denton noted in a specially convened news conference, steps had been taken. While it was too soon to see much progress, the reactor was still in a relatively safe condition.

President Carter, realizing the need to calm the citizens of the area who remained in their homes, decided on a course of action late Saturday night. In a pre-midnight announcement, he stated his intention of visiting Three Mile Island personally, to see for himself how the matter stood. The impact of this on the communities in central Pennsylvania, as they heard about it the next morning, was a stabilizing force.

Early on the morning of Sunday, April 1, monitoring teams went out into the surrounding region and into the air above the plant. They wanted samples to reinforce available readings from sites scattered throughout the countryside. Radioactive levels were normal, or close enough to cause no concern, so the White House was notified.

Shortly after 12:30 PM, a green and white helicopter, with the president and his wife aboard, circled the plant noisily for an aerial view. It then flew about fifteen miles up-river to the Harrisburg airport. After landing and a security check by agents assigned to the president's party, they drove off in a long black limousine. At the gates of the plant, Mr. Carter and his wife donned plastic overshoes and were issued radiation badges. Following a short walk across the gray concrete, they were ushered into the control center for an on-the-spot briefing.

Within an hour, the president went to a Middletown gymnasium to discuss his observations with the press. He stated that the situation, while still not under full control, was stabilizing. In his soft Georgia accent, he noted any errors that might be made should be on the side of "caution and extra safety."

The presence of the president seemed to restore confidence to those who had remained inside the fallout area. There was a general realization that Carter would not have come in person, much less have brought his wife, if there were imminent signs of danger. The mass evacuation that had been taking place for days slowed, then halted altogether.

Scientists and technicians, who had been working around the

clock, were, by late Sunday evening, able to see progress in diminishing the size of the bubble. For the first time, it looked as if the reactor might be coming back under control.

In the early dawn on Monday, April 2, highways on both banks of the river were almost vacant. An occasional truck passed, but there was no sign of the usual rush hour traffic created by busy people on the way to their jobs in Harrisburg and other communities.

Lending an official air to the unusual holiday, Gov. Thornburgh authorized excused absences for state workers. Retail stores, both in the suburbs as well as downtown, remained closed, as owners and others who had not fled stayed in their homes.

Small gatherings of people, however, could be found clustered around radios and television sets awaiting the next news report. After the brief bulletin was over, especially if it contained previously unannounced statements, there would be renewed intensity in conversation about the problem and the question of leaving or staying.

Shortly after noon, tension, which had been building for days, found a release and started to falter. Techniques used to shrink the bubble had worked better than anyone had hoped. Although the period of maximum risk was over, it would take months to find a solution to the remaining problems and bring the reactor to a full cold shutdown. Core damage would require more months to assess and clean up. Thousands of gallons of highly radioactive water from the broken cooling system, which had been pumped into holding tanks, would present a disposal problem that might take years to solve.

How close did the reactor on Three Mile Island come to a core melt? No one knows. Expert opinion has been offered by both sides. Some hold that a meltdown occurred. The operators consider that possibility remote. Others feel it was averted by a hair's breadth.

There are, however, certain factual findings that bear no argument. First, the plant was poorly situated. Its position on the island was fine from a standpoint of security, water supply, or power transmission, but its location in the middle of a busy area of almost a million people did not make good sense.

Secondly, it was virtually impossible to get accurate information during early and middle stages of the event. Conflicting reports came from plant operators, NRC staff, local officials, and the state and federal governments. This has been a consistent difficulty during nuclear incidents. Some of the inaccurate reports were due to a reporter's need for a story. An interviewer, who knows little or nothing about the processes, questions a non-qualified person who will talk. The result is a hodgepodge of misinformation. The main barrier to direct, factual communiqués is more pervasive and harder to handle. Pro- and antinuclear groups use the same facts to present conflicting sides of the story to the press. Spin makes it difficult for people to obtain objective, hard facts.

Third is a lesson repeated over and over again. When plant operators are faced with a choice between a possible meltdown or a release of radioactive emissions into our environment, they will inevitably opt for the voluntary release.

Fourth, even the most sophisticated experts were surprised by the presence of the hydrogen bubble that formed during the problem period. None of the theoretical analyses of possible reactor incidents included a rapid buildup of hydrogen gas to the point where pressures inside the vessel would not allow water to be pumped in. Yet, until this event, individuals were willing to stake their reputations on their work and believed they had successfully theorized every contingency. It is clear there was still a lot to learn.

The biggest lesson from the accident on Three Mile Island is contained in some informal remarks made by an engineer from Westinghouse. While disturbed by the accident, he was pleased, naturally enough, that there had been no serious consequences. Looking on the bright side, he saw the incident as an excellent "testing ground," where full-sized systems were run through a series of exercises, and experts in the nuclear field gained "empirical" experience about equipment in use. He was, of course, sorry the experience had to be gained in such a manner, but nonetheless grateful for it.

Three Mile Island was not the first serious nuclear accident and won't be the last. It's a stunning realization to comprehend the fact that many emergency systems that will be called upon to save the public have never been subjected to full-size, in-the-field, life-situation testing. There may be more surprises in store for us next time.

SIXTEEN

Chernobyl, Russian Military Reactor Dangers, and Soviet Secrecy

On April 26, 1986, at 1:23 AM, an accidental steam explosion damaged the No. 4 reactor of the V. I. Lenin Memorial Chernobyl Nuclear Power Station in the town of Pripyat, Ukraine. The initial blast started a fire. There were additional explosions. The result was an atomic meltdown that belched an astounding amount of radioactive particles and gas into the atmosphere. Following prevailing winds, there was fallout over the Soviet Union, Europe, Britain, Scandinavia, and parts of eastern North America.

On the International Nuclear Event Scale (INES) used to classify the severity of nuclear accidents, Chernobyl was labeled Level 7. It would have been rated higher, but Level 7 is the worst score ("major accident") in the measurement system.

What went wrong? Almost everything. Consider these facts.

The facility director and the chief engineer both had worked in coal-fired electrical plants and had limited experience with nuclear-power generation. The deputy chief engineer for reactors 3 and 4 had dealt only with small units made for nuclear submarines.

The reactor, an RBMK (reaktor bolshoy moshchnosti kanalniy) design, is a type of reactor built only in the Soviet Union. It is now considered flawed and outdated by international experts, who call for all remaining RBMKs to be shut down. The RMBK was intended to produce plutonium for nuclear weapons as well as provide electricity. Components required for this dual role made it too large to be housed in a reasonably sized containment shell, which can keep a lid on radioactive material in case of an accident. So the pressure vessel was exposed. When it broke there was no protection against spewing radioactive materials into the environment.

The RBMK reactor had serious design defects. Pockets of steam, called "voids," tended to form in the water used to cool the nuclear pile. Steam voids allowed the reactor to produce more energy. Producing more energy created more steam and therefore more voids, which made the reactor harder to manage since there was less water to slow reactions. The problem with the RBMK was more prevalent at low power settings, a fact not understood by its operating crew.

The control rods that slid in and out of the nuclear pile to speed or retard the reaction were of an unusual design. Made from graphite, boron carbide, and containing water, the rods actually increased the nuclear reaction for seconds after insertion. Reactor operators were unaware of this.

The operating team did not communicate effectively with safety personnel when performing a test maneuver with the pile. In spite of facility guidelines, they switched off many of the reactor's protection systems. The team also removed all but seven control rods in spite of directives prohibiting pile operation with less than fifteen rods in the core.

Cost savings realized by not constructing a containment vessel were nullified by the amount of radioactive contaminants released when the pressure vessel burst. In-rushing air allowed a graphite fire to flare. In the end, there was nothing to stop the outpouring of dangerous contaminants.

The situation was made worse by a lack of preparation of local officials and inadequate equipment in the reactor No. 4 control room. Dosimeters didn't work so the crew could not accurately measure levels of radioactivity. A reading from a replacement dosimeter was ignored because the instrument was considered defective. This led, despite hunks of graphite and reactor fuel scattered around the building, to the conclusion that the reactor was undamaged. The crew in the reactor building wore no protective suits or breathing devices. Most died from radiation within weeks of the disaster. The first firefighting team was not advised that smoke and debris were highly radioactive. The team leader died, and many of the firemen received extreme doses of radiation.

The explosive release of radioactive materials was so powerful that residents of Pripyat reported seeing a glowing cloud against the dark morning sky. Immediate response to the disaster came close to making matters much, much worse. Water pumped in to quench the fire ran underneath the reactor floor into an enclosed space. Smoldering nuclear fuel was burning its way through the floor. Attempts to dampen the blaze by dumping suppression material from helicopters intensified the problem. Had the seething mass dropped into the trapped water, the resulting explosion would have, according to many estimates, contaminated land for hundreds of miles around the plant.

The list goes on.

Even today, after studying the accident, holding various review boards, and with enough time to look back impartially, there is some question as to what actually happened. The International Atomic Energy Agency (IAEA) at first centered the main cause on the actions of the operators. Then, years later, the IAEA revised its position and placed the blame on reactor design.

As was not uncommon in the old Soviet Union, ruling bodies acted to put the best possible face on the accident. No report of the event was made public until detection of fallout from the explosion by Swedish scientific teams made keeping the secret impossible.

Even then, the cover-up eventually went so far as to include a government mandate to physicians prohibiting their naming "radiation" as cause of death.

On the evening of April 26, just hours after the disaster, a government committee arrived on-site. They found two workers dead and fifty-two others hospitalized. Then the number in the hospital jumped to two hundred with thirty-one deaths. After a few hours' study, authorities realized the reactor was destroyed and ordered evacuation of the city of Pripyat. That involved some fifty thousand people. Another eighty-five thousand in the vicinity were also included, which jumped the total to one hundred thirty-five thousand. Eventually, some three hundred thousand individuals were resettled.

To speed up the depopulation, many residents in the first wave were led to believe they were being temporarily relocated to other sites and would return home in about three days. Belongings left behind in the town still remain. The people never came back.

Soldiers and workers sent to clean the site were called "liquidators." One of their first tasks was to release water trapped under the reactor floor to prevent a catastrophic explosion. Three courageous men, two dressed in rubber wetsuits, were sent to do the job. One held a lamp so the pair could see while working their way through a dark tunnel to the valves that controlled a spillway. When opened, the spillway would allow the water to flow out. The lamp died, leaving the two men with no light. They felt their way through the wet blackness by following a pipe. After completing their mission, they returned to discover they had been exposed to intense radiation.

Typical of Soviet estimates during that period, it is unclear how many liquidators were involved in the mop-up operation. Numbers range from three hundred thousand to six hundred thousand. Many received exposure to radioactive elements and gases.

Years later, vehicles used by liquidator teams remain in the area where drivers left them.

Through hard work in a dangerous environment, the most deadly debris was dumped into the remains of the reactor. Helicopters were then used to deposit untold tons of sand, lead, and boric acid on the rubble. Then concrete was poured over the resulting mess. When hardened, this formed a massive shield that sealed away the entire reactor site.

That woeful piece of cut-and-fit engineering was supposed to last twenty-five years. In that time span, a true mausoleum was to have been designed and installed. Twenty years later, the concrete temporary shell is cracked in many places and leaks radiation. There is no sign of the replacement container.

With the breakup of the old Soviet Union, no one knows what effects the Chernobyl disaster will have on the people of that area in the coming years. Thousands upon thousands in Russia, Belarus, and Ukraine still live in what are considered zones of contamination. Various studies are conflicting, but none is positive. One notes that ten thousand people have developed thyroid cancer and anticipates another fifty thousand will do so.

One of the gravest facts about the Chernobyl catastrophe is that it was not the first serious nuclear disaster in the Soviet Union. As outlined in Chapter 3, during the 1940s and 1950s a worse series of atomic cataclysms took place in the Ural Mountains.

What compounds this tragedy is that in the more than half century between the two worst atomic catastrophes in history, little had been done by the government to better protect its people. In both cases, ill-equipped workers were allowed into extremely toxic areas without proper protection. A high degree of secrecy was maintained. Massive evacuations were conducted with no regard to informing those being relocated about the severity of their situation. The root cause of both incidents stemmed from unskilled personnel taking unauthorized actions without proper communications with experts. Winging it is not conducive to a positive relationship with atomic energy.

Both accidents are directly attributable to a rather cavalier attitude toward nuclear safety. A large part of that outlook was caused by budgetary shortages. A lack of money is the key reason given for the shocking state of nuclear power generation in Russia today.

In 2006, Russia possessed ten operating nuclear power stations with thirty-one reactors that deliver 15 percent of the nation's electricity. Experts on the international scene have indicated half of those reactors are at best in risky condition. No less than eleven of the reactors are the RBMK type that contributed to the Chernobyl incident. And a number of other units are operating beyond their designed years of production, after having received engineered upgrades to prolong useful life.

All this leads to some question about Russia's ability to decommission reactors in such a way as to ensure public safety. Indeed, how they have disposed of radioactive materials in past years is an issue of international concern.

The subject of waste storage is especially troubling for methods currently in use by the Russian Navy. Murmansk is a city of about a half million people. It is the largest Russian seaport on the Arctic Ocean and is largely ice-free year-round. Radiation counters are located at many busy intersections. Radio stations often include reports on radiation levels in newscasts. Why this strong interest in atomic matters? There are a number of exhausted nuclear reactors from military ships that have been sunk in shallow offshore waters while awaiting proper deactivation. When will that be? No one is certain.

Through 1996, the Russian Northern Fleet decommissioned about ninety of its nuclear submarines. A quarter of the subs have had their atomic fuel removed. The rest are afloat at various bases on the Kola Peninsula. These are being joined by more obsolete boats each month. Reportedly dump sites for spent nuclear fuel are above maximum capacity. In some cases, those locations are also in dubious repair.

In addition to the above problems, from 1959 through 1991 the Soviet Union dumped radioactive waste, six submarine reactors, and material from an ice breaker with spent fuel into the Barents and Kara Seas. Solid wastes and reactors were disposed of in the Novaya Zemlya fjords and the Kara Sea, at depths from 40 to 450 feet.

Those areas, plus a trough almost one thousand feet deep in Novaya Zemlya, have been examined by joint Norwegian-Russian specialist groups and found to be acceptable in terms of levels of contamination. However, controls regulating the use of beaches and marine resources are still in place near the coasts of Novaya Zemlya.

Report after report recounts serious Russian naval problems with nuclear materials. Later accounts indicate the degree of government desire to keep these events from making international news.

Based on past performance, and given the fact that little seems to have been learned from experience, it is difficult to predict an accident-free future for Russian use of nuclear energy. Sergei Kiriyenko, who served as President Boris Yeltsin's prime minister and is now head of Russia's Federal Agency for Nuclear Power, stated that Russia planned to construct forty-two to fifty-eight nuclear power plants by 2030 and forty to fifty units abroad in the next thirty years. Time will tell, but in the first decade of the twenty-first century, it is clear the Russians have not made a great contribution to a safer nuclear world.

SEVENTEEN

Japanese Accidents

Japan has few natural resources. After the oil crisis in 1973, the island nation decided to decrease its reliance on foreign imports. Successive governments have been determined to become self-sufficient and have embraced nuclear power. A sound argument can be made that Japan, of all nations on earth, has the greatest vested interest in commercial applications of atomic energy.

It is more than just the number of electricity-producing reactors in that country. As of June 2006, Japan has fifty-five reactors in operation. The nation ranks third highest in number of reactors worldwide, behind the United States (103) and France (59). In terms of square miles, Japan is about two-thirds the size of France and only one-twenty-fifth as large as the United States. So Japan is at the top of the list in nuclear reactors per square mile of territory.

As of 2006, a total of thirty nations possess at least one power-plant nuclear reactor. The world total is 442. Of all commercial reactors operating outside the United States, 16 percent are in Japan. And nuclear power plants produce a full 35 percent of Japan's electric energy. The Tokyo Electric Power Company (TEPCO) is the largest investor-owned power company in the world, a remarkable situation considering Japan's diminutive geographic size.

The Japanese connection to nuclear power, however, is not based on the number of its reactors alone. Another important link stems from a fact of history.

Starting in the late 1940s and continuing through the 1960s, the United States was leader in all forms of nuclear technology. From reactor design through containment engineering and safety measures, the United States offered what was state of the art for two decades. That was forty years ago. In the interval, no new nuclear electricity-producing plants (aside from the TVA's Watt's Bar unit) were erected in the United States. Nuclear engineers who were in their twenties during that period of dominance have retired or moved into other fields. In short, if a company desired to build a new nuclear power plant, a large American talent pool of those with hands-on experience no longer exists. Military applications are another matter, but in the commercial field, the United States is no longer preeminent.

Between the 1960s and the turn of the century, however, about three hundred new plants were constructed in various nations around the world. Who did the engineering? Who had the expertise? Clearly it was not the United States.

French firms filled part of the need. But Japanese companies quickly came to the forefront and earned international respect. In addition to updates and improvements to the basic Westinghouse reactor design, they brought new thinking to materials as well as methods used in constructing plants.

In 2006, the Japanese firm Toshiba bought Westinghouse from the British government for almost $5 billion. Westinghouse, an American leader in nuclear engineering, had been acquired by the British government agency BNFL in 1998. Toshiba's acquisition significantly strengthens Japan's position as a supplier of nuclear technology at a time when, worldwide, nuclear power delivers as much energy as was produced from all sources combined in 1960.

Considering the heavy reliance on atomic power, Japan's record for nuclear accidents was better than average until the 1990s. A notable incident occurred in April 1981, when more than forty workers were exposed to radiation during maintenance of a facility.

Throughout the 1990s, the nation's safety record deteriorated. In December 1995, the secondary cooling system of a prototype fast-breeder reactor leaked tons of sodium, causing a fire at Tsuruga. The reactor was closed for a year. In 1997, thirty-five workers were exposed to radiation at Tsuruga; steel barrels leaked radioactive waste at Tokaimura; there was a fire at a uranium-enrichment lab near Tokyo; and a TEPCO power-generating reactor leaked small amounts of radiation. In 1998, a TEPCO reactor shut down when a cooling pump failed.

Then, on September 30, 1999, Japan's worst accident to that time happened without warning. Tokaimura is a village on the Pacific about eighty miles north of Tokyo. The sister city of Idaho Falls, Idaho—a place also associated with atomic energy—Tokaimura is noted for its expanse of beaches, not to mention what is known as a "reconversion plant." This type of operation reprocesses nuclear fuel.

What happened at 10:35 AM was caused by human error. No machinery was involved. No elaborate control systems malfunctioned. On that day, uranium was to be purified to be made into a fuel for use at an experimental reactor. Members of a team of three were involved in an unfamiliar procedure, utilizing an unapproved method, with equipment not designed for the process, and were unaware of the danger that using too much of a particular type of uranium could result in criticality, a self-sustaining chain reaction.

The technique required mixing powered uranium oxide with nitric acid to produce uranyl nitrate. Three different tanks, each for a specific step, were needed. These were: a dissolving tank, a buffer tank with a particular design to prevent criticality, and a water-jacketed precipitation tank, where the final product would be formed into a solid.

A report attributed to the *Asahi Shimbun* newspaper indicated a supervisor, who wanted to get off work early, instructed a pair of workers to add the uranium oxide in a larger amount than normal to speed up the process. Another report stated that the team wanted to complete the operation before a new crew came on.

Whatever their reasons, two workers mixed small amounts of uranium oxide powder and nitric acid in a ten-liter stainless steel bucket rather than in the dissolving tank. Then they poured that mixture directly into the last-step precipitation tank, skipping the first two tanks.

Normally, the procedure called for adding about five pounds of uranium oxide to the acid. The technicians added more than thirty-five pounds directly into the precipitation tank. That was seven times more than could be safely processed.

As the final bucket was poured in, disaster struck. A blue flare, silently indicating the start of an uncontrolled chain reaction, was seen. In seconds, the two received high doses of radioactivity and experienced vomiting, pain, and shortness of breath.

In a criticality accident, the most dangerous radiation to individuals is in the immediate vicinity. With distance from the nuclear reaction, the threat decreases quickly. But gases given off contain harmful isotopes. No one noticed that an exhaust fan, venting radioactive gases, was open until twelve days after the accident.

As radiation alarms began sounding, the pair and their supervisors hastened from the room and left the building. The two technicians, whose error caused the disaster, received immediate medical attention, but both died within seven months of the accident.

It took only minutes after the 10:35 AM mistake for reports of the incident to reach news media. The regional government (prefecture) was notified by fax in an hour. Sixty minutes later, local village authorities were asked to call for an evacuation, which took another hour. Relocated immediately were 150 people who lived within a 0.2-mile radius of the facility. Shortly, roads were closed and experts were on the scene. Plans were set for additional evacuations, if necessary, and schools and twelve large manufacturing plants were closed so students, teachers, and ten thousand workers could go home.

On-site, radiation levels climbed to ten thousand times higher than normal. Over a mile away, the figure was ten times the norm.

The final precipitation tank, where criticality occurred, was encased in a cooling water jacket. The surrounding water reflected neutrons back to the center, accelerating the reaction. A method to stop the process was quickly agreed upon, and necessary gear was brought to the site. TEPCO rushed more than eight hundred pounds of sodium borate from its nuclear plant sixty miles away. Boron, which is used in control rods in nuclear reactors, slows nuclear reactions.

Small crews of courageous technicians and supervisors were organized. Their task was to enter the building and flush the water from the cooling jacket around the tank. Then the contents of the tank could be brought under control.

Photographs were made of the valve that would release the water. Several attempts were made before one team of two successfully drained the water away. Then the boron was added to ensure that the critical event was terminated. Minutes later radiation levels began declining.

A number of workers engaged in trying to halt the chain reaction received exposures equal to the amount of radiation permitted for an entire year. And one took almost twice that level.

From the initiation of the accident to the end of the critical period took twenty hours. It was rated Level 4, later upgraded to

Level 5, on the International Nuclear Event Scale. By some reports, fifty-five individuals were exposed to radiation. That total included forty-five employed on the site, three firemen, and seven workers at a golf course not far from the facility. Others accounts list as many as eighty-three persons exposed.

The aftermath of this terrible event, as has come to be expected, brought forth anger, accusations of government laxity, and indignation. The police were inclined to charge both the company that owned the facility and its management with criminal behavior. The news media found countless errors and asked embarrassing questions. An immediate investigation was begun at some twenty nuclear fuel processing facilities in Japan.

Before the flurry of resentment caused by the accident was over, there were the confessions of wrongdoing that so typify Japanese scandals, demands that the government tighten controls over the entire nuclear industry, and wide-scale fault-finding inspections.

Despite claims and counter-claims, charges, leaked news stories, speeches, and promises, in the end, one issue was made very clear. Many serious breeches of safety regulations had occurred in many operations.

Following the investigation, TEPCO was forced to temporarily shut down all seventeen of its nuclear power plants for falsifying safety records.

Five years after the Tokaimura incident, Japan suffered its worst accident, in terms of deaths, at a nuclear power station in the town of Mihama, situated on the Sea of Japan about forty miles north of Kyoto. In August 2004, a steam generator pipe broke. Non-radioactive steam killed five and burned several workers who were delivering tools to the facility in preparation for its annual inspection. Officials stated that no radiation leaked from the plant and that there was no danger to the public.

All this aside, the Japanese government has shown no intention of abandoning its unique position in the international nuclear industry. And there has been no official desire to lessen Japan's use of nuclear energy. It is clear plans to construct an additional twenty new reactors by the year 2010 remain unchanged.

EIGHTEEN

Disaster Planning

On August 29, 2005, a natural disaster of unprecedented ferocity destroyed much of the city of New Orleans, Louisiana. Wind-driven storm surge from Hurricane Katrina broke through levees and inundated the metropolitan area. The much-touted pumping systems, which were intended to drain away flood waters, failed to do so. In the course of only a few hours one of America's grandest cities was largely destroyed. Virtually all emergency response systems failed. Ranks of police and firefighters were decimated. There was open looting of stores. Many hundreds of people were forced onto elevated freeway sections of Interstate 10 to escape rising torrents. Some were there for days with little food or water and no shelter from the sun or elements. Thousands more took refuge from the storm in the Superdome, where social and survival services failed, the electricity went off, and part of the roof blew away.

In the aftermath of that cataclysmic event, it was clear that the many plans for just such an eventuality were worthless. In fact, they were harmful in that they promoted a false sense of security.

Just twenty-seven days later and three-hundred-odd miles to the west, a massive attempt was made to evacuate part of

Houston, Texas, the nation's fourth-largest city. Another hurricane, Rita, was the cause. Again, chaos, confusion, and loss of life reigned. Tens of thousands of cars and trucks poured onto major highways, filling them to such an extent that traffic could only inch forward. After a few hours, vehicles began running out of gasoline and were pushed off the pavement. Entire families were stranded without water or sanitary facilities amid a sea of cars. As more gas tanks emptied, ribbons of vehicles, some almost a hundred miles long, staggered to a complete halt.

Towns along clogged routes blocked freeway exits so evacuees would not stream into their streets. State troopers and then Texas National Guard units were called to assist. But traffic congestion was so extreme that their mobility was hindered to the point of rendering them almost useless. Three full days were required to restore a modicum of order. Again, all of the preparation for evacuations, federally funded planning agencies, inter-county safety councils, emergency programs, and so many other services failed.

In both of the above cases, evacuees were running from wind and water. What if they'd been fleeing radioactive contamination? People understand natural phenomena. Potential exposure to radiation is another matter entirely and would have added panic and hysteria to an already dire situation.

What can average members of our society do to protect themselves and their loved ones during such an incident?

This is an important question to ask, but the answers are nebulous. Inured as we are to the possibility of catastrophe in daily life, we give little thought and less action to such events. There are several things, however, that any of us might do, if we are so inclined.

First, we can examine the planning done for us by others. In 1979, following the Three Mile Island accident, the U.S. Nuclear Regulatory Commission (NRC) began a serious evaluation of all existing emergency plans for the 103 nuclear power reactors licensed to operate at sixty-five sites in thirty-one states. Roles of the Federal Emergency Management Agency (FEMA) and the NRC were more closely defined, with FEMA as the lead agency for planning and response. The NRC was charged with assisting FEMA. The outcome of these changes was a studied improvement in all plans.

Every nuclear power plant has an Emergency Preparedness Plan. Local and state governments must also have emergency procedures that mesh with those of the nuclear facility. Plants are required to test their plans in realistic drills. These exercises include plant managers, employees, and local, state, and federal officials. If the outcome of the drill is not favorably evaluated by officials, the plant will not be able to continue operating.

This is well and good. But there are three problems with all such predetermined programs.

First, individuals charged with plan implementation may hesitate to act soon enough to achieve maximum benefit. It is a fearsome responsibility to cause hundreds of thousands of people to leave their homes. Ordering an evacuation will result in injuries and deaths. Vacillation is therefore normal. Delay, in a nuclear event, can be disastrous. Past experience shows there will be delays due to a desire for more information, indecision, and fear of making the wrong call.

Second, the very fact a plan exists is somewhat of a problem for plant owners because their public stance must be one of safety. The existence of an emergency program does not speak of secure operating conditions. Rather, to many people, an emergency plan implies there will be an emergency. If processes are safe, then a backup emergency program is superfluous. If, however, there is any degree of uncertainty about their safety or any question as to whether or not an adverse series of events might finally climax in harm to our society, a plan is a necessity. But it is also proof that mechanisms designed in those facilities are fallible.

Third, and most telling, unlike a hurricane that comes after days of warnings and cautions, a nuclear event happens suddenly. Alarms that have been silent for years suddenly scream into life, and the emergency is upon us.

Even the best of plans require response time. Texas and FEMA officials learned the impossibility of demanding or advising an evacuation without first establishing refueling capabilities, rest stops, and other essential services along evacuation routes. It takes days, not hours, to have everything in place. In the case of a nuclear mishap, there may be only minutes.

Individuals who will be affected, therefore, need to look at these plans and consider how they might actually work as opposed to how they are supposed to work. No great expertise is required. Anyone who drives on a freeway during rush hour becomes acquainted with the problems of traffic and periodic standstills. From this experience comes sufficiently practical knowledge to review and determine the feasibility of at least the evacuation phase of these predetermined action programs.

A key part in almost every instance of disaster programming is the use of city, county, and state emergency-response facilities. Local fire and police departments will be called to assist. State agencies will be notified and placed on standby.

Where the incident demands action inside the confines of an installation, these civil units are generally required to obey the commands of the nuclear facility's managers, no matter how inexperienced these individuals might be in combating or facing a dangerous situation. As the Browns Ferry crisis revealed, the local county fire chief was better informed and more capable of determining how to extinguish the blaze than engineers on the operator's staff.

Outside an installation, civil authorities will take charge through regular channels of command. These officials are trained

in many of the activities required to, say, evacuate a neighbor-
hood. But this training, in most cases, falls far short of moving a
city of one million people from where they are at 7:00 on a given
evening to somewhere else in a matter of hours. It is an impossible
task, and no amount of advance preparation will produce enough
roadway and mobility to get the job done.

Large cities will be better prepared, but it appears that far too
few local police or fire departments have sufficient programs to
familiarize all personnel with the difficulties peculiar to a nuclear
contamination threat. Nor do they have an ample amount of the
specialized equipment to detect various forms of radiation and
protect themselves from contamination, or the medical knowledge to render first assistance to victims who have been exposed.

Nuclear power plant emergency plans specify two "Emergency
Planning Zones." The first zone covers a circle within ten miles of
the power plant, where the greatest possibility of direct exposure to
radiation occurs. The second zone encompasses a larger area,
within a fifty-mile radius. In the second zone, food, water, animals,
and crops could be contaminated in the event of an accident.

Each person with an interest has access to a nuclear facility's
NRC-approved Emergency Preparedness Plan. If you live close to
a nuclear power plant, radioactive storage site, or waste disposal
area, you need to be aware of hazards connected with that particular facility. If you live in the ten-mile zone, you need to check
yearly for emergency information from the power company that
operates the nuclear power plant nearby. Attend local public
information meetings.

To locate the emergency plan, search online for the name of
that nuclear facility. Under "Emergency Plans," you'll find that your
plant has procedures that comply with local, state, and federal regulations. There will be warning sirens and other emergency alert
methods, such as specialized radios and computerized telephone

calling systems, to notify residents within the ten-mile Emergency Planning Zone.

About three million people live within ten miles of a nuclear power plant. Many millions more live within fifty miles. Those who live within fifty miles of a nuclear facility might well familiarize themselves with the emergency preparedness plans of their community.

The Federal Emergency Management Agency (FEMA) has fact sheets concerning nuclear hazards on its website (www.fema.gov). In short, FEMA recommends that you: attend public information meetings; learn your city's warning systems; find out about emergency plans for schools, work place, nursing homes, or wherever a family member might be; create a family plan, which includes a place to meet and a way to communicate; have a disaster supplies kit; check evacuation routes for your area and be prepared to evacuate or shelter at home; have an emergency communication plan, which includes designating an out-of-state contact if family members cannot connect immediately; listen to the radio or TV for official instructions.

Radiological emergency plans that deal with ways to minimize radiation exposure list three important guidelines: distance, shielding, and time.

1. Distance

The greater the distance from a source of radiation, the less exposure you will receive. If you are caught outside during a radiological incident, cover your mouth and nose. Seek shelter immediately. When coming indoors, remove clothing and shoes. Place articles in a plastic bag and seal it. Shower to wash off any particles.

2. Shielding

After distance, heavy material between you and the source of radiation is next most important. As soon as possible, shelter indoors. Close windows and vents and shut off the air-conditioning/furnace to minimize indoor contamination.

If advised to evacuate, be sure your home is closed up well. Turn off the air-conditioning/furnace, shut vents, lock windows and doors. Listen to announcements on radio or TV for information on evacuation routes.

Take disaster supplies. When leaving, remember to close your car's air vents, turn off the air-conditioning/heating, and keep windows rolled up.

3. Time

The less time spent near a source of radiation, the less exposure you will receive. And radioactive materials lose strength over time.

Expect confusion because it will be everywhere. Pay no heed to rumors. Official news broadcasts will tell things pretty much the way they are. Don't expect special treatment. For babies, young children, those who are pregnant, seriously ill, or who have some distinct reason to believe there has been exposure to radiation, tell someone in charge. But be ready to do the military "hurry-up-then-wait" routine, because the chaos of the moment will prohibit anyone from giving immediate attention.

The simple rule all specialists reiterate is: Don't panic. No matter what your personal feelings may be, the odds are against being in a situation of immediate, instant danger. There will be more than enough time to do anything within reason that needs to be done.

After a radioactive release, you must remember that water, foods, and animals may be contaminated. You will have to follow instructions from local authorities. If you experience unusual symptoms after exposure, such as headache, fatigue, nausea, vomiting, diarrhea, thermal-like burns, bruising, bleeding, or hair loss, you should seek medical attention as soon as possible.

For more detailed information and specifics regarding your city, county, or region's emergency plan, phone your local Office of Emergency Management or search online using these keywords: [name of your city] Office of Emergency Management. Phone numbers will be listed. Many cities offer handbooks. These will include preparedness for your region's most likely catastrophes (hurricane, tornado, earthquake, flood, etc.).

Prepare a disaster supplies kit with these items:
Cash and credit cards
Portable battery-operated radio with extra batteries
First aid kit
Flashlight and extra batteries
Bottled water
Packaged food and manual can opener
Essential medicines
Extra pair of eyeglasses
Changes of clothing (long-sleeved shirts and long pants to protect skin)
Sturdy walking shoes (an additional pair)
Copy of important documents
Emergency supplies for the car include:
Flashlight and extra batteries
Jumper cable
Tire repair kit
Gas can
Fire extinguisher
Blanket
Bottled water
Packages of high-energy food
Maps

The likelihood of needing these kits is not great—especially for a radiological event. However, the old adage "An ounce of preparedness is better than a ton of regret" remains true. It is always better to be prepared than sorry.

NINETEEN

What We Must Do

Sixty-odd years into the nuclear age two facts are stunningly clear.

First, global demand for electric energy is not going to diminish. Year by year our need will grow.

Second, the supply of coal, oil, and natural gas is not limitless. If the entire earth were made of those materials we would eventually use them all. So burning coal, natural gas, oil, and other combustibles to generate electric energy is not a long-term solution to the energy problem. Neither is harnessing the sun, wind, geothermal heat, water, tides, and all of the other sources of energy. These are aids but not solutions.

There has been enormous progress in the nuclear field since the embryonic days of the 1940s. We have come a long way. During that time, especially compared to mining, drilling, and refining, few people have been injured. The amount of radioactivity in our environment has increased, albeit slightly. But this has largely come from the explosion of military devices, not from nuclear power stations.

Our technology and understanding of the equipment needed to harness the atom as a heat source for generating electricity safely has improved annually. But there is a lot we still do not know, a lot we still need to learn.

In America, we are facing a time limit. If we continue to import hydrocarbons at the present rate, we are going to have to face some hard decisions—and make big changes in our basic lifestyles.

Atomic energy can pull us out of the hole and keep us out long enough to work on an alternative nuclear process. Fusion, for instance, is far cleaner than the fission technique used today. But nuclear energy is not going to save us unless we act now. The price of every facility under construction has increased, year by year. Plants designed in the '60s cost several hundred million. By the 1980s, projected costs for a facility neared a billion dollars. Just rebuilding the Browns Ferry No. 1 reactor, which is scheduled to go on line in 2007, has cost $1.8 billion for repairs and upgrades.

Aside from initial costs, other problems are present. Existing nuclear piles developed by companies to operate economically based on specific prices for uranium have troubles. In many cases they are unable to purchase the fuel unless they are willing to pay three or four times original estimates. In one case, costs skyrocketed over 500 percent! And to date, we have really just begun to address the financial aspects involved in closing down a reactor site after its operational life comes to an end. Estimates indicate it might take four or five times the original construction price to decommission an average-size station and pile.

There are also too many unanswered questions about equipment safety and operational durability, not to mention waste disposal, transportation, and power generating technology.

We require a way out. We need a way for nuclear power stations to produce the energy we need—energy to make new jobs and assure continued employment. But we have to do it with minimum risk to our society and to our world.

In the 1950s, the Soviet launching of Sputnik I astounded the United States and damaged American egos. Rallying to President

John F. Kennedy's clarion call, the challenge was met. Within a decade an astronaut walked on the moon.

Federal funds, allotted by contract to private companies for research and development of the necessary hardware, put us there. It was an outstanding example of how the U.S. government can work with industry and science to attain a predetermined goal.

A safe reactor, or at least a safer reactor with even lower emissions, is a goal we must accept as a challenge. Along with the other problems of a nuclear society, this should become the impetus for a national achievement program. It would cost far less in the end than sending men into space, and like the space program, it could produce an amazing amount of "fall-out" technology, which could be used in a vast number of fields. It is also a giant step toward solving one of the most serious situations in the world today.

Somehow, it would be fitting for the largest user of energy in the history of man to be the developer of a clean, safe, and efficient source of atomic power. It is possible. The attainment of this goal is a greater challenge for the twenty-first century than space flight was in the late 1950s. But it is within our grasp. And the U.S. Nuclear Power 2010 Program is just one of the initiatives we have undertaken.

Work is now in progress on Generation 4 nuclear reactor designs. One, the Pebble Bed Modular Reactor (PBMR), holds promise because of size and control over the fissionable material. Others represent strides forward as well.

Work is also underway to create new sites to receive nuclear waste. This is vital—and more reactors will make it even more so. Reluctance to act has resulted in over-storage of spent radioactive materials on nuclear power plant sites. That solution is archaic.

Along with this program ought to come the necessary revisions to the Price-Anderson Act to assure each citizen of proper redress if the ax does fall.

Accompanying that should be, as discussed earlier, some form of small annual tax. Collected through the federal or state government for every current and new hookup or installation, this money would fund individual states to purchase, train, and maintain adequate nuclear emergency teams.

If we start now, we have time. How much time, no one really knows. There is going to be a nuclear accident of major proportions. It may not be anybody's fault, and it will not stem from any one cause. But sooner or later, it will happen. No responsible, informed person disagrees with this simple fact: When it hits, we have to be ready.

Our immediate action is vital. Monies expended will be returned many times over to millions of Americans who will be able to continue their lifestyles and provide for their families.